P9-EFI-747

WOMEN AND LEADERSHIP

WOMEN AND LEADERSHIP

DEBORAH L. RHODE

OXFORD
UNIVERSITY PRESS

OXFORD

UNIVERSITY PRESS

Oxford University Press is a department of the University of Oxford. It furthers
the University's objective of excellence in research, scholarship, and education
by publishing worldwide. Oxford is a registered trade mark of Oxford University
Press in the UK and certain other countries.

Published in the United States of America by Oxford University Press
198 Madison Avenue, New York, NY 10016, United States of America.

© Oxford University Press 2017

All rights reserved. No part of this publication may be reproduced, stored in
a retrieval system, or transmitted, in any form or by any means, without the
prior permission in writing of Oxford University Press, or as expressly permitted
by law, by license, or under terms agreed with the appropriate reproduction
rights organization. Inquiries concerning reproduction outside the scope of the
above should be sent to the Rights Department, Oxford University Press, at the
address above.

You must not circulate this work in any other form
and you must impose this same condition on any acquirer.

Library of Congress Cataloging-in-Publication Data
Names: Rhode, Deborah L., author.
Title: Women and leadership / Deborah L. Rhode.
Description: New York : Oxford University Press, 2016.
Identifiers: LCCN 2016016714 (print) | LCCN 2016028435 (ebook) |
ISBN 9780190614713 (hardback) | ISBN 9780190614720 (E-book) |
ISBN 9780190614737 (E-book)
Subjects: LCSH: Leadership in women. | Women executives. | Leadership. | Sex role. |
BISAC: LAW / Discrimination. | LAW / Gender & the Law.
Classification: LCC HQ1233. R463 2016 (print) | LCC HQ1233 (ebook) |
DDC 305.43/30334—dc23
LC record available at https://lccn.loc.gov/2016016714

3 5 7 9 8 6 4

Printed by Sheridan Books, Inc., United States of America

For Barbara Kellerman

CONTENTS

WOMEN AND LEADERSHIP

INTRODUCTION

In the heat of the 2016 presidential campaign, Frank Bruni wrote a *New York Times* op-ed under the title, "If Trump Changed Genders." Bruni concluded the thought experiment with the observation that a "woman with his personal life, public deportment and potty mouth wouldn't last a nanosecond in a political campaign—or for that matter in a boardroom." This campaign speaks volumes about what Bruni called the "utterly and unjustly dissimilar" standards confronting male and female leaders.[1]

Those double standards are longstanding. For most of recorded history, women were largely excluded from leadership positions. A comprehensive review of encyclopedia entries published just after the turn of the twentieth century identified only about 850 eminent women throughout the preceding two thousand years. In rank order, they included queens, politicians, mothers, mistresses, wives, beauties, religious figures, and "women of tragic fate."[2] Few of these women had acquired leadership positions in their own right. Most exercised influence through relationships with men.

Since that publication, we have witnessed a transformation in gender roles. Women now exercise leadership in virtually every part of the private and public sectors. Yet progress is only partial. Despite a half century of equal opportunity legislation, women's leadership opportunities are far from equal. The most comprehensive survey finds that women occupy less than a fifth of senior leadership positions across the public and private sectors.[3] In politics, women constitute over half the voting public, but only 19 percent of Congress, 12 percent of governors, and 19 percent of mayors of the nation's one hundred largest cities.[4] From a global perspective, the United States ranks ninety-seventh in the world for women's representation in political office, below Slovakia, Bangladesh, and Saudi Arabia.[5] In academia, women account for a majority of college graduates and postgraduate students but only about a quarter of full professors and university presidents.[6] In law, women are almost half of law school graduates but only 18 percent of the equity partners of major firms, and 21 percent of Fortune 500 general counsels.[7] In the nonprofit sector, women constitute three-quarters of staff positions but only a fifth of the leaders of large organizations.[8] In business, women account for a third of MBA graduates, but only 4 percent of Fortune 500 CEOs.[9] At current rates of change, it could take more than a century for women to reach parity in the C suite.[10]

This book seeks to advance our understanding of why women remain so underrepresented in leadership roles, what strategies are most likely to change that fact, and why it matters. The discussion is aimed at several audiences: women interested in leadership positions, organizations interested in increasing their proportion of women leaders, and readers interested in the status of women. To make significant progress, the book argues that we must confront second-generation problems of gender inequality that involve not deliberate discrimination but unconscious bias, in-group favoritism, and inhospitable work-family structures. And it claims that those barriers should be dismantled, both because a just society is committed to equal opportunity and because a competitive economy cannot afford to undervalue half its talent pool.

Unlike much of the popular literature concerning women and leadership, this analysis suggests that the problem cannot be resolved at the individual level; structural and cultural solutions are essential. Although women's choices help account for women's underrepresentation in leadership positions, conventional wisdom too often underestimates the extent to which these choices are socially constructed and constrained.

Because context matters in shaping leadership challenges, constraints, and strategies, subsequent chapters explore in detail the challenges in particular fields.[11] After this overview chapter describes the barriers confronting women in leadership and the societal stakes in addressing them, Chapter 2 reviews obstacles for women in politics and how best to respond. Chapter 3 focuses on women and management, Chapter 4 on women in law, Chapter 5 on women in academia, and Chapter 6 on women on corporate boards. To fill in gaps in the existing research, the discussion draws on data from a survey of approximately a hundred prominent women leaders in academia and the nonprofit sector.[12] To situate the analysis, this introductory chapter explores the rationale for greater gender equity, the reasons for women's underrepresentation in leadership, and the strategies most likely to remedy it.

Equal Opportunity as a Public Good

Women's unequal representation in leadership positions poses multiple concerns. For individual women, the barriers to their advancement compromise fundamental principles of equal opportunity and social justice. These barriers impose organizational costs as well. Women are now a majority of the most well-educated Americans, and a growing share of the talent available for leadership. Organizations that lack a culture of equal opportunity are less able to attract, retain, and motivate the most qualified individuals.[13] Obstacles to women's success also decrease employees' morale, commitment, and retention, and increase the expenses associated with recruiting, training, and mentoring replacements.[14]

A second rationale for ensuring equal access to leadership positions is that women have distinct perspectives and capabilities to contribute. For effective performance in an increasingly competitive and multicultural environment, workplaces need individuals with diverse backgrounds, experiences, and styles of leadership.[15] The point is not that there is some single "woman's point of view," or woman's leadership style, but rather that gender differences matter in ways that should be registered in positions of power.

A wide array of research underscores the value of diversity in leadership contexts. For example, some studies indicate that diverse viewpoints encourage critical thinking, creative problem solving, and the search for new information; they expand the range of alternatives considered, and counteract "group think."[16] Men's and women's differing knowledge and experience can affect how they seek and evaluate information, which affects their decision-making processes and "collective intelligence."[17] When individuals hear dissent from someone who is different from them, it provokes more thought than when it comes from someone who looks the same.[18]

Some studies also find a correlation between diversity and profitability in law firms as well as in Fortune 500 companies.[19] Having more women in top management is associated with greater market revenue.[20] Of course, correlation does not establish causation. Financial success may do as much to enhance gender equity as gender equity does to enhance financial success. Organizations that are on strong economic footing are better able to invest in diversity initiatives that promote both equity and profitability.[21] But whichever way causation runs, there are strong reasons to support gender equality. Inclusiveness in leadership signals a credible commitment to equal opportunity and responsiveness to diverse perspectives.[22] As subsequent discussion makes clear, many policies that level the playing field for women, such as those involving work-family accommodations, mentoring, and equitable work assignments, are all likely to have other organizational payoffs.

The societal stakes are substantial. More than three-quarters of Americans say that the country has a crisis in leadership, and confidence in leaders has fallen to the lowest level in recent memory.[23] The nation can ill afford to exclude so many talented women from positions of influence, particularly given the growing body of evidence suggesting that women bring distinctive strengths to these roles.

The Difference "Difference" Makes

Assumptions about gender differences in leadership styles and effectiveness are widespread, although as Alice Eagly's pathbreaking work notes, the evidence for such assumptions is weaker than commonly supposed.[24] Reviews of more than forty studies on gender in leadership find many more similarities than differences between male and female leaders.[25] Not only are those gender differences small, they are smaller than the differences among women.[26] So too, in the Pew Research Center's recent survey on women and leadership, a large majority of the American public sees men and women as similar on key leadership traits such as intelligence, honesty, ambition, decisiveness, and innovation.[27] The main differences that emerged were compassion and organization, and on those traits women were rated as superior to men.[28] The only gender differences that are consistently supported by evidence on performance are that female leaders are more participatory, democratic, and interpersonally sensitive than male leaders.[29] Eagly notes that women "attend more to the individuals they work with by mentoring them and taking their particular situations into account."[30] Leaders interviewed for this book often spoke of being more collaborative than their male counterparts.[31] According to Debora Spar, president of Barnard College, "recent research shows that as women, we are more likely to help out in the workplace . . . [and] that helping behaviors can greatly improve business outcomes."[32]

In effect, women are more likely than men to engage in transformational leadership, which stresses inspiring and enabling followers to contribute to their organization.[33] This approach holds advantages over traditional transactional leadership, which focuses on exchanges between leaders and followers that appeal to followers' self-interest. Women tend to use a transformational style because it relies on skills associated with women, and because more autocratic approaches are viewed as less attractive in women than in men.[34] A transformational style has obvious advantages because it enables women to establish a level of trust and cooperation that is essential to effectiveness. Janet Napolitano, former Arizona governor, cabinet secretary, and currently president of the University of California, notes that one critical leadership characteristic is helping others accomplish their mission: "People need to know you are investing yourself in doing what you need to do so they can succeed. It is a big mistake to parachute in with a prepared plan about who will do what. I've seen guys do this all the time."[35] Although transformational leadership is generally viewed as the most effective approach, it does not fit all organizations.[36] Some highly male-dominated settings invite a top-down style, and women who were firsts in those settings, such as Margaret Thatcher, Golda Meir, and Indira Gandhi, led in ways that were as commanding as those of men.[37]

Similar points are applicable to gender differences in leadership priorities. Women are particularly likely to cite assisting and empowering others as leadership objectives, along with promoting gender equality.[38] In a 2015 Pew survey, 71 percent of women believed that having more women in top leadership positions in business and government would improve the quality of life for all women.[39] Of course, not all female leaders are advocates on women's issues. Some are at pains to distance themselves from gender concerns. As Marissa Mayer famously put it, "I'm not a girl at Google, I'm a geek at Google."[40] Other women have internalized the values of the culture in which they have succeeded, and have little interest in promoting opportunities that they never had. They have "gotten there the hard way," and they have "given up a lot"; if they managed, so can everyone else.[41] On the whole, however, women's greater commitment to women's issues emerges in a variety of contexts. For example, most evidence indicates that female judges are more supportive than their male colleagues on gender-related issues.[42] And many women judges, both through individual rulings and collective efforts in women's judicial organizations, have addressed women's concerns on matters such as domestic violence, child support, and gender bias training.[43] The same is true of women in management and public service. For some female leaders, their own experiences of discrimination, marginalization, or work-family conflicts leave them with a desire to make life better for their successors.[44] Because these women have bumped up against conventional assumptions and inflexible workplace structures, they can more readily question gender roles that men take for granted.[45] Their perspective deserves a hearing in leadership contexts.

As to leadership effectiveness, most research reveals no significant gender differences. Success in leadership generally requires a combination of traditionally masculine and feminine traits, including vision, ethics, interpersonal skills, technical competence, and personal capabilities such as self-awareness and self-control.[46] Contrary to popular assumptions, large-scale surveys generally find that women perform equally with or slightly outperform men on all but a few measures.[47] One recent study found that women scored higher than men on twelve of sixteen leadership competencies.[48] Some evidence also suggests that women are less subject than men to the arrogance and overconfidence that contributes to leadership failures, and are better decision makers under stress.[49] Such differences prompted the quip by the International Monetary Fund's managing director, Christine Lagarde, that the global financial crisis would have played out quite differently "if Lehman Brothers had been 'Lehman Sisters.' "[50] However, women cannot be effective unless others accept their leadership—and context matters. One meta-analysis found that men's effectiveness as leaders surpassed women's in roles that were male-dominated, but that women's effectiveness surpassed men's in roles that were less masculine.[51]

Taken as a whole, these findings on gender differences should come as no surprise. Gender socialization and stereotypes play an obvious role; they push women to behave in ways that are consistent with traditional notions of femininity. Yet these differences in leadership contexts are generally small because advancement often requires conformity to accepted images of leadership. And some traditional differences have been blurred by recent trends in leadership development, which have encouraged both sexes to adopt more collaborative, interpersonally sensitive approaches.[52] It is also unsurprising that some studies find superior performance by women leaders, given the hurdles that they have had to surmount to reach upper-level positions and the pressures that they have faced to exceed expectations.[53] To the extent that female leaders gravitate toward a collaborative, interpersonally sensitive approach, it is because that style proves an asset in most leadership settings. Whatever else can be inferred from this research, it is clear that a society can ill afford to exclude so many talented women from its leadership ranks.

Women's Underrepresentation and Women's Choices

What accounts for this underrepresentation of women in leadership roles? One common explanation involves women's choices. As Sheryl Sandberg has famously put it, not enough women "lean in."[54] In a widely cited cover story in the *New York Times Magazine*, Lisa Belkin claimed that women's underrepresentation is less because "the workplace has failed women" than because "women are rejecting the workplace." "Why don't women run the world?" asked Belkin. "Maybe it's because they don't want to."[55] Harvard professor Barbara Kellerman similarly raises the possibility that many women "do not want, or at least they do not badly want what men have . . . Work at the top of the greasy pole takes time, saps energy, and is usually all-consuming. Maybe the women's values are different from men's values. Maybe the trade-offs [that] high positions entail are ones that many women do not want to make."[56]

Such observations capture a partial truth. Women, including those with leadership credentials, do on average make different choices from men. In a 2015 study by McKinsey & Company and Leanin .org of nearly thirty thousand workers, 54 percent of men but only 43 percent of women wanted to be a top executive.[57] In a 2015 *Time* magazine poll, only 38 percent of women, compared with 51 percent of men, described themselves as very or extremely ambitious.[58] Another 2015 study by Harvard Business School researchers found that compared to men, women had more life goals, placed less importance on power, associated more negative outcomes with high-power positions, and were less likely to take advantage of opportunities for professional advancement.[59]

More women than men also cut back on paid employment for at least some period. In a study by the Center for Work-Life Policy of some three thousand high-achieving American women and men (defined as those with graduate or professional degrees or high-honors undergraduate degrees), nearly four in ten women reported leaving the workforce voluntarily at some point over their career. The same proportion chose a job with lesser compensation and fewer responsibilities than they were qualified to assume, in order to accommodate family responsibilities. By contrast, only one in ten men left the workforce primarily for family-related reasons.[60] Although other surveys vary in the number of women who opt out to accommodate domestic obligations, all of these studies find substantial gender differences.[61] Almost 20 percent of women with graduate or professional degrees are not in the labor force, compared with only 5 percent of similarly credentialed men. One in three women with MBAs are not working full-time, compared with one in twenty men.[62] The overwhelming majority of these women do, however, want to return to work, and most do so, although generally not without significant career costs and difficulties.[63] Increasing numbers of women appear ready to make that sacrifice. More married millennial women (42 percent) planned to interrupt their careers than baby boomers (17 percent).[64]

Yet women's choices are an incomplete explanation of women's underrepresentation in leadership positions. Most surveys of men and women in comparable jobs find that they desire leadership opportunities equally.[65] In one recent study, almost the same percentage of mid- or senior-level women wanted to reach top management as men (79 vs. 81 percent).[66] Moreover, to blame women's choices for women's underrepresentation ignores the extent to which those choices are socially constructed and constrained. Before they have substantial caretaking responsibilities, women are not significantly less ambitious than men. In a recent study of Harvard MBA graduates, women's career aspirations did not substantially differ from men's.[67] Pew survey data found that more women than men age eighteen to thirty-four say that having a successful, high-paying career is very important or the most important thing in their lives.[68] In a McKinsey survey of workers age twenty-three to thirty-four, 92 percent of women and 98 percent of men expressed a desire to advance professionally. But by middle age, only 64 percent of women, compared with 78 percent of men, expressed such a desire.[69] Similarly, a Bain & Company survey of one thousand women and men in a mix of American companies found that women started out with slightly more ambition than men, but for those with more than two years on the job, aspiration and confidence among the female workers plummeted.[70]

What happens in the intervening years is often a combination of women's disproportionate family responsibilities and a workplace unwilling to accommodate them. In the Harvard study, many women who expected to have careers of equal priority with their spouses, and to share child care responsibilities equally, ended up with less egalitarian arrangements.[71] Yet even for Harvard MBAs, differences in family arrangements and the extent of labor force participation did not explain women's lower number of leadership positions compared to men.[72] Only 11 percent were full-time stay-at-home parents.[73] And even the women who did leave their jobs after becoming mothers did so "reluctantly and as a last resort, because they [found] ... themselves in unfulfilling roles with dim prospects for advancement."[74]

One woman's experience was typical: she quit after being "mommy tracked" when she came back from maternity leave.[75] As Anne-Marie Slaughter notes, "Plenty of women have leaned in for all they're worth but still run up against insuperable obstacles created by the combination of unpredictable life circumstances and the rigid inflexibilities of our workplaces, the lack of a public infrastructure of care, and cultural attitudes that devalue them the minute they step out or even just lean back from the workplace."[76] Explanations that focus solely on women's choices obscure the influence of men's choices as husbands, policy leaders, and managers. As subsequent discussion indicates, if women aren't choosing to run the world, it may in part be because men aren't choosing to share equally in running the household.

Gender Bias

> Men are too aggressive when they bomb countries. Women are too aggressive when they put you on hold on the phone.

> —Laura Liswood[77]

One of the most intractable barriers to women's advancement is the mismatch between the qualities associated with leadership and the qualities associated with women. Most of the traits that people attribute to leaders are those traditionally viewed as masculine: dominance, authority, assertiveness.[78] These do not seem attractive in women.[79] Four fifths of Americans think decisiveness is essential for leaders, and over a quarter believe that women are less decisive than men (a belief unsupported by research).[80] Although some evidence suggests that these stereotypes are weakening, people still more readily accept men as leaders.[81] Women, particularly women of color, are often thought to lack "executive presence." In studies where people see a man seated at the head of a table for a meeting, they typically assume that he is the leader. They do not make the same assumption when a woman is in that seat.[82]

Most individuals prefer a male to a female boss.[83] In one study, not a single legal secretary preferred working with female attorneys over their male counterparts. Half preferred working with men. Some believed that female lawyers were harder on their female assistants because these law-yers "feel they have something to prove to everyone."[84] Women often in-ternalize these cultural biases, which diminishes their sense of themselves as leaders and their aspirations to positions of influence.[85] Women under-estimate (while men overestimate) their leadership abilities compared to ratings received from colleagues, subordinates, and supervisors.[86]

Women who do seek leadership positions are subject to double stan-dards and double binds. What is assertive in a man seems abrasive in a woman, and female employees risk seeming too feminine, or not feminine enough. On the one hand, they may appear too "soft"—unable or unwill-ing to make the tough calls required in positions of greatest influence. On the other hand, those who mimic the "male model" are often viewed as stri-dent and overly aggressive.[87] In the words of a Catalyst research report, this competence-likeability trade-off means that women are " 'damned if they do and doomed if they don't' meet gender-stereotypic expectations."[88] An overview of more than a hundred studies finds that women are rated lower as leaders when they adopt authoritative, traditionally masculine styles, particularly when the evaluators are men, or when the role is one typically occupied by men.[89] Autocratic or power-seeking behavior that is accept-able in men is penalized in women.[90] Female supervisors also are disliked more than male supervisors for giving negative feedback.[91] Women who come on too strong evoke labels such as "bitch," "ice queen," and "iron maiden."[92]

The intersection of racial and gender stereotypes compounds the problem. As one Asian woman explained, "I am frequently perceived as being very demure and passive and quiet, even though I rarely fit any of those categories. When I successfully overcome those misperceptions, I am often thrown into the 'dragon lady' category. It is almost impossible to be perceived as a balanced and appropriately aggressive lawyer."[93] This double bind was apparent in the unsuccessful 2015 lawsuit brought by Ellen Pao against a leading Silicon Valley venture capital firm. Pao was faulted both for being too "passive and reticent" in board meetings, and for speaking up, demanding credit, and "always positioning" herself.[94] Such assertiveness was not viewed as disabling in a male colleague who was promoted. As she testified at trial, "The frustration I have is that be-haviors that were acceptable by men were not acceptable by women."[95]

Attitudes toward self-promotion and negotiation reflect a related mismatch between stereotypes associated with leadership and with femininity. Women are expected to be nurturing, not self-serving, and entrepreneurial behaviors viewed as appropriate in men often seem distasteful in women.[96] Self-promoting behaviors provoke backlash.[97] They appear "tacky and shameless" and "leave a bad taste in people's mouth."[98] Women are also penalized more than men for attempting to negotiate favorable employment treatment.[99] The result is to discourage women from engaging in conduct that is useful in obtaining leadership opportunities.[100] In effect, women face trade-offs that men do not. Aspiring female leaders may be liked but not respected, or respected but not liked, in settings that require individuals to be both in order to succeed.[101]

Many women also internalize these stereotypes, which creates a psychological glass ceiling. On average, women appear less willing to engage in self-promoting or assertive behaviors.[102] And as one comprehensive overview of gender in negotiations puts it, "Women don't ask."[103] Numerous studies have found that women negotiate less assertively on their own behalf.[104] An unwillingness to seem too "pushy" or "difficult," and an undervaluation of their own worth, often deters women from bargaining effectively for what they want or need.[105] In workplace settings, the result is that female employees are less likely than their male colleagues to gain the assignments, positions, and support necessary to advance. A wide array of evidence also documents the effects of what psychologists label "stereotype threat." Awareness that others are evaluating them based on stereotypes can focus individuals' attention on the negative aspects of those stereotypes and undermine achievement.[106]

So too, despite recent progress, women, particularly women of color, often lack the presumption of competence enjoyed by white men, and must work harder to achieve the same results.[107] In one Gallup poll, only 45 percent of women believed that the sexes have equal job opportunities; in a 2015 Pew survey, four in ten Americans thought that women seeking to climb the ladder in business or politics have to do more than their male counterparts to prove themselves.[108] Leaders interviewed for this book often offered variations on the quip that women have to "work twice as hard to get half as far."[109] Research confirms what these perceptions suggest. Studies in which participants evaluated job applications that were the same except that some had female names and others had male names find that men are preferred for masculine and gender-neutral jobs, women for feminine jobs such as secretary.[110] The role of bias in orchestra auditions became apparent when screens were introduced to shield the identity of musicians; women's success rate after that change rose by 50 percent.[111]

Women's work is also held to higher standards than men's.[112] In one study, half of participants evaluated the resumes of a female applicant with more education and a male applicant with more work experience, and the other half evaluated a male applicant with more education and a female applicant with more work experience. Participants gave less weight to whichever credential the female applicant had.[113] To overcome these presumptions, people must receive clear and unambiguous evidence of a woman's substantial superiority over men before judging the woman to be better at a task.[114] So too, male achievements are more likely to be attributed to individual capabilities such as intelligence, drive, and commitment, and female achievements are more often attributed to external factors such as chance or preferential treatment, a pattern that social scientists label "he's skilled, she's lucky."[115] In a recent example, a *New York Times* profile of Sheryl Sandberg wrote that "everyone agrees she is wickedly smart. But she has also been lucky."[116] The more subjective the standard for assessing qualifications, the harder it is to detect such biases. Because subjective criteria are particularly significant in upper-level positions, women are particularly likely to be underrepresented at the top. Gender stereotypes are especially strong when women's representation does not exceed a token level, and too few counterexamples are present to challenge conventional assumptions.[117] In contexts where men can be promoted based on potential, women must show performance.[118] They are also more likely than men to be punished for mistakes, which may discourage them from taking risks that would demonstrate leadership abilities.[119]

Women of color are particularly likely to have their competence questioned and their authority resisted, resented, undermined, or ignored.[120] In one Catalyst survey, 56 percent of African Americans, 46 percent of Asians, and 37 percent of Latinas believed that racial or ethnic stereotypes existed at their organization.[121] Sixty-six percent of African American women, and 40 percent of Asians and Latinas, believed that diversity policies have failed to address racial bias, and a wide array of research finds a basis for this perception.[122] In one study involving identical resumes, an applicant named Lakisha was less likely to get callbacks for interviews than an applicant named Emily.[123] Lakisha had to have eight additional years of experience in order to get the same number of callbacks as Emily.[124] Another study found that whites are judged as being more effective leaders and as possessing more leadership potential than individuals of color.[125] A common assumption is that women of color are the beneficiaries of affirmative action rather than merit selection.[126] So too, black women are rated more harshly when things go awry than either black men or white women.[127] Asian American women are thought to be too demure and submissive to exert leadership authority.[128] Backhanded compliments speak volumes about the lingering effects of racial assumptions. One black woman was told that she spoke so well that no one would have known that she was African American.[129] Latinas report similar experience with their competence being questioned, or being greeted with surprise. One recalled a colleague who "went on and on about how authoritative and articulate I was at a meeting. It was the funniest thing, and I mean funny in a sad, sad way."[130]

Many women report such "microindignities" or "microaggressions," the terms that researchers use to describe commonplace behaviors, whether intentional or unintentional, that communicate "hostile, derogatory or negative... slights and insults."[131] The cumulative effect of these incidents is to lower self-esteem, increase frustration, and compromise morale.[132] Janet Napolitano recalls a typical example. In an out-of-court legal proceeding, the opposing lawyer "was being very dismissive and condescending, and at one point said something like, 'Well, little girl, that's not a real objection.'"[133] Targets of such indignities often face a catch-22 in determining whether to respond. If they object, they may be seen as confrontational and overly sensitive; if they remain silent, they may experience guilt and resentment. African Americans are particularly wary of the need to avoid being seen as an "angry black woman."

Devaluation of women's competence is also particularly pronounced for mothers. Having children makes women, but not men, appear less qualified and less available to meet workplace responsibilities. In one experimental setting, a consultant who was described as a mother was rated as less competent than a consultant described as not having children.[134] In a related study, subjects evaluated applications from equally qualified candidates who differed only in parental status. Mothers were penalized on a host of measures, including perceived competence, commitment, and starting salary. Fathers suffered no penalty and on some measures benefited from parental status.[135] When résumés were sent to employers who advertised job openings, mothers were called back half as often as childless women.[136] Even when mothers were described as exceptional performers, they were rated lower in likeability, which produced fewer job offers.[137] Like mothers, pregnant women are often viewed as ill-suited for managerial positions.[138] It is revealing that the term "working" is rarely used and carries none of the adverse connotations of working mother.

Other cognitive biases compound the force of these traditional stereotypes. People tend to notice and recall information that confirms their prior assumptions; they filter out information that contradicts those assumptions.[139] For example, when employers assume that a working mother is unlikely to be fully committed to her career, they more easily remember the times when she left early than the times when she stayed late. So too, those who assume that women of color are beneficiaries of preferential treatment, not merit-based selection, will recall their errors more readily than their insights. Similar distortions stem from what psychologists label a "just world" bias.[140] People want to believe that individuals generally get what they deserve and deserve what they get. To sustain this belief, people will adjust their evaluations of performance to match observed outcomes. If women, particularly women of color, are underrepresented in positions of prominence, the most psychologically convenient explanation is that they lack the necessary qualifications or commitment. These perceptions can, in turn, prevent women from getting assignments that would demonstrate their capabilities, and a cycle of self-fulfilling predictions results.[141]

In-Group Favoritism

A further problem involves in-group favoritism. Extensive research documents the preferences that individuals feel for members of their own
groups. Loyalty, cooperation, favorable evaluations, and opportunities
all increase in likelihood for in-group members.[142] Women in traditionally male-dominated settings often remain out of the loop of mentoring
and professional development opportunities.[143] Lack of information can
leave women blindsided by office politics.[144] Aspiring female leaders are
also less likely than their male colleagues to feel that their supervisors
support their career aspirations.[145] In one representative survey, 43 percent of African American women cited not having an influential sponsor or mentor as a major barrier to achievement; a third cited exclusion
from informal networks.[146] A typical example emerged in Pao's lawsuit
against Kleiner Perkins. According to the plaintiff, a partner explained
that women weren't invited to a networking dinner at Al Gore's home
because they would "kill the buzz."[147] Pao also was denied a seat at the
center table during key meetings. When asked about the exclusion at
trial, Kleiner Perkins's managing partner observed that "I really don't
think it was a very big deal to us who sits at a table or who does not."[148]
Women who have experienced or witnessed marginalization think otherwise. One chapter in Sheryl Sandberg's bestseller, *Lean In,* is titled "Sit
at the Table."[149]

Such in-group bias prevents women from developing the "social
capital" and sponsorship necessary for success in many workplaces.[150]
The relatively small number of women in positions of power often lack
the time or the leverage to mentor all who may hope to join them.
Moreover, recent research suggests that women and minorities who
push for other women and minorities to be hired and promoted may
be penalized in their own performance reviews, which may erode their
leverage or deter them from exercising it.[151]

Women who have only token status in upper-level positions also
experience heightened visibility along with weaker social networks,
organizational support, and peer assistance.[152] This in turn can impair
performance and job satisfaction.[153] Even a woman as talented as
Madeleine Albright recalls that early in her career before becoming

secretary of state, she was sometimes reluctant to speak when she was the only woman in the room.[154]

Differences across race, ethnicity, and culture compound the problem. Men who would like to fill the gaps in mentoring often lack the capacity to do so or are worried about the appearance of forming close relationships with women.[155] In one *Harvard Business Review* study, close to two-thirds of men acknowledged that they avoided sponsoring junior women out of concern that their attention would appear inappropriate.[156] Women of color experience particular difficulties of isolation and exclusion.[157] Individuals in senior positions are sometimes reluctant to provide any negative feedback for fear of seeming racist.[158]

Although a growing number of organizations have responded by establishing formal mentoring programs and women's networks, not all programs are well designed to level the playing field. Part of the problem is a lack of incentives. Mentoring activities are not adequately rewarded in many workplaces, and programs that randomly assign relationships may make such activities less pleasant or comfortable, particularly when cross-gender or cross-racial pairings are involved.[159] Too many individuals end up with mentors with whom they have little in common. Senior men often report discomfort or inadequacy in discussing "women's issues," and minorities express reluctance to raise diversity-related concerns with those who lack personal experience or empathy.[160] The result is a "culture of caution," in which individuals in organizations that need change feel unable to talk openly about how to achieve it.[161]

Work-Family Conflicts

When I was a law student interviewing for summer jobs in the late 1970s, a partner told me that there was no "woman problem" at his firm. One of the firm's sixty-some partners was a woman, and, he assured me, she had no difficulties reconciling her personal and professional lives. The preceding year she had given birth on a Friday and was back in the office the following Monday. These "faster than a speeding bullet" maternity leaves have not entirely vanished. Marissa Mayer, who was appointed CEO of Yahoo while pregnant, received front-page news coverage for taking only two weeks of maternity leave and committing to "work throughout it."[162] Mayer's experience is in some sense emblematic of our partial progress. Three decades ago, hiring a female head of a Fortune 500 company, much less a pregnant one, would have been almost unthinkable. But the pressures she faces to shortchange her family, and the criticism she confronts for appearing to do so, suggest progress yet to be made. So too, Patricia Woertz, CEO of Archer Daniels Midland, recalled how one of her first bosses warned her that children would ruin her career. His advice was, "Get yourself fixed and put it on your expense report."[163] Pregnant women are still sometimes greeted with advice to have an abortion, and with questions such as, "Do you feel you're up to this project?"[164] Rhea Suh, president of the Natural Resources Defense Council (NRDC), recalls that the first question in a recent job interview was about her ability to combine having young children and a really demanding job. It was not a question asked of fathers.[165]

In principle, the vast majority of men support gender equality, but in practice, many fail to structure their family lives to promote it. Despite a significant increase in men's family responsibilities over the last three decades, women continue to shoulder the major burden. Unlike same-sex couples, where paid and unpaid work tend to be more evenly shared, most heterosexual couples still divide many tasks along traditional gender lines.[166] Women spend over twice as much time on child care and household tasks such as food preparation, cleaning, and laundry.[167] Women also provide more than twice as much elder care, not only for their own parents but for their in-laws as well.[168] Even in families where both husbands and wives are employed full-time, the mother does about 40 percent more child care and 30 percent more housework than the father.[169] Although most millennial men do not believe in the traditional allocation of child care roles, they seldom entirely escape them on becoming parents.[170] So too, in one study of well-educated professional women who had left the paid workforce, two-thirds cited their husbands' influence on the decision, including their lack of support in child care and other domestic tasks, and their expectation that wives should be the ones to cut back on employment.[171]

Gender disparities are especially pronounced among those who opt out of the labor force. According to Census Bureau data, about a quarter of married women with children under fifteen are stay-at-home mothers;

fewer than 1 percent of married men with children of that age are stay-at-home fathers.[172] Although a larger number of fathers stay at home due to illness, disability, or unemployment, the disparity in caregiving remains dramatic.[173] The reasons for that disparity are deeply rooted in cultural attitudes. According to Pew Research, a majority of Americans think that children are better off if the mother stays home, but only 8 percent believe that children are better off if the father does.[174]

When researchers ask full-time mothers about their choice, only a minority, typically 20 to 30 percent, cite "a longstanding desire to be a stay-at-home mom" or the "pull" of family. Other common reasons are the cost of child care, the needs of elderly parents or a disabled family member, the expectations and unavailability of a partner, and the lack of meaningful part-time options, manageable hours, or a flexible schedule.[175] In Pamela Stone's study of high-achieving professional women who opted out of the workforce for some period of time, 90 percent gave work-related reasons, although the gendered division of family responsibilities also played a significant role. Over half mentioned their husband as a key reason for their decision to quit.[176] In couples where both partners were working long hours, women came to realize that something had to change and their spouse "wasn't going to."[177] At times, this made economic sense, given the differences in earning power between members of dual-earning couples. As one stay-at-home professional put it, there was "too much money at stake" for her husband to reduce his schedule.[178] In other cases, it was a matter of preferences; men couldn't imagine cutting back, and women felt that "*Somebody's* got to be there."[179]

Most male leaders in business and professional positions have spouses who are full-time homemakers, or who are working part-time. The same is not true of female leaders, who, with few exceptions, are either single or have a partner with a full-time job.[180] In one survey of four thousand executives, 60 percent of men had wives who did not work full-time outside the home, compared with only 10 percent of the women.[181] Far more mothers than fathers are single parents, and this is particularly true of women of color, who often assume additional caretaking obligations for their extended family.[182]

Double standards in domestic roles are deeply rooted in cultural attitudes and workplace practices. Working mothers are held to higher standards than working fathers and are often criticized for being insufficiently committed, either as parents or as professionals. Those who seem willing to sacrifice family needs to workplace demands appear lacking as mothers. Those who take extended leaves or reduced schedules appear lacking as leaders. These mixed messages leave too many women with the uncomfortable sense that whatever they are doing, they should be doing something else.[183] The problem is compounded by society's devaluation of caretaking. It speaks volumes about our cultural attitude that leaving a job to "spend more time with my family" is often a euphemism for being fired.

The gender imbalance in family roles reinforces gender inequalities in career development. Women with demanding work and family responsibilities often lack time for the networking and mentoring activities that are necessary for advancement. As former Catalyst President Sheila Wellington notes, at the end of the day many "men head for drinks. Women for the dry cleaners." Men pick up tips; women pick up kids, laundry, dinner, and the house.[184] Although women on the leadership track can often afford to buy their way out of domestic drudgery, not all family obligations can be readily outsourced.

Gender inequalities in family roles pose a particular challenge for women in leadership positions, which typically require highly demanding schedules. Hourly requirements in most professions have increased dramatically over the last two decades, and what has not changed is the number of hours in the day.[185] For leaders in business, politics, and the professions, all work and no play is fast becoming the norm rather than the exception; a sixty-hour workweek is typical.[186] Technological innovations that have solved some problems have created others. Although it is increasingly possible for women to work at home, it is increasingly impossible not to. Many high-achieving women remain tethered to their office through emails and cell phones. Unsurprisingly, most women in upper-level professional and business positions report that they do not have sufficient time for themselves or their families.[187] Many aspiring leaders express frustration with workplace demands that compete not only with families but also with commitments to community, religious, and other voluntary organizations that are important in their lives.[188]

Part of the problem is the wide gap between formal policies and actual practices concerning work-family conflicts. Although most women in top managerial and professional positions have access to reduced or flexible schedules, few of these women feel able to take advantage of such options. As they suspect, even short-term adjustments in working schedules such as leaves or part-time status for under a year result in long-term reductions in earnings and advancement.[189]

The stress, inflexibility, and unmanageable time demands that result from workplace norms play a major role in women's decision to step off the leadership track.[190] Although many of these women return to a high-powered career, others find their reentry blocked, or see a leadership position as less appealing than volunteer work, or starting their own small-scale business in which they can control their hours.[191] Some of these options offer leadership opportunities of another sort, but far too much talent falls by the wayside.

The fact that caretaking is still considered primarily an individual rather than a social responsibility adds to women's work in the home and limits their opportunities in the world outside it. The United States has the least-family-friendly policies in the developed world. It stands alone in not guaranteeing paid maternity leave.[192] American policies concerning part-time work and flexible schedules are far less progressive than Western Europe's.[193] Quality, affordable child care and elder care are also unavailable for many women attempting to work their way up the leadership ladder.[194] Although these are not only women's issues, women have paid the highest price for the failure to address them.

The Limits of Law

Part of women's progress in reducing the gender gap in the workplace is attributable to the passage of equal employment opportunity legislation. Title VII of the Civil Rights Act bars discrimination on the basis of sex as well as other prohibited characteristics, including race, religion, and national origin.[195] States generally have comparable statutes. But as ways of equalizing women's treatment in the workplace, these laws fall short.

Employment discrimination cases are, as research demonstrates, "exceedingly difficult to win."[196] They are also difficult to settle on terms that adequately compensate for the costs of complaining. Fewer than 20 percent of sex and race discrimination claims filed with the federal Equal Employment Opportunity Commission result in outcomes favorable to the complainant.[197] Settlements in these cases are generally modest, and only 2 percent of complaints result in victory at trial.[198] About 40 percent of trial wins are only temporary; they are reversed on appeal.[199]

These sobering statistics do not include the vast number of cases in which individuals may have been subject to discrimination but lacked the information or inclination to challenge it. Often, the subjectivity of standards and insufficient transparency surrounding hiring, promotion, and compensation decisions, particularly in upper-level employment, make it difficult for individuals to know that they have been subject to bias. Unless and until they assume the costs of suing, women may have little idea of whether they have a suit worth bringing. They don't know what is being said about them in contexts that exclude them. Not all differential treatment leaves a paper trail, and colleagues with corroborating evidence are often reluctant to expose it for fear of jeopardizing their own positions.[200] Women who are denied promotions seldom know until after they initiate litigation how closely their files resemble those of successful candidates.

Ann Hopkins, an accountant who successfully sued Price Waterhouse after it denied her partnership, had no specific proof that "sexist comments" had been made about her or any other woman at the firm at the time she filed her complaint.[201] Yet the record ultimately revealed ample evidence of gender stereotypes. Female accountants were faulted for being "curt," "brusque," or "women's libber[s]," or for acting like "one of the boys."[202] Hopkins herself was characterized as someone who "overcompensated for being a woman" by acting "macho" and "overbearing," and who needed "a course at charm school."[203] But several male accountants who achieved partnership had been characterized as "abrasive," "overbearing," and "cocky."[204] No one suggested charm school for them.

Nancy Ezold, the associate who unsuccessfully sued the Philadelphia law firm of Wolf, Block, Schorr, & Solis-Cohen for discrimination after being denied a partnership, learned only after filing suit how her performance evaluations stacked up against those of male colleagues who were promoted. She had been characterized as "assertive," preoccupied with "women's issues," and lacking in analytic ability.[205] Yet some of the male associates who became partners had been described as "not real smart," overly "confrontational," "very lazy," and "more sizzle than steak."[206] Ellen Pao, the woman who unsuccessfully sued Kleiner Perkins, was faulted for having "sharp elbows" and inadequate "interpersonal skills." A male colleague who was promoted was characterized as "brash," "arrogant" and "overbearing."[207] As her lawyer noted, "The comments are similar; the results are different."[208]

Even individuals with convincing evidence of bias are often reluctant to challenge it. One national survey of a thousand workers found that a third of those who reported experiencing unfair treatment did nothing. Only a fifth filed an internal complaint, and only 3 percent took legal action.[209] Other studies find similarly low rates of legal responses.[210] The reluctance to bring formal claims reflects multiple factors. Social science research finds that most individuals deny being subject to discrimination that they know affects their group.[211] People do not like to see themselves as victims; it undermines their sense of control and self-esteem, and involves the unpleasantness of identifying a perpetrator.[212] Other individuals are deterred by the high cost of legal action and the low probability of winning any substantial judgment.[213] The price of a discrimination case can be substantial, both in financial and psychological terms. Ann Hopkins's legal fees for her seven-year suit against Price Waterhouse totaled more than $800,000 in current dollars.[214] Even if a plaintiff finds an attorney to take the case on a contingent fee basis, the out-of-pocket litigation expenses can be steep; Nancy Ezold estimated hers at more than $225,000, and Ellen Pao was held liable for $276,000.[215]

Plaintiffs also are putting their professional lives on trial, and the profiles that emerge are seldom entirely flattering. In listening to defense witnesses, Hopkins "felt as if my personality were being dissected like a diseased frog in the biology lab."[216] In some cases, complainants' foibles become fodder for the national press. The lead plaintiff who sued Sullivan and Cromwell in one of the nation's first law firm sex discrimination cases had her "mediocre" law school grades aired in the *Wall Street Journal*.[217] In Ezold's case, a Wolf Block senior partner told the *American Lawyer* that she was like the proverbial "ugly girl. Everybody says she has a great personality. It turns out that [Nancy] didn't even have a great personality."[218]

Many women also resist bringing claims of discrimination out of concerns of reputation and blacklisting. Complaining about bias risks making an individual seem too "aggressive," "confrontational," or "oversensitive"; she may be typecast as a "troublemaker or "bitch."[219] Advice from colleagues regarding discrimination based on sex or sexual orientation is generally to "let bygones be bygones," "let it lie," "[d]on't make waves, just move on."[220] Those who ignore this advice frequently experience informal retaliation and blacklisting; "professional suicide" is a common description.[221] Studies find that formal complaints of discrimination generally result in worse outcomes than less assertive responses.[222] As one plaintiff's lawyer put it, a "mid- or high-level attorney who decide[s] to sue in connection with a cutback or firing may never eat lunch in [this] town again."[223] Reported cases often bear this out. Hopkins found herself "a pariah in the Big Eight" accounting firms.[224]

Another part of the problem is that courts accept even small differences in duties or responsibilities as proof that women's jobs are not substantially equal to those held by men, or accept other excuses for differential treatment. The difficulties of proving that positions are equal emerged clearly in a case in which the plaintiff was a vice president in charge of her employer's largest division. Her managerial functions were the same as those of other division heads. Although she was among those with the greatest seniority, she was paid significantly less than the other male vice presidents, and less than several other men who were neither division heads nor corporate officers. The court, however, accepted the company's justification that the other male vice presidents performed work that was "substantially more important to the operation of the company."[225] In another similar case, the trial court dismissed out of hand the notion that a female vice president was underpaid in comparison with other male vice presidents because each was in charge of "different aspects of Defendant's operation; these are not assembly line workers."[226]

Many cases reflect a mismatch between legal definitions of discrimination and the social patterns that produce it. To recover damages, the law forces a choice between two overly simplistic accounts of workplace decision making. The basis for an employer's decision must be judged either biased or unbiased, its justifications sincere or fabricated. Yet in life rather than law, legitimate concerns and group prejudices are often intertwined, and bias operates at an unconscious level throughout the evaluation process rather than overtly at the time a decision is made.[227] Most of what produces different outcomes, particularly in upper-level employment contexts, is not a function of demonstrably discriminatory treatment that leaves a paper trail. Rather, these outcomes reflect interactions shaped by unconscious assumptions and organizational practices that "cannot be traced to the sexism [of an identifiable] bad actor."[228] Even when a plaintiff locates direct evidence of bias, courts sometimes dismiss it as "stray remarks," which are insufficient to establish liability if the employer can demonstrate some legitimate reason for unfavorable treatment. So, for example, in one case a court found no discrimination where a supervisor stated, "Fucking women. I hate having fucking women in the office." In the trial court's view, this remark, though inappropriate, seemed directed at "women in general" rather than the plaintiff in particular. Her claim failed because she could not establish that gender was the only reason for her lack of promotion and training opportunities.[229]

Nor are many outcomes so blatantly unjust as to satisfy courts' demanding standard that disparities in treatment be "overwhelming" or so apparent as "virtually to jump off the page and slap you in the face."[230] Rather, the subtle, often unconscious forms of bias that constitute "second generation" discrimination problems are often beyond the reach of legal remedies.[231] To address the underrepresentation of women in leadership positions, the discussion below suggests responses at both individual and organizational levels.

Strategies for Individuals

Popular how-to books for women give contradictory advice. Some counsel women to act more like men. *Why Good Girls Don't Get Ahead But Gutsy Girls Do: Nine Secrets Every Woman Must Know* claims, "A gutsy girl breaks the rules"; "A gutsy girl doesn't worry whether people like her."[232] *Nice Girls Don't Get the Corner Office* similarly counsels women to "man up."[233] By contrast, *How to Succeed in Business Without a Penis: Secrets and Strategies for the Working Woman* suggests, "Women can silently rule with their innate mommy-nurturing skills."[234] *Taming Your Alpha Bitch* similarly wants women to become "femininely empowered."[235] Even reputable research reports sometimes give conflicting signals. One Catalyst publication suggests both that women should "learn to ignore gender and act in gender-neutral ways" and that they should "acknowledge the elephant in the room," and "immediately confront an inequitable situation and clearly communicate . . . concerns."[236]

The most systematic research on women in leadership does, however, offer some consistent advice. The first involves competence. Leaders and aspiring leaders need a strong work ethic. Some describe being consistently willing to exceed expectations—to "go above and beyond to get the job done."[237] Congresswoman Marsha Blackburn advises women: "Under promise. Over perform. Do not whine. Do the job."[238] Former GE CEO Jack Welch similarly told women that all they had to do to succeed was "overdeliver."[239] Christine Lagarde, chair of the International Monetary Fund, has compensated for feelings of insecurity by being "overprepared." When asked if that was a problem, she acknowledged, "Well, it's very time-consuming."[240] Women can also benefit from using a strategic "yes" to occasional extra work if they "make sure that yes is heard loud and clear for maximum professional capital."[241] The "yes" should be combined with a strategic "no" to tasks that do not lead to advancement. Current research finds that women are less likely than men to decline such dead-end work and that aspiring female leaders often end up bearing disproportionate burdens.[242]

Women also need to strike the right balance between "too assertive" and "not assertive enough" and to combine warmth and friendliness with a forceful approach.[243] They need, as Janet Napolitano put it, to walk the line between being strong and strident.[244] Ninety-six percent of Fortune 1000 female executives reported that it was critical or fairly important that they develop "a style with which male managers are comfortable."[245] That finding is profoundly irritating to some women. At one national Summit on Women's Leadership, many participants railed against asking women to adjust to men's needs. Why was the focus always on fixing the female? But as others pointed out, this is the world that women inhabit, and it is not just men who find overly authoritative or self-promoting styles off-putting. To maximize effectiveness, women need ways of projecting a decisive and forceful manner without seeming arrogant or abrasive. Some experts suggest being "relentlessly pleasant" without backing down, and demonstrating care and competence.[246] Strategies include expressing appreciation and concern, invoking common interests, emphasizing others' goals as well as their own, and taking a problem-solving rather than critical stance.[247] Successful women leaders such as Sandra Day O'Connor have been known for that capacity. In assessing her prospects for success, one political commentator noted that "Sandy . . . is a sharp gal" with a "steel-trap mind . . . and a large measure of common sense. . . . She [also] has lovely smile and should use it often."[248] She did.

What women should *not* do to temper their assertiveness is use a tentative speaking style. They need a tone that will command respect. Yet when men are around, many women tend to fall back on deferential speech norms, such as verbal hedges and disclaimers ("I'm not sure this is correct, but . . .").[249] In mixed groups, women talk less, use more tentative speech patterns, and are less influential than men.[250] Peggy McIntosh, a sociologist at Wellesley College, recalls a conference in which seventeen women in a row spoke during the plenary session, and all seventeen started their remarks with some sort of apology or disclaimer, such as "I've never thought about this very much," or "I really don't know whether this is accurate." And this was a women's *leadership* conference.[251]

Formal leadership training and coaching can help in developing interpersonal styles, as well as capabilities such as risk taking, conflict resolution, and strategic vision. Effective leadership requires a repertoire of approaches, adapted to what the context demands, and training can help individuals acquire the range of skills required.[252] Leadership programs designed for women or minorities can address their special challenges.[253] Profiles of respected leaders can also provide instructive examples of the personal initiative that opens professional opportunities. Successful women generally have not just waited for the phone to ring. They have ventured out of their comfort zone, volunteered for tough assignments, and asked for opportunities that will help them advance.[254] This is, to be sure, not a risk-free strategy; as noted earlier, women are punished more than men for mistakes. But neither will it be possible for many women to develop and demonstrate their leadership potential without looking for stretch assignments. Even if they don't fully deliver, they can benefit by "failing forward"; early missteps can teach lessons that pave the way to future success.[255]

Women also need to identify long-term goals and those who can assist in advancing them.[256] They should not be shy in asking for mentoring and especially sponsorship.[257] Deborah Gillis, president of Catalyst, notes the difference: "A mentor talks *to* you, offering advice and sharing experiences. A sponsor talks *about* you, advocating on your behalf, lending ... [his or her] reputation and credibility."[258] As one leader noted, cultivating sponsors is a way to build respect and "investment in my success."[259] To forge such strategic relationships, women should recognize that those from whom they seek assistance face competing demands. The best mentoring generally goes to the best mentees: people who are reasonable and focused in their concerns and who make sure the relationship is mutually beneficial. Because self-promotion often seems unattractive in women, they should find others to promote them.[260] And they should do their part in supporting others. Marie Wilson, former president of the Ms Foundation for Women and founder of the White House Project, advises women interested in leadership to "encourage each other ... and tell each other the truth, even when it's painful.[261]

Aspiring leaders also need what psychologist Carol Dweck terms "a growth mindset." Women should be continually trying to improve, confronting their deficiencies, and identifying any blind spots.[262] Perseverance in the face of adversity and criticism is equally important.[263] Angela Duckworth's research documents the crucial role of "grit"—a combination of passion and perseverance—in accounting for professional achievement.[264] Oprah Winfrey is a case study in such resilience; she was once fired from a television reporter job with the observation, "You're not fit for TV."[265]

Setting priorities and managing time are also critical leadership skills. As NRDC President Rhea Suh put it, mothers need to "raise their hands" for senior positions and insist that the workplace adapt.[266] Women with substantial family commitments need to establish boundaries, delegate domestic tasks, and give up on perfection; "done is often better than perfect."[267] "Let it go," says Anne-Marie Slaughter.[268]

In negotiating workplace accommodations, women should emphasize that they will be "flexible with [their] flexibility . . . [and will] offer contingency plans for possible conflicts."[269] Once they have secured a reasonable arrangement, women should not "slip into balanced bliss" and assume that they "can park [their] . . . schedule in the DONE file."[270] Women need to take initiative about regularly checking in with supervisors to ensure they're still on board. The challenge is to let everyone "know you're available and committed—without being available and committed the whole time."[271] Women who step out of the labor force should find ways of keeping professionally active. Volunteer efforts, occasional paying projects, continuing education, and reentry programs can all aid the transition back.

Women who seek committed relationships also need to find the right partner. For many individuals, say the authors of *Getting to 50/50*, "the most important career decision you make is whom you marry. (And the deals you make with him [or her])."[272] Interviews with leaders consistently emphasize the importance of equality in intimate relationships.[273] Jennifer Granholm, a former governor of Michigan, notes that "my best 'strategy' for success was marrying a man who was unabashedly encouraging and unafraid to be the primary parent. Whenever young women ask for my advice I tell them to 'marry well'. And by that, I mean find a spouse that will allow you to soar."[274]

So too, women must be self-reflective about their own goals and values. Just because there is a hoop on the road to advancement, women don't always need to jump through it. Leadership experts Herminia Ibarra, Robin Ely, and Deborah Kolb emphasize the importance of anchoring their efforts to a sense of larger purpose.[275] When asked what advice she would give to aspiring women, Patricia Harrison, president of the Corporation for Public Broadcasting, responded: "Know yourself and ask why do you want to lead. What do you want to do as a leader? Who are you? What are your values?"[276]

Finally, women who have reached leadership positions need to focus on empowering other women. Former secretary of state Condoleezza Rice notes that a key leadership characteristic is the ability to identify leadership qualities in others.[277] As Ilene Lang, former president of Catalyst, puts it, women should "be sure to pay it forward and advocate for others as well." Even from a purely self-interested perspective, this commitment makes sense. Catalyst research finds that leaders who support others "are more successful, for themselves and for their teams, in terms of advancement and compensation . . . Paying it forward pays back."[278] Obvious though this might seem in principle, it is complicated in practice by what is variously labeled the "leadership paradox" or the "paradox of power." This paradox arises from the disconnect between the qualities that enable individuals to achieve leadership positions and the qualities that are necessary for individuals to succeed once they get there.[279] People who reach top positions are generally propelled by a high need for personal achievement. Yet to perform effectively in these positions, they must focus on creating the conditions for achievement of others. Successful leadership requires subordinating their own self-interest to a greater good. As the philosopher Laotse famously put it, "A leader is best when people barely know he exists. When his work is done, his aim fulfilled, they will say: 'we did it ourselves.'"[280]

Strategies for Organizations

The most important strategy for organizations in ensuring equal access to leadership is a commitment to that objective, which is reflected in organizational policies, priorities, and reward structures.[281] That commitment must start at the top. An organization's leadership needs not simply to acknowledge the importance of diversity, but also to establish structures for promoting it, and to hold individuals accountable for the results. Performance on diversity-related issues should be part of the job evaluation process.[282] But it is not enough to include diversity in performance appraisals if no significant rewards or sanctions follow as a consequence.[283] A commitment to gender equity should figure in promotion and compensation decisions.[284]

Successful leadership initiatives often involve task forces or committees with diverse members who have credibility with their colleagues and a stake in the results.[285] The mission of that group should be to identify problems, develop responses, and evaluate their effectiveness.

Institutional self-assessment should be a critical part of all diversity initiatives.[286] Leaders need to know how policies that influence inclusiveness play out in practice. This requires tracking progress on key metrics and collecting both quantitative and qualitative data on matters such as advancement, retention, assignments, satisfaction, mentoring, and work-family conflicts.[287] The importance of self-evaluation was apparent at one of my recent presentations on diversity in the legal profession. After my keynote address, a young woman came to the podium and told me how well my description of gender barriers matched her experience. But what depressed her the most was that she had come to the program with her firm's managing partner, who had leaned over during my comments and whispered, "Aren't you glad we don't have those problems at our firm?"

All too often, leaders are ill-informed about the gap between their organization's formal commitments and daily realities. As earlier discussion indicated, many organizations have official policies on flexible and reduced schedules that are unworkable in practice. Periodic surveys, focus groups, interviews with former and departing employees, and bottom-up evaluations of supervisors can all cast light on problems disproportionately experienced by women. Some organizations have created outside advisory councils that meet with leaders to review progress on key inclusion measures.[288] Monitoring can be important not only in identifying challenges and responses but also in making people aware that their actions are being assessed. Requiring individuals to justify their decisions can help reduce unconscious bias.[289] And requiring leaders to quantify their results can prevent complacency. As Barnard President Debora Spar puts it, for an effort to advance women to be truly effective, it needs to be "reflected in cold hard numbers."[290]

Whatever oversight structure an employer chooses, a central priority should be ensuring equitable allocation of professional development opportunities. Women with leadership potential need access to job assignments that will promote career advancement.[291] Women should also have more than token representation in key positions such as members of management committees.[292] Critical mass helps prevent marginalization of diversity concerns.[293]

Well-designed training programs on leadership and bias can also be useful, although many existing programs fail to satisfy that description.[294]

U.S. companies spend almost $14 billion on leadership development, but as a McKinsey report notes, many of these initiatives are neither adequately evaluated nor effectively structured to provide core competencies and on-the-job learning.[295] Accordingly, Harvard Professor Iris Bohnet advises organizations to "avoid showering women with generic leadership development" programs of unproven success.[296] Rather, as she and other experts suggest, leaders need to invest in initiatives that have a demonstrated track record in advancing those they serve.[297]

Diversity training requires similar evaluation. As Alexandra Kalev and Frank Dobbin note, such training consumes "the lion's share of the corporate diversity budget yet studies suggest that it may do little to change attitudes or behaviors."[298] One review of close to a thousand published and unpublished studies of interventions designed to reduce prejudice found little evidence that training reduces bias.[299] In a large-scale review of diversity initiatives across multiple industries, training programs did not significantly increase the representation or advancement of targeted groups.[300] Part of the problem is that such programs typically focus only on individual behaviors and not institutional problems; they also provide no incentives to implement recommended practices, and can provoke backlash among involuntary participants.[301] As Bohnet points out, just telling people to resist stereotypes can "have the opposite effect—by making those stereotypes more salient."[302]

That is not to suggest that all diversity training programs are doomed to failure. Some smaller-scale research offers a more optimistic picture. One survey of managing partners and general counsel of law firms reported largely positive responses to unconscious bias training. As participants put it, many people "don't know what they don't know," and education can be helpful in "opening dialogue and making people aware."[303] So too, training programs can be useful in making people conscious of stereotype threat and how to give performance evaluations that do not trigger it. For example, critical feedback should be coupled with expressions of confidence that the employee can meet the expected standards.[304]

Another common strategy is networks and affinity groups for women and minorities. These vary in effectiveness. At their best, they provide useful advice, role models, contacts, and development of informal mentoring relationships.[305] By bringing women together around common interests, these networks can also forge coalitions on diversity-related issues and generate useful reform proposals.[306] Yet the only large-scale study on point found that networks did not significantly advance career development; they increased participants' sense of community but did not do enough to put individuals "in touch with what or whom they ought to know."[307] Such research counsels against complacency. Organizations need not just to establish a woman's network; they need also to monitor its effectiveness and to devise strategies for improvement.

One of the most demonstrably successful interventions involves mentoring and sponsorship, which directly address women's difficulties in obtaining the support necessary for career development. Many organizations have formal mentoring programs that match employees or allow individuals to select their own pairings. Well-designed initiatives that evaluate and reward mentoring and sponsorship activities can improve participants' skills, satisfaction, and advancement.[308] However, many current programs are not effectively structured. Often they do not specify the frequency of meetings, set goals for the relationship, or require evaluation.[309] Instead, they rely on a "call me if you need anything" approach, which leaves too many women reluctant to become a burden.[310] As noted earlier, ineffective matching systems compound the problem; women too often end up with mentors with whom they have little in common.[311] Other programs demand a minimum amount of contact and "reams of reports," which may make the relationship seem like one more pro forma administrative obligation.[312]

Formal programs also have difficulty inspiring the kind of sponsorship that is most critical. Women need advocates, not simply advisors, and this kind of support cannot be mandated. The lesson for organizations is that they cannot simply rely on formal structures or "paper mentors."[313] They need to cultivate and reward sponsorship of women and to monitor the effectiveness of mentoring programs. Identifying and nurturing high performers should be a priority, as should training of potential sponsors.[314] Some successful programs pair high-potential women with senior managers and hold those managers accountable for making women ready for promotions within a specified time period.[315] In short, organizations need to create a culture of sponsorship, in which upper-level leaders are expected to support women for career development opportunities.[316]

Designing effective work-family programs also should assume higher priority. Four out of five women say they need more flexibility at work.[317] The solutions are obvious in principle but elusive in practice. Promising approaches include expanding the number of upper-level positions that are eligible for extended parental leave, part-time work, and flexible schedules, ensuring that such positions have adequate responsibility and potential for advancement, and spotlighting the success of those with alternative work arrangements.[318] Also critical is extending the time for caretakers to be evaluated for higher-level positions and providing pathways back to the fast track for those who step off temporarily. More organizations should follow the lead of those that have established "career customization," which enables individuals to dial back (or dial up) their commitments without penalty.[319] Such family-friendly policies improve recruitment, retention, and morale. One survey of seventy-two companies found that these policies increased the proportion of women in senior management five years later, controlling for other variables.[320] As Slaughter notes, organizations also need to rethink expectations of 24/7 availability for everyone on the leadership track.[321]

To make all these reforms possible, they must be seen not as "women's" issues but as organizational priorities in which women have a particular stake. Men must be allies in the struggle. As diversity experts note, "Inclusion can be built only through inclusion. . . . Change needs to happen in partnership *with* the people of the organization, not *to* them."[322] The challenge remaining is to create that sense of unity and to translate rhetorical commitments into organizational priorities.

WOMEN IN POLITICS

During one of the 2012 presidential debates, Mitt Romney famously emphasized his efforts while Massachusetts governor to identify qualified women to serve in his administration. In his recollection, his staff collected "binders full of women."[1] Romney's inartful phrase reflects a longstanding problem of women's underrepresentation in political leadership. How to get women out of binders and into office, and what difference that would make, are questions central to the women's movement.

Increasing women's representation in top political offices is also critical to advancing women's representation in leadership more generally. Political leaders are role models for the nation and play crucial policy roles in addressing gender inequality. Other countries have done better than the United States in securing women's leadership in politics, and have reaped the rewards on "women's issues."

The Underrepresentation of Women in Political Leadership

Until the last several decades, women in political office were notable for their absence. The only positions in which they held significant representation were on library and school boards.[2] Overt prejudice was pervasive.

When the Gallup poll began asking whether voters would support a qualified woman for president in 1937, only a third said yes.[3] In 1932, Hattie Caraway, who had been appointed to fill the Senate vacancy left by her deceased husband, became the first woman elected to the U.S. Senate. The *Washington Post* noted that she joined a "phalanx" of female Congressional colleagues, seven to be exact, and thus "the era of women is really upon us."[4] Almost thirty years later, when the nation's third elected woman senator was opposed by another woman, *Time* magazine announced that "women permeate U.S. politics."[5] Yet in the 1970s, only two women served as governors and one as a senator. About 90 percent of state legislatures and more than 95 percent of Congress were male.[6] Until the late 1970s, women's representation in the federal cabinet was less than 1 percent.[7] Almost half of the first sixty women to win congressional elections were widows who filled their husbands' seats.[8] In explaining his reluctance to appoint women, President Richard Nixon told an aide, "I'm not for women, frankly, in any job. I don't want any of them around. Thank God we don't have any in the cabinet."[9]

When women ran for office, the tendency was to describe them in terms of their family status. For example, the *Washington Post* characterized opponents in the 1990 Texas gubernatorial race as "A 57-year-old white-haired grandmother, Ms. Richards," and "Mr. Williams, a West Texas oil man."[10] Women who achieved political leadership faced questions about their domestic responsibilities. Newly elected Congresswoman Pat Schroeder was asked by a male colleague how she could handle being both a mother and a member of the House. Schroeder reassured him that "I have a brain and a uterus and I use both."[11] For women lacking a spouse or children, some explanation was necessary. A profile of Attorney General Janet Reno in the *New York Times* noted that she "has never married or had children . . . She remains close, however, to her two brothers Robert . . . and Mark; her sister Maggy . . . and various nieces and nephews."[12] Stereotypical characterizations of women politicians were common: "tart-tongued," "screechy," "shrill," and "hectoring."[13] Outside the United States, descriptions of women leaders were similar. Indira Gandhi of India was a "dumb doll," Gro Harlem Brundtland of Norway was "nagging," and Helen Clark of New Zealand was a "political dominatrix."[14]

Today, the political landscape looks quite different. Voters no longer report discriminating against women.[15] Ninety-five percent of Americans say that they would vote for a qualified woman for president.[16] Three-quarters believe that men and women are equally qualified for political leadership, and of the remainder, 11 percent of women and 7 percent of men think women make better leaders.[17] Most Americans think that the country should have more women in elective office.[18] In commenting on women's progress, Hillary Clinton noted that she may have lost the 2008 presidential nomination, but her eighteen million votes made it a close race: "Although we weren't able to shatter that highest hardest glass ceiling this time . . . it's got about eighteen million cracks in it."[19]

Despite this progress, gender disparities in political leadership remain persistent and pervasive. Women account for just 19 percent of Congress, 25 percent of state legislatures, 12 percent of governors, and 19 percent of mayors of the nation's one hundred largest cities.[20] Women of color constitute just 6 percent of Congress, 5 percent of state legislators, 4 percent of governors, and 6 percent of the mayors of the one hundred largest cities.[21] Almost half the states have yet to elect a woman governor or U.S. senator.[22] Three states have never elected a black woman to their legislature, and only two women of color have ever served in the Senate.[23] There has never been a female secretary of defense or treasury, two of the most powerful cabinet positions.[24] Given current rates of change, it would take close to one hundred years to equalize men's and women's representation in Congress.[25] As Chapter One noted, the United States ranks ninety-seventh in the world for women's representation in national legislatures, below Bangladesh, Bulgaria, and the United Arab Emirates.[26]

At the local and party levels, women's underrepresentation can be just as bad. A profile of Los Angeles leadership found that men occupied seven out of eight of the city's top positions.[27] In political parties, the Republicans confront a shortage in female leadership. Only about a quarter of women in Congress are Republican, and only one woman figured among a long list of potential 2016 GOP presidential contenders.[28] Only seventeen Republican women have served in the Senate in its entire history.[29] When Senate Speaker John Boehner announced an all-male list of 2012 committee chairs, the ensuing outcry forced an appointment—of just one woman, to head a relatively inconsequential committee on which she had never served.[30]

The problem is not performance. Researchers consistently find that when women run for office, they are just as effective in terms of fundraising and electability.[31] They also receive about the same amount of media coverage.[32] In experimental situations, Americans rate female candidates no worse than males, and in opinion surveys, women are rated equal to or better than men on seven of eight traits useful in politics.[33]

What then, accounts for women's underrepresentation? The discussion that follows explores a number of difficulties. The first is that women are less likely than men to run for office. Other difficulties involve the political and personal challenges that discourage women from running and undermine their performance. One major obstacle is the advantage of incumbency. The overwhelming majority of incumbents in state and federal legislative positions are men, most of whom successfully seek reelection.[34] Another problem is that when women do run, they face a more challenging political landscape than men, which is partly due to the gender-related issues discussed below.[35] Women also tend to run later in life because of family responsibilities, which makes it difficult to gain the experience necessary for the highest offices.[36] Some evidence suggests that local party leaders are less likely to recruit women than men as candidates, particularly women of color, and that women are much less likely to consider running unless they are asked.[37] Twice as many female as male legislators report that they "had not seriously thought about running until someone else suggested it."[38] A final problem is that certain structural features of the American political system are not conducive to women's representation.

In accounting for why women are less likely than men to run for political office, political scientists Jennifer Lawless and Richard Fox surveyed some thirty-nine hundred potential candidates and identified recurring barriers:

- Women perceive the electoral environment as highly competitive and biased against female candidates
- Women are much less likely than men to see themselves as qualified for office

- Potential female candidates are less competitive, less confident, and more risk-averse than their male counterparts
- Women are less likely than men to receive suggestions and encouragement to run for office
- Women react more negatively than men to many of the demands of modern campaigns
- Women have disproportionate family responsibilities that interfere with the time required for successful political careers.[39]

Other research suggests women are still underrepresented in occupations such as law that are launching pads for politics, although this disparity is declining.[40] So too, although party officials (who are predominantly men) no longer display overt gender bias, they often recruit candidates from their own male-dominated networks.[41]

Although women in fact do as well as men when they run for office, the perception among women is otherwise. Seven out of ten women in Lawless and Fox's study thought that female candidates did not raise as much money as similarly situated males, and a majority thought that women did not win as often.[42] Among state legislators, only a minority of women, compared with 90 percent of men, believed that raising campaign funds money was equally difficult for men and women.[43] Sixty-two percent of Americans believe that one reason women are underrepresented in political leadership is that they are held to higher standards.[44] Many female politicians believe that they need to work harder than men to be taken seriously by colleagues and constituents, and that they face less tolerance for mistakes.[45] Congresswoman Virginia Foxx recalls in her early years in local elective office, making a motion and not having it seconded, and then watching when fifteen minutes later, a man made essentially the same motion and it passed unanimously.[46] Almost all female senators have stories of being kept out of rooms, clubs, and caucuses, and of being patronized, propositioned, and scolded for abandoning their children.[47] Women of color are particularly likely to report political marginalization.[48]

Campaign experts similarly note that female candidates face more questions of credibility and credentials. As one consultant put it, "This is just the world we live in."[49] Some research has found that female congressional candidates had to be more qualified than male opponents in order to succeed or to receive the same vote share, although recent research suggests that this qualification gap is fading.[50] Still, many female politicians agree with Charlotte Whitman, the first female mayor of Ottawa, who famously maintained: "Whatever women do, they must do twice as well as men to be thought half as good. Luckily, this is not difficult."[51] Most American women think she's right, except for the part about it not being difficult.

So too, women are more likely than men to understate their competence and qualifications.[52] Despite similar credentials, men in the Lawless and Fox study were 60 percent more likely than women to assess themselves as "very qualified" to run for office, and women were more than twice as likely as men to rate themselves as "not at all qualified."[53] Women also rated themselves lower on character traits of political relevance such as being confident, competitive, risk-taking, entrepreneurial, and thick-skinned.[54] Compared with men, women were less likely to receive encouragement to run for political office, both from political officials and activists, and from family and colleagues.[55] In addition, women had more negative feelings than men did toward certain aspects of campaigning, such as fundraising, going door-to-door to meet constituents, possibly needing to engage in negative campaigning, losing privacy, and sacrificing time with family.[56]

In commenting on these obstacles, some female politicians regret not being more proactive in their formative years. Former Michigan governor and attorney general Jennifer Granholm observed: "The most significant obstacle has been my own foot on the brakes, especially when I was younger. I was not as aggressive as I might have been in pursuing positions; indeed, I was rather passive and was fortunate that others approached me."[57] So too, when asked about the barriers to women in politics, former Arizona governor and U.S. cabinet secretary Janet Napolitano noted that "when you are in elected politics, you have to develop a thick skin pretty fast and give up a lot of personal privacy. I don't think we prepare women to do that and to let things roll off their backs."[58]

Women also walk a difficult line in coping with gender stereotypes. Voters have traditionally associated characteristics of toughness and strength with men, and many have favored these traits in political leaders over characteristics associated with women, such as compassion and morality.[59] Sixty-one percent of Americans believe that a male candidate is better equipped to handle military crises; only 3 percent think that a female candidate is.[60] However, Katherine Dolan's recent research on congressional races suggested that this maybe changing; voters did not evaluate male and female candidates differently on trustworthiness, competence, and leadership, and that gender stereotypes were not a significant influence on voter behavior.[61] Nor did women and men politicians position themselves to capitalize on stereotypical expectations.[62] Party affiliation and incumbency were much more critical than gender in determining the outcomes of House and Senate races.[63]

Yet as other evidence suggests, female candidates confront challenges that men do not. As one researcher notes: "Women politicians and leaders often experience double binds because they encounter conflicting expectations. On the one hand, they are supposed to comply with the female role by promoting women's demands and being cooperative, warm and altruistic. On the other hand, they are supposed to comply with the role of politician by . . . being self-assertive, competent and competitive."[64] Kim Campbell, Canada's first female prime minister, noted the problem: "I don't have a traditionally female way of speaking. . . . I'm quite assertive. If I didn't speak the way I do, I wouldn't have been seen as a leader. But my way of speaking may have grated on people not used to hearing it from a woman. It was the right way for a leader to speak, but it wasn't the right way for a woman to speak. It goes against type."[65] In the 2013 New York mayoral race, lesbian Christine Quinn was described as "bossy," "combative," and not "feminine" enough.[66] Other women candidates similarly report being derailed for being too "tough."[67]

The result is to leave women facing a double standard and a double bind. What is "hard hitting" in a male candidate can look "shrill" in a woman, and female candidates can face charges that "they're not tough enough to be in charge or they're too bitchy to be."[68] In Kelly Dittmar's recent survey of campaign behavior, consultants believed that female candidates confronted conflicting demands to fit a masculine ideal while upholding femininity.[69] As one consultant wrote, "To ignore gender in strategy, message, and how one deals with an opponent is malpractice."[70] In commenting on women's challenge, one pollster quipped that the ideal female candidate for president would be a "combination of Jack the Ripper and Mother Teresa."[71]

The double standard has been on display in recent presidential campaigns. In 2011, when Michele Bachmann was seeking the Republican nomination for president, *Time* magazine put an unflattering picture of her on its cover over a headline that labeled her "The Queen of Rage."[72] Hillary Clinton has long been dogged by concerns that she is "cunning," "savage," and "pushy"—a "lady Macbeth in a headband."[73] In 2008, Obama famously dismissed Clinton's challenges in negotiating the toughness-likeability tradeoff with the comment, "You're likable enough, Hillary."[74]

The double standard figured in the 2016 race as well. Trump denounced Clinton as "shrill."[75] He also claimed that if she were a man and she was "the way she is, she would get virtually no votes."[76] This prompted the observation by *New York Times* columnist Gail Collins, "Do not ask yourself how many votes Donald Trump would get if he were a woman and he was the way he is. Truly, you don't want to go there."[77] Commentators similarly observed that if Bernie Sanders were a woman, he couldn't get away with "shouting constantly. Scowling on TV. Sounding grumpy. Looking frumpy."[78] When told that one young voter liked Sanders because his hair was a mess and he yelled a lot, Clinton commented, "Boy, that would really work for any women we know."[79] In another interview, Clinton noted that she and other female politicians fret about how to "navigate what is still a relatively narrow path, to express yourself, to let your feelings show, but not in a way that triggers all of the negative stereotypes . . . You have to be aware of how people will judge you for being, quote, 'emotional,' and so it's a really delicate balancing act."[80] When asked more generally about gender bias in political campaigns, Hillary Clinton responded: "Sexism is maybe less pronounced, less obvious, but it is still prevalent in our political scene. . . . [T]here's still a double standard, there's no doubt about that. I see it all the time where women are just expected to combine traits and qualities in a way that men are not. And it does make running for office for a woman a bigger challenge."[81]

Women also shoulder disproportionate family obligations, which affects their political aspirations. As Chapter One notes, those disparities persist in dual career couples. Women are six times more likely than men to bear responsibility for the majority of household tasks, and about ten times more likely to be the primary child-care provider.[82] The demands of politics, such as travel, irregular hours, and evening and weekend events, are hard to reconcile with significant caretaking responsibilities.[83] The perception lingers in some quarters that, as Bella Abzug once told Representative Patricia Schroeder, "You have little kids. . . . You won't be able to do this job."[84] In recent congressional and mayoral races in New Hampshire, Illinois, and California, female candidates were asked whether being elected would leave them with enough time to be a good mother to their children.[85] During her vice-presidential campaign, Sarah Palin was widely criticized for subordinating the needs of her child with Down's syndrome.[86]

To be sure, those criticisms are declining as more women with young children are seen as successful in the political arena. Some female candidates have effectively capitalized on the image of "Mamma Grizzly" that Sarah Palin popularized.[87] New Hampshire Senator Kelly Ayotte cast herself as the Granite Grizzly and portrayed her motherhood as a qualification for office.[88] Yet the problems in juggling obligations persist. New Hampshire Senator Jeanne Shaheen recalls that she was once asked to address a group of women on work-life balance. And after a few days of work on the speech, she realized she couldn't deliver it, because she didn't have a real strategy. "My idea of work/life balance has been learning to live with the guilt."[89] But just as having a family presents problems, so too does being unmarried or childless. In the view of some voters, a woman who does not choose to have children does not seem quite normal.[90] So whatever their family situation, traditional gender expectations make running for office more challenging for women.

Comparative research also reveals structural features of the American political system that work against women. Female candidates do better in nations that have systems of proportional representation, which allocate legislative seats on the basis of the number of votes each party received. Women also do better where party control is strong and politicians are "more or less interchangeable representatives of party platforms."[91] By contrast, the United States has a simple majoritarian system and politicians depend more on personal visibility and credibility. Seniority is often critical in establishing those credentials. Women do less well in part because they suffer greater penalties for interrupting their political career or starting it later due to family responsibilities.[92]

In addition, women face more primary opposition, perhaps because they are perceived as more vulnerable than men.[93] Whatever the reason, women confront a more difficult primary terrain, which may discourage some from running for office.

Some women are also deterred or undermined by the heightened scrutiny and gendered barbs that they encounter as politicians.[94] In commenting on the "excess[ive] criticism and sharper microscope" turned on women, Sarah Palin maintained that to "whine" about it did no good. "Fair or unfair, it is there. I think that's reality, and it think it's a given . . . [that women need to] work harder."[95] During debate in the New York senatorial race, Senator Kirsten Gillibrand and Republican candidate Wendy Long were asked whether they had read *Fifty Shades of Grey*. The *Atlantic's* David Graham commented, "Yes that's right, when you get two powerful women together for their one and only political debate, they're forced to discuss S&M erotica. . . . Would anyone ask two male candidates if they had subscriptions to *Playboy*?"[96]

The particular venom directed at Hillary Clinton is a cautionary tale. Neil Cavuto of Fox News *Your World* declared, "Men won't vote for Hillary Clinton because she reminds them of their nagging wives. And when Hillary Clinton speaks, we hear 'Take out the garbage.' "[97] Other commentators criticized her "cackle," and her "abrasive," "irritating," "scolding," and "Hitlerian" manner.[98] References to her as a "ball breaker" and "castrator" aired on cable television, and a Hillary nutcracker was sold as a novelty item.[99] Tucker Carlson claimed that "when she comes on television, I involuntarily cross my legs."[100] Other commentators criticized her for enabling her husband's sexual misconduct and demonizing his victims. Chris Matthews of MSNBC claimed that the only reason Hillary Clinton was a U.S. senator and candidate for president was "that her husband messed around . . . She did not win . . . on her merit.[101] That journalists felt entitled to make such comments speaks volumes about the differential tolerance of racism and sexism in political campaigns. After two men at a Clinton rally yelled out, "Iron my shirts," Anna Quindlen observed that the most striking aspect of the incident was that the "jeers got little coverage. If someone at an Obama rally had called out a similar remark based on racial bigotry—'shine my shoes,' perhaps—not only would it have been a story, it would have run on page one."[102]

Women's appearance also attracts special scrutiny. The problem is longstanding. When Geraldine Ferraro stood before the Democratic national convention, anchor Tom Brokaw announced, "The first woman to be nominated for vice president . . . Size six."[103] Hillary Clinton's occasional show of cleavage and her preference for pantsuits has received widespread comment, including television star Tim Gunn's observation that she "dresses like she's confused about her gender."[104] A YouTube video of a Kentucky Fried Chicken bucket featured "Hillary Meal Deal: 2 Fat Thighs, 2 Small Breasts, and a Bunch of Left Wings." That image figured on buttons during the 2016 presidential campaign.[105] Clinton herself claimed that during her time as First Lady, "If I change[d] my hairstyles I [could] knock anything off the first page of the paper."[106] Even interviews with her hair stylist received prominent media coverage.[107]

Other women have faced similar scrutiny. Wisconsin Congressman Jim Sensenbrenner chastised First Lady Michelle Obama because "she lectures us on eating right while she has a large posterior herself."[108] Representative Michele Bachmann was criticized for wearing too much makeup to a political debate.[109] Congressional candidate Krystal Ball was condemned for sexually suggestive college pictures.[110] Elizabeth Warren was told that she had a "school marm" appearance, and that she came across in ads as a "smarter than thou older woman sporting granny glasses and sensible hair."[111] President Obama gave Kamala Harris the backhanded compliment of being the "best looking attorney general in the country."[112] Donald Trump asked about Carly Fiorina, "Look at that face! Would anyone vote for that?"[113] (He later implausibly claimed that he was talking about her "persona," not her looks).[114] Vice presidential candidate Sarah Palin received extensive attention for her beauty pageant history as well as severe criticism for the cost of her campaign-financed wardrobe.[115] It speaks volumes about our culture's misplaced priorities, as well the pressures facing female candidates, that Palin's campaign spent more on her makeup specialist than on her foreign policy advisor.[116]

Comments about women's appearance are often trivialized, and women who call them out are often criticized as whiny or humorless. Yet studies show that any comments made about a female candidate's appearance, regardless of their content, negatively influence public opinion.[117] Even if those opinions do not drive political behavior, demeaning press coverage may contribute to women's reluctance to expose themselves to potentially bruising political campaigns.

Women may also be deterred or undermined by media portrayals of female candidates as less intelligent or mainstream than male candidates. Sarah Palin, Nancy Pelosi, and Hillary Clinton have been characterized as "crackpot," "lunatic," "diva," "wackjob" "air head," "dilettante" and "feminazi."[118] A *Saturday Night Live* parody famously summarized Palin's foreign policy experience as "being able to see Russia from my house."[119] To survive in politics, women need a thick skin. As one leader put it, "The first time I was called an idiot, it was really upsetting. Now I just think, 'You're an idiot, too.'"[120]

The Difference "Difference" Makes

These gender barriers take on special importance if, as noted earlier, most Americans believe that having more women in office would be better for the country. Claims about the difference that gender difference makes in politics are longstanding. A century ago, Rheta Childe Dorr's *What Eight Million Women Want* envisioned a world in which women's "special capabilities" were fully realized in the work of governing. The result, she asserted, would be that the "city will be like a great, well-ordered comfortable sanitary household. There will be no slums, no sweatshops, no sad women and children toiling in tenement rooms. . . . All the family will be taken care of, [and] taught to take care of themselves. . . ."[121] Supporters of women's suffrage similarly cast women as municipal housekeepers, whose "high code of morals" would "purify politics."[122] Disillusionment quickly set in, but convictions that women bring special strengths to the political process persist. In announcing her candidacy for the U.S. Senate, Blanche Lambert Lincoln explained that she was running because "nearly one of every three senators is a millionaire, but there are only five mothers."[123]

The argument for women's increased representation in political leadership rests on two premises. The first, based on descriptive representation, is that the presence of women is important in and of itself on symbolic grounds. It helps confer legitimacy on governing institutions and provides female role models. The more women who are visible at various leadership levels, the more likely girls are to indicate an interest in becoming politically active as adults, which will broaden the nation's pool of potential leaders.[124] A second premise, based on substantive representation, is that the participation of women increases the likelihood both that women's interests will be adequately represented and that governing institutions will function more effectively due to women's distinctive backgrounds and governing styles.

The assumption that women would and should represent women's special interests is a relatively recent phenomenon. Early female politicians tended to avoid identification with women's issues.[125] California Senator Barbara Boxer wryly described the traditional approach of female candidates: "You never mentioned being a woman . . . you hoped nobody noticed."[126] Contemporary female politicians are more likely to see themselves as representing women, but with limited consensus on what that representation entails.[127] Women do not speak with a single voice, and what constitutes "women's interests" is not always self-evident. Yet even if, as I have argued elsewhere, it is possible to find common ground around many issues central to women's well-being, the question remaining is whether putting more women in office is a reliable way of advancing that agenda.[128]

Although it obviously depends which women are elected, most evidence suggests that their greater presence in political leadership makes a difference, particularly in getting women's issues onto the agenda. Both in Congress and in state legislatures, women are more likely than men to address women's issues, to rank them as priorities, and to spend political capital on their behalf.[129] Some studies also suggest that greater women's representation leads to more women-friendly policies in state-by-state comparisons.[130] Female legislators also have closer ties to women's organizations, connections that cross party lines and increase the likelihood that women's interests will be considered.[131] Women of color are particularly likely to champion issues of special concern to women and communities of color.[132] A case in point on the difference that difference makes is the national Women's Health Initiative. Women in Congress asked the General Accounting Office to audit spending by the National Institutes of Health. The audit revealed that only 13 percent of funds were spent on women's health. As a result, congressional women on both sides of the aisle successfully pushed for greater funding for women's health care and research.[133]

So too, many women in the executive branch here and abroad have made major strides in advocating women's concerns. As secretaries of state, Madeleine Albright and Hillary Clinton made women's rights a priority. In the 1980s, Norway's first woman prime minister, Gro Harlem Brundtland, caused a worldwide sensation when she championed reproductive rights and appointed women as 44 percent of her second cabinet.[134] In Chile, Michelle Bachelet appointed a cabinet that was half women and put forward an array of women-friendly proposals.[135] New Zealand Prime Minister Helen Clark pushed for measures such as paid parental leave, child care, and a unit for gender equality in the Human Rights Commission.[136]

Yet gender differences in political priorities should not be overstated. Researchers frequently find no consistent relationship between greater gender equality in political representation and greater gender equality in social policies or outcomes.[137] In the United States, party affiliation is more important than gender in predicting legislators' votes on women's issues, and ideology is more important than gender in predicting sponsorship of legislation on these issues.[138] As researchers note, the number of women in legislatures matters less than the extent to which the women members identify with women's issues.[139]

Conservative Republican women often play a leading role in opposing legislation on matters such as reproductive rights and equal pay. When asked if Congress would be more likely to pass the Paycheck Fairness Act if there were more women members, Representative Rosa DeLauro's short answer was "No." It matters who those women are. "We've never been able to engage the Republican women," DeLauro explained. "As a matter of fact, they're the people who get up on the floor and speak against [the act.]"[140] As politics has grown more polarized in recent years, it has become increasingly difficult to get women to cross party lines in support of women's issues. Coalitions are likely only on uncontroversial proposals, such as expanded treatment for autistic children of armed service members or violence against women in the military.[141] Moderate Republican women are in a particularly difficult position; it is hard to advance within the party and influence its agenda without toeing the conservative line on gender-related matters.[142] It was no coincidence that Carly Fiorina, the only female Republican candidate in the 2016 presidential race, was adamantly prolife and opposed to funding for Planned Parenthood.[143]

Many female politicians also want to avoid too much affiliation with women's issues "both because they want to be recognized as representing all the people . . . and [because] they believe that it undermines their potential power in the institution."[144] As one Senate staffer noted, "You don't want to scare off men or have them be threatened by you. You do not wave the banner of women's rights in their face."[145] For this reason, some female legislators prefer committee assignments that aren't aligned with "soft" issues associated with women.[146] Women also worry about accusations that they are playing the "gender card." The charge has dogged Hillary Clinton, and has come not only from Donald Trump, but even from other women, including Carly Fiorina, who also faced the claim.[147] "People should not be voting for candidates based on their gender," said Bernie Sanders, and his supporters lambasted Clinton advocates for "voting with their vaginas."[148]

Clinton herself has been clear that "I'm not asking people to support me because I'm a woman [but because] I'm the most qualified, experienced and ready person to be the president."[149] But she also has embraced women's issues, and responded to one of Donald Trump's charges with the acknowledgment, "Well, if fighting for women's health care and paid family leave and equal pay is playing the 'woman card,' then deal me in."[150] Clinton has further claimed that women bring special strengths to public office. As she told one interviewer, "I just think women in general are better listeners, are more collegial, more open to new ideas and how to make things work in a way that looks for win-win outcomes."[151]

Evidence on that point is mixed. Some research finds few gender differences in political leadership style or approach.[152] Although female politicians often claim that women are more likely than men to be collaborative and conciliatory, profiles of major women leaders here and abroad do not always bear this out.[153] Margaret Thatcher, Golda Meir, and Indira Gandhi were not known for conciliatory styles. Thatcher was famous for her arrogance and intolerance of dissent.[154] "I am not a consensus politician," she once declared. "I am a conviction politician."[155] As one historian noted, "Mrs. Thatcher simply didn't behave as men thought a woman should behave. She was rude, she shouted, she interrupted, she was tough, she was ruthless. . . ."[156] This assisted her because many men in her cabinet "simply didn't know how to deal with an assertive woman, especially one in a position of political superiority."[157] Thatcher embraced the label of Iron Lady, and distanced herself from women's issues. As she once put it, "I don't notice that I'm a woman." She also claimed that the "battle for women's rights has been largely won. The days when they were demanded and discussed in strident tones should be gone forever. And I hope they are. I hated those strident tones you hear from some 'women's libbers.'"[158] A biographer described her as an "honorary man."[159] Similarly, Indira Gandhi had an authoritarian approach and did little to advance gender equality.[160] Golda Meir's domineering style led her to be described as "the only man in the Ben Gurion government."[161] In her autobiography, Meir assigns gender a minor role. She was not a "great admirer of the kind of feminism that gives rise to bra burning," and believed that "being a woman has never hindered me in any way at all."[162] These women exemplified the view that Eleanor Roosevelt once expressed: if women wanted to succeed in politics, they had to "learn to play the game as men do."[163]

Yet more recent examples suggest that many American women politicians are interested in playing a different game. As Jay Newton-Small's profile put it, they "tend to compromise more and grandstand less. They are better at building consensus" and putting "ego aside in search of a greater goal."[164] Forty percent of American voters believe that female politicians are better able to develop consensus.[165] Women's tendency toward participatory styles of leadership is an asset in many political contexts such as budget processes and bipartisan coalition building.[166] It is widely reported that female state legislators adopt more-collaborative, consensual styles than men and that women in Congress have an approach that is "more collaboration, less confrontation; more problem-solving, less ego; more consensus building, less partisanship."[167] For example, during the government shutdown in the fall of 2013, congressional women played a pivotal role in brokering a solution. A cottage industry of commentary echoed the views of a *Time* magazine article titled "Women Are the Only Adults Left in Washington."[168] French Finance Minister Christine Lagarde famously claimed that "women inject less libido and less testosterone into the equation."[169] Many Americans watching the 2016 Republican presidential debates undoubtedly agreed. No woman leader has come close to the female equivalent of Donald Trump's reassurance to the nation about the size of his penis.[170]

Strategies for Change

To identify strategies for change, an obvious first step is to clarify the kind of change the nation is looking for. Is the goal simply to increase the number of women in political leadership? Or is it to advance women's interests more generally, and to develop women's leadership as a means to that end? Placing more women in power, regardless of their styles or ideologies, can have some benefit by creating role models for the next generation. But in the long run, the best way to achieve gender parity in political leadership is through recruitment and support of female candidates who will make gender equity a policy priority.[171] Expanding women's political opportunities will require addressing the broader sources of sex-based inequality, such as gender stereotypes and gender disparities in family responsibilities. Examples such as Margaret Thatcher remind us that simply putting women in power does not necessarily empower women as a group. To advance gender equality, more votes and dollars must be targeted at politicians committed to that objective.

Strategies for increasing women in political leadership fall into two general categories. The most effective but least politically plausible are structural changes in the political system, such as switching to a system of proportional representation or imposing quotas for women's representation. As noted earlier, women do better under proportional representation systems.[172] They also benefit from quotas, which about a hundred countries have adopted in some form, although not all are sufficiently ambitious or well enforced to make a difference.[173] Some quotas reserve a certain percentage of seats in the governing body for women, and some require all parties to field a certain percentage of female candidates or nominees. In many countries, quotas have brought substantial progress.[174] Persistent exposure to female politicians has increased voters' willingness to support them.[175] Globally, women's representation in parliaments has more than doubled since the mid-1990s.[176] This growth has, in turn, helped expand the pool of women qualified to serve as cabinet ministers, whose representation has also more than doubled.[177] However, in this country, quotas and proportional representation have been nonstarters, and Americans do not seem likely to change that view.

Accordingly, attention should focus on strategies designed to increase women's willingness and capacity to run for office, and to remove obstacles that stand in the way. For example, more support should go to organizations that provide mentoring and resources for aspiring women politicians. Former Michigan governor Jennifer Granholm did not find local mentors, but was fortunate to "team up with an organization [the Barbara Lee Foundation in Massachusetts] that provided me with strategies and recommendations for success, and connected me with other elected women. That exposure was terrific."[178] A growing number of nonprofit groups are available to provide such assistance.[179] Examples include: Ready to Run, VoteRunLead, Political Institute for Women, Yale Women's Campaign School, Emerge America, Project GoPink, She Should Run, and the National Federation of Republican Women.[180] The Center for American Women and Politics' Ready to Run Diversity Initiative offers specific workshops for African American women, Asian American women, and Latina women. These workshops help women of color build networks, identify role models, and develop campaign strategies.[181] However, many of these initiatives are grossly underfunded.[182] They deserve greater financial support from those who care about women's leadership.

More initiatives should target younger women as well. Differences in political ambition start early. In high schools, more than twice as many male as female students indicated that they would consider running for office when they were older.[183] A case history that attracted national attention is Phillips Exeter Academy, an elite prep school that has had only four girls as president of the student body in forty years.[184] On college campuses, women are a majority of students but hold only a minority of student leadership positions.[185] At Princeton, for example, women constituted 50 percent of undergraduates, but held only 14 percent of the top leadership positions.[186] Male college students are twice as likely as female students to report that they definitely plan to run for office at some point in the future, and are also substantially more likely to be open to upper-level political offices (president, member of Congress, and mayor).[187] The problem is not lack of interest in politics. Female students score higher in political knowledge than their male counterparts.[188] The main difficulties, rather, are that female students are not encouraged and socialized to think about a political career, and they lack confidence in their qualifications and ability.[189] As one young woman put it, "I just don't feel smart enough regarding politics."[190]

More efforts could focus on encouraging and training this next generation of women leaders. So, for example, the Girl Scouts' national organization has partnered with congressional offices and federal agencies to run an internship program for high school students. It has also launched other initiatives that enlist girls in solving local community problems.[191] The Center for American Women and Politics has established "Teach a Girl to Lead, a national education and awareness campaign that makes resources available to parents, teachers, librarians, and students.[192] The center also runs the NEW Leadership program, which offers summer institutes for college women. These institutes emphasize the value of civic engagement and the importance of having women in positions of political leadership.[193] Elect Her: Campus Women Win is an initiative that attempts to convince more female college students to run for student government. Additional funding and outreach by such programs could feed the pipeline for future office holders. It could also help address the gender gap in political advisory positions. Women are underrepresented among congressional staff and consultants working on federal and gubernatorial campaigns.[194] Opening more opportunities for women in these roles could expand the pipeline for leadership positions.

So too, political parties could do more to recruit women and to dispel the myth that they are less electable. More individuals could contribute to funds such as Emily's List, which provides support to Democratic female candidates, and to other initiatives that equip women for office.[195]

More positive, less gendered portrayals of female politicians in the press and entertainment media could also encourage women's political ambition. Efforts such as Name It. Change It, a nonpartisan project of She Should Run, the Women's Media Center, and Political Parity, can help monitor coverage of sexism in political campaigns and call out those responsible.[196] Candidates and their supporters need to do the same. Examples of effective responses include Washington Senator Patty Murray's decision to turn an insult from a state legislator into a campaign slogan. She embraced the label of a "mom in tennis shoes."[197] During Kathleen Sebelius's campaign for governor of Kansas, her campaign protested when a reporter described her pink toenail polish and her opponent's policy positions. Sebelius's press secretary called the reporter and asked how he would feel if his own daughter were treated that way.[198] Hillary Clinton has similarly responded to sexism with a mix of humor and stoicism. Her website offers a hot pink "women's card" and totebag proclaiming "Girls Just Wanna Have a Fun-da-mental Rights."[199] When a male pundit accused her of "shrieking" during her speech following the 2016 Iowa caucus, Clinton observed, "We are still living with a double standard, and I know it. Every woman I know knows it. . . . I don't know anything other to do than to just keep forging through it and just taking the slings and arrows that come with being a woman in the arena."[200]

To make that arena more welcoming, we also need a strong women's movement. Activism is essential to build support for gender equity initiatives and the women politicians who support them.[201] Cross-national research finds that the presence of such a movement is a better predictor of women's rights policies than the proportion of women's representation in legislatures.[202] A revitalized movement must more effectively respond to the needs of particularly disadvantaged subgroups. Research confirms what common sense suggests: women's groups, like other public interest organizations, tend to focus on the concerns of their funding base. Less attention goes to issues that disproportionately affect those disadvantaged by race, class, sexual orientation, or related factors.[203] In one study of women's rights organizations, an interviewed staff member put it bluntly: welfare reform is "really just not our cup of tea."[204] To alter those priorities, women's organizations need to find more ways of making issues that are of concern to the disadvantaged also of concern to more women leaders.

The women's movement also needs to do a better job in connecting with young women about the importance of gender in political contexts. The 2016 presidential campaign drew attention to the generational schism among women, particularly among those who support a progressive agenda.[205] The problem was captured by one African American female college student who explained her support for Bernie Sanders over Hillary Clinton with the observation, "I don't find gender that important."[206] Feminists need to do better in addressing those views and communicating the case for more women in political leadership.

None of this will be easy. But the last half century has witnessed dramatic changes in the nation's willingness to elect women leaders. When women run, women can win. The challenge now is to convince more women of that fact, to address the obstacles in their way, and to support those who make gender equity a political priority.

WOMEN IN MANAGEMENT

A half century ago, the *Harvard Business Review* ran a survey of leaders titled "Are Women Executives People?" It found that 41 percent were "anti-woman executive" in principle, and only about a quarter would be comfortable working for a woman.[1] Around the same time, some recruiters on college campuses posted signs, "No women need apply."[2] In 1969, when Katharine Graham became the first woman CEO of a Fortune 500 company, a position she inherited at the *Washington Post* after the death of her husband, she was totally unprepared. Not only was she unable to understand a balance sheet, she had not anticipated the sexism she encountered. Early into her role, when asked to speak on the status of women, she responded that the subject was one in which she was "honestly not interested or educated."[3] Later, as she grew more aware that the business world "was essentially closed to women," she thought "things would grow better with time ... particularly when there were more women involved and less notice was given to any single one of us, but it didn't happen that way. For one thing, there never were that many more of us—and still aren't, at least not at the highest levels."[4]

Graham's assessment is still correct. The facts are frustratingly familiar. As Chapter One noted, women constitute a third of MBA graduates, but only 4 percent of Fortune 500 CEOs.[5] There are more men named John running S&P 1500 companies than there are women.[6] In finance and insurance, women are almost half of middle managers but only 17 percent of senior managers in the largest firms.[7] Globally, women hold less than a quarter of senior management roles, the stepping-stone to CEO positions.[8] And in the United States, women of color account for 19 percent of the population but only 4 percent of the executives or senior-level management in S&P companies.[9] A Catalyst report summarized the situation in its title: *Still No Progress After Years of No Progress.*[10] At current rates of change, Chapter One pointed out that it could take more than a century to achieve parity in executive suites.[11]

Gender Bias

How much of women's underrepresentation is attributable to gender bias is a matter of dispute. On being appointed as CEO of Hewlett Packard in 1999, Carly Fiorina famously said, "I hope that we are at the point that everyone has figured out that there is not a glass ceiling."[12] After being fired from that position, Fiorina saw things differently: "After striving my entire career to be judged by results and accomplishments, the coverage of my gender, my appearance and the perceptions of my personality would vastly outweigh anything else."[13]

Fiorina is not alone in her perceptions. To be sure, the workplace has improved considerably over the last quarter century, and female managers are no longer routinely asked to make copies or coffee.[14] In a 2015 Pew Research Center study, four out of five Americans say that men and women make equally good business leaders. And substantial minorities believe that women are better in some respects: they are more honest and ethical, and better mentors.[15] Yet only a quarter of women in upper management and executive positions believe that they have an opportunity to be promoted on the same timeline as men.[16] Half of Americans think that a reason more women are not in top business positions is that women are held to higher standards and have to do more to prove themselves; half think businesses aren't ready to hire women for those positions.[17] A wide variety of research suggests that these perceptions are well founded. Objective qualifications alone cannot account for women's underrepresentation at the top.[18] Differences in promotions persist even after controlling for relevant factors such as education and work experience.[19] Indeed, in one survey of more than seven thousand executives, women rated higher than men on twelve of sixteen traits identified as important to leadership.[20] In another survey of feedback data on sixteen thousand leaders, women were rated above men on overall effectiveness.[21] Yet those capabilities have not been matched by leadership opportunities. A survey of more than four thousand MBAs found, after controlling for relevant factors, that men started at higher levels than women and received higher pay and more promotions.[22] It takes greater education and experience for women to become CEOs than for men.[23] In experimental situations in which participants receive written descriptions of managerial behavior that differ only in the sex of the leader, women are evaluated less favorably than men, particularly for male-dominated leadership roles.[24] In one Harvard Business School experiment, MBAs were given two case studies, identical except that in one the CEO was named John and in the other was named Jane. Students rated Jane more negatively.[25] In other research, male MBAs perceived men as more likely than women to possess management characteristics.[26] So too, credit for team success is more often given to male than female members.[27]

In large-scale surveys of senior executive women, the most frequently cited obstacle to advancement is "male stereotyping and preconceptions."[28] The force of these stereotypes is apparent in experimental situations where male and female performance is objectively equal, but women are held to higher standards, and their competence is rated lower.[29] Resumes are rated more favorably when they carry male rather than female names.[30] Subjects who receive identical employee profiles except for gender give men higher bonuses even if meritocratic values are stressed.[31] These biases are particularly acute for women of color. Asians are often thought technically competent, but lacking in leadership potential, and other minorities are assumed to be beneficiaries of special treatment rather than meritocratic selection.[32]

Many women recount examples of lacking the presumption of competence enjoyed by white men. Carly Fiorina recalls the time when a male boss told her flat out that, although people assumed that *he* must be pretty good or else he wouldn't be in the job he was in, they didn't assume that about *her*. "You have to convince them. . . . [T]his was the first time it ever occurred to me that my gender alone could deny me the presumption of competence."[33] The absence of that presumption helps account for why 61 percent of female executives reported having been mistaken for a secretary at a business meeting.[34] At a small dinner Steve Jobs hosted for then-President Bill Clinton, one of the guests asked Carol Bartz, former CEO of Yahoo, to get him a cup of tea.[35] Deborah Gillis, president of Catalyst, recalls being at a meeting in which the organization's leader mistook a prominent international trade attorney for a secretary who could bring him a glass of water. On being told of his mistake, he paused, "and without missing a beat replied, 'It's so tough these days, the lawyers look like secretaries, and the secretaries look like lawyers.' "[36]

So too, in managerial contexts, decision makers generally see women as more suited for jobs involving human relations than those involving high-visibility projects and line responsibilities for profits and losses.[37] The absence of such line experience is the major reason given by CEOs for women's underrepresentation in leadership positions.[38] Women are also assigned a disproportionate share of what Harvard Professor Rosabeth Moss Kanter labeled "office housekeeping"—tasks that have low visibility, status, and rewards, such as committee work and informal advising. Research shows that, as Sheryl Sandberg and Adam Grant observed, "women help more but benefit less from it." Men get more credit for taking on office housekeeping than women, and face less backlash for saying no. "A man who doesn't help is 'busy' "; a woman is "selfish."[39]

Moreover, for women, effective performance does not necessarily suggest leadership potential. In one recent study of twenty-eight hundred managers, supervisors who rated female subordinates somewhat higher than men in current competence still rated the women lower in long-term leadership potential.[40]

Lack of tolerance for mistakes also impedes women's advancement and makes them more risk-averse than men.[41] A *Harvard Business Review* survey reports that women leaders are more isolated than men and often "find it impossible to rally support in the wake of failure. More so than men, they crash and burn."[42] As one manager noted, "In my company, mistakes and missteps are rarely tolerated to the same degree for women as for men. A promising male may have two to three opportunities . . .

and will be tagged as 'ballsy' for taking on a difficult project, even if he fails. Women will be tagged as incapable or 'not yet ready' when they fail in the same situation."[43] As Gail McGovern, president of the American Red Cross, puts it, women leaders are "in a fishbowl. They are held to higher standards."[44]

Partly as a response to these gender biases, men consistently overestimate their abilities and performance, and women underestimate both.[45] A Hewlett-Packard study found that women applied for promotions only when they believed that they met 100 percent of the qualifications necessary for the job; men were willing to apply when they met 60 percent.[46]

Women also suffer from the mismatch between the qualities associated with leadership and the qualities viewed as attractive in women.[47] The "great man" model of leadership is still with us, and the term has seldom been used generically. Most characteristics associated with leaders are masculine: dominance, authority, assertiveness, and so forth.[48] In recent years, this disjuncture between traditional femininity and leadership has lessened somewhat. Women are becoming more like men in their career aspirations and achievements.[49] More women now occupy highly visible leadership roles, and recent theories of leadership have stressed the importance of interpersonal qualities commonly attributed to women, such as cooperation and collaboration.[50]

Yet despite these trends, traditional gender stereotypes still leave women with a double standard and a double bind. As Chapter One noted, behavior that is assertive in a man seems abrasive in a woman, and women risk seeming too assertive or not assertive enough. Aggressive women are viewed as unpleasant to work with or for, and have difficulty enlisting respect, support, and cooperation from coworkers.[51] "Attila the Hen" and "the Dragon Lady" are common labels.[52] Only two women appear on a list of the fifty-one rated CEOs that employees enjoy working for.[53] Indeed, some executive coaches have developed a market niche in rehabilitating "bully broads," female managers who come across as insufficiently feminine.[54] Carly Fiorina recalls that when she was the CEO of Hewlett-Packard, she was routinely referred to as a " 'bimbo' or a 'bitch'—too soft or too hard, and presumptuous besides."[55] Sally Krawcheck, former head of wealth management at Bank of America and former chief financial officer at Citigroup, notes that "men can show temper and people do a 'mental eye roll' and move on." But she can "count on one hand, on one finger, the number of tantrums I've seen a woman have. As she was having it, I remember thinking to myself, Bitchy. . . . Women need to operate in narrower emotional channels than men."[56] A marketing communications manager for a major international firm was told that she was a "bitch" but that if she were a man, it "wouldn't be a problem."[57] At a global retail company, when women spoke up to defend their turf, "they were vilified. They were labeled 'control freaks'; men acting the same way were called passionate."[58]

In environments where men are dominating and confrontational, women risk being dismissed as "pushy" if they try to be heard by engaging in similar behavior.[59] Male CEOs who speak up often in meetings are rated higher in competence than female counterparts who do the same.[60] A study of performance reviews in the tech field found that negative comments about personality—such as being too abrasive— showed up in only twice in eighty-four critical reviews received by men and seventy-one of the ninety-four critical reviews received by women.[61] Other research on the tech field found that 84 percent of women had gotten feedback that they were too aggressive, 53 percent that they were too quiet, and 44 percent that they were both.[62] Similarly, in a study by Stanford's Clayman Institute for Research on Women and Gender, female employees received two and a half times the amount of feedback as their male colleagues concerning an aggressive communication style.[63] Men's reviews had about twice as many positive comments related to assertiveness and self-confidence. When study participants were asked which of two candidates they would pick for a top position, about 90 percent selected the person described in terms related to individual initiative, the same terms that turned up more often in the men's performance reviews.[64] Geraldine Laybourne, president of Disney/ABC Cable Networks, asked whether men calling Mattel CEO Jill Barad too abrasive "have . . . met Ted Turner? Have they met Michael Eisner? Compared to most CEOs she is not abrasive. But maybe compared to their wives she is."[65]

Self-promotion is also disproportionately punished in women.[66] A telling business school experiment illustrated the problem. It gave participants a case study about a leading venture capitalist with outstanding networking skills. Half the participants were told that the individual was Howard Roizen; the other half were told that the individual was Heidi Roizen. The participants rated the entrepreneurs as equally competent but found Howard more likeable, genuine, and kind, and Heidi more aggressive, self-promoting, and power-hungry.[67] Even talking too much can penalize women. Yale School of Management Professor Victoria Brescoll asked male and female participants to rate a hypothetical CEO who talked more than others. Both sexes viewed a female CEO as less competent and less suited to leadership than a male CEO who talked for the same amount of time. When the fictitious female CEO was described as talking less than others, her perceived competence shot up.[68]

Even the most accomplished women are subject to the double standard. One leader now widely acclaimed for her efforts to regulate high-risk derivatives while chair of the Commodity Futures Commission, was dismissed at the time as "strident."[69] Jill Abramson, former executive editor of the *New York Times*, was widely reported to have lost her job because she was "pushy," "brusque," and difficult to work with.[70] The publisher who let Abramson go insisted that gender had nothing to do with it; the dismissal, he said, was attributable to arbitrary decision making, failure to consult, and public mistreatment of subordinates.[71] Many knowledgeable observers were unconvinced. If Abramson were a male, they asked, would the story be the same? "Would there even be a story?"[72]

The backlash women experience makes them less willing to negotiate for opportunities or engage in self-promoting behaviors that may be necessary for leadership roles.[73] People are less likely to hire or want to work with women who negotiate than with men who do so.[74] Those reactions can deter female managers from asking for what they need for career development.[75] Because women often internalize gender stereotypes, they generally see themselves as less deserving than men for rewards for the same performance and less qualified for key leadership positions.[76]

Many women also are reluctant to raise gender-related issues because those who do are often branded as "extremist," "militant," "strident," "oversensitive," "abrasive," "disruptive," or "difficult to work with."[77] Even if they express such concerns in gentle, nonconfrontational terms, women may worry that they will be viewed as "self-serving" "whiners" who are unable to compete without special treatment.[78] These risks may not seem worth taking if women lack confidence that their efforts will do much good. For women of color, who are often especially isolated in upper-level positions, the pressures to avoid divisive issues can be intense.[79]

In male-dominated settings, aspiring female leaders are also subject to special scrutiny and polarized assessments. Gender stereotypes are particularly strong when women's representation does not exceed a token level, and too few counterexamples are present to challenge conventional assumptions.[80] A small number of superstars will attract special notice and receive higher evaluations than their male counterparts, but women who are just below that rank tend to get disproportionately lower evaluations.[81] At the same time, the presence of a few highly regarded women at the top creates the illusion that the glass ceiling has been shattered for everyone else. And when superstars fail or opt out, their departures attract particular notice and reinforce stereotypes about women's lesser capabilities and commitment.[82]

Gender stereotypes also affect socialization processes that steer women away from leadership positions, particularly in tech fields. Young women are often discouraged by geek culture from taking an active interest in computer science.[83] Gender socialization similarly points women towards staff positions in human relations and marketing, rather than line positions having profit-and-loss responsibilities, from which promotions to top leadership are made.[84]

Some research also suggests that women may be sabotaged by what researchers label the "glass cliff" phenomenon: the tendency to promote female leaders to high-risk positions.[85] Several factors contribute to this tendency. Women may face less competition from men for these positions and may face more pressure to accept in order to demonstrate their ability. Organizations that are struggling may also value qualities that are disproportionately associated with women, such as interpersonal skills and collaborative leadership styles. A high-risk situation may also motivate decision makers to promote a nontraditional candidate in order to signal to stakeholders that the organization is headed in a bold new direction.[86] Such high-risk positions may pose particular challenges for women because they have less peer support and fewer work-related resources than similarly situated men.[87]

Research on the glass cliff in American organizations is mixed, but the best recent study finds evidence of the phenomenon.[88] That survey looked at all women who served as Fortune 500 CEOs and a corresponding matched sample of male Fortune 500 CEOs. Researchers found that the women were far more likely to be appointed in an organization that was struggling; 42 percent of the women compared to 22 percent of the men were appointed in high-risk circumstances. Women were also more likely to be forced to step down than men (32 percent vs. 13 percent) and were less likely to continue to serve on corporate boards (27 percent vs. 67 percent).[89]

In-Group Favoritism

So too, women in traditionally male-dominated settings often lack access to the support, mentoring, and sponsorship that are available to their male colleagues.[90] Even CEOs acknowledge the persistence of an unintended and unconscious "old boy's network."[91] The relatively small number of women who are in positions of power may not have the time or the leverage, or in some cases the inclination, to assist all who hope to join them. Men who would like to fill the gaps in mentoring frequently lack the capacity to do so or are worried about the appearance of forming close relationships with women.[92] One study found that almost two-thirds of senior men admit that they're hesitant to initiate any one-on-one contact with an up-and-coming woman.[93] Few companies are as insensitive as Wal-Mart once was, in holding executive retreats over quail hunting at Sam Walton's Texas ranch and having middle managers' meetings include visits to strip clubs.[94] But in many corporate settings, even women in senior leadership roles have found themselves on the "outside looking in" when it comes to the inner circle where decisions are made.[95] In a 2016 survey of women in Silicon Valley, two-thirds felt excluded from key social networking opportunities because of gender.[96]

Moreover, not all mentoring is created equal. As Chapter One noted, what aspiring leaders most need is not simply mentors but sponsors—those who will support them for prominent positions and assignments. Research consistently finds that women in management are overmentored and undersponsored relative to their male peers.[97] A Catalyst study looked at more than four thousand high-potential men and women with excellent credentials. Women reported getting more mentoring, but men's mentors were more senior.[98] Two years later, in a follow-up study, business school professor Herminia Ibarra asked how many of the women had been promoted since the Catalyst survey. She found there was no significant relationship between having had a mentor and receiving a promotion. One woman explained why: "I'm going to get mentored to death before I'm promoted."[99] Sallie Krawcheck notes: "if you look around Wall Street and corporate America, we're putting women . . . in mentoring programs, we're giving them special leadership training, telling them how to ask for promotions—but we are *not* promoting them. . . . We are just making them busier."[100] As another leadership study concluded, all too often "women have mentors up the wazoo. But they have little to show for it in terms of money, promotions, and satisfaction."[101]

Differences across race and ethnicity can compound the problem. Women of color experience particular difficulties of isolation and exclusion.[102] Nearly half of black women and a third of white, Hispanic, and Asian women say that they haven't received senior-level support in advancing their careers.[103] In cross-racial mentoring relationships, candid dialogue may be particularly difficult. Minority protégés may be reluctant to raise issues of bias for fear of seeming oversensitive. White mentors may be reluctant to offer candid feedback to minorities for fear of seeming racist or of encouraging them to leave.[104]

In-group favoritism is also apparent in allocation of work and client development opportunities. Women often encounter greater difficulty than men in obtaining important assignments that enable them to showcase or develop their talents.[105] A Catalyst survey of sixteen hundred "high potential" business school graduates found that men received assignments with higher budgets, responsibility, and visibility than comparably situated women.[106] Unsurprisingly, given these patterns, only 28 percent of senior-level women, compared with 40 percent of men, say they are very happy with their career.[107]

Work-Family Conflicts

When Jamie Clark, the first female head of the federal Fish and Wildlife Service, became pregnant in 1999, the expectation was that she would resign. A biologist by training, she finally reminded her colleagues that pregnant women "get fat, they don't get stupid." Her situation was sufficiently novel that when she gave birth, the *Washington Post* ran a story under the caption, "Fish and Wildlife Service Lands an Eight Pounder."[108]

Although female leaders with children are no longer uncommon, the challenges they face remain. According to a recent Pew Research Center survey, more than half of Americans believe that women's family responsibilities are a reason they are not in top business positions.[109] In another Pew study, 58 percent of millennial mothers said that being a working mother made it harder for them to advance in their career.[110] Jack Welch, former CEO of General Electric, once voiced common views with uncommon candor: "There's no such thing as work-life balance. There are work-life choices, and you make them, and they have consequences." Women who take time off can still "have a nice career," but their chances of reaching the top decline.[111] According to the president of a New York executive search firm, "employers would love to hire more senior women but they can't change the reality of the jobs that they're filling. It's very work-intensive, the hires are grueling. A lot of women are raising families. It's not as attractive to them."[112] In one study of Harvard Business School alumni, nearly half of those who were married had chosen a job with more flexibility, and a quarter had slowed down the pace of their career; four in ten planned to interrupt their career for their family.[113]

Although work-family policies are not just women's issues, women pay a disproportionate price because, as Chapter One noted, they still assume a disproportionate share of family obligations. Even in households where parents have similar career demands, a LeanIn.Org and McKinsey & Company study found that 41 percent of mothers reported doing more child care than their spouses and 30 percent reported doing more domestic chores.[114] Five times as many senior men as women had a stay-at-home partner.[115] Other studies find similar disparities. In one, three-quarters of male executives had a stay-at-home spouse; three-quarters of female executives had a spouse who worked full-time.[116] In another survey of nearly four thousand executives, only 10 percent of the women but 60 percent of the men had a spouse who didn't work full-time outside the home.[117] Consistent with these findings, a recent study of millennials found that 37 percent of women but only 13 percent of men said they planned to interrupt their career for children. A third of the women did not expect their career to be equal to that of their spouse.[118] A majority of Harvard male MBAs expected that their career would take precedence over their partner's career, and that their partner would assume primary child-care responsibility.[119]

Women with substantial caretaking commitments face workplace challenges on several levels. The most obvious involves the lack of time to put in the extra hours that may be critical for demonstrating excellence or for building sponsorship and mentoring relationships.[120] In a Bain & Company survey, when employees were asked to rank the most important characteristics for promotion, the second most common one was willingness to put in extra hours.[121] Sixty percent agreed that a key trait was an "unwavering commitment to long hours and constant work."[122] A McKinsey study found most men and women agreed that a top-level career implies "anytime, anywhere" availability to work, and that this imposes a particularly severe penalty on female managers. When asked whether having children is compatible with a top-level career for women, more than a third of those surveyed thought it was not.[123] Of Harvard MBA graduates, 73 percent of men and 85 percent of women believed that "prioritizing family over work" is the top barrier to women's career advancement.[124] Some research also suggests that when workplaces demand total availability, women are more likely than men to request formal accommodations and suffer the marginalization that results. Men are more willing and able to "pass" by looking for ways to curtail their hours under the radar and retain a formal posture of total commitment.[125] In a comment that signaled the priorities of many organizations, Mark Zuckerberg, the founder and CEO of Facebook, told a group of would-be entrepreneurs that young people without families had an advantage because they "just have simpler lives . . . Simplicity in life allows you to focus on what's important."[126]

A related problem is that having children makes women, but not men, appear less competent and less available to meet workplace responsibilities.[127] Managers who take leaves receive significantly fewer promotions and smaller salary increases. They are regarded as less than fully committed.[128] The term "working father" is rarely used and carries none of the adverse connotations of "working mother." When General Motors President Mary Barra appeared on the *Today* show during the company's ignition-switch scandal, Matt Lauer asked whether, as the mother of young children, she could do "both [jobs] well."[129] Lauer himself is the father of three children, which apparently hasn't stopped him from doing his job. Wharton Business School's Monica McGrath similarly recalls an example of motherhood bias in an executive management meeting that she attended as a consultant. One of the managers present suggested that the woman who was the most qualified candidate for an overseas post probably would not want the job because she had two small children. Meeting participants "actually thought that this was a sensitive remark."[130] Screenwriter Terri Minsky remembers telling an executive she worked for that she was pregnant. He responded: "You are as useful to me now as if you had a brain tumor."[131]

A final set of problems stems from the stigma incurred by those who seek accommodations for family responsibility. This stigma discourages women from taking advantage of flexible working schedules. As one female manager put it, "In my organization, everyone knows that taking up the offer of flextime means giving up any chance of being considered leadership potential."[132] In one McKinsey survey of some four thousand employees, only 3 percent of managers and fewer than 1 percent of senior executives worked part-time.[133] In another McKinsey study of about thirty thousand workers, 90 percent thought taking an extended leave would hurt their position.[134] Part-time status and time out of the workforce generally results in long-term losses in earnings as well as lower chances for promotion.[135] A sex discrimination case against the pharmaceutical company Novartis found that women who took advantage of the company's work-family policies were penalized, and sometimes actively pushed out.[136] Women who return from maternity leave or who opt for reduced or flextime often fall victim to the assumption that they won't have sufficient time available for demanding assignments.[137]

Working mothers' determination to display commitment has often reached ludicrous levels. One head of government and community relations got a call from her boss in her hospital room hours after her first child was born. "There's a doctor walking into the room. I'll have to call you back," she said. "All right. Well, try to call me by 10:00 a.m.," he responded. "I said 'Okay'. If I look back, it's one of the conversations I would most love to have a do-over on. . . ."[138]

Strategies for Individuals

According to Sheila Wellington, former president of Catalyst, the most important advice from successful women is to "perform beyond expectations . . . This is how you counter the 'competency' barrier that women tell us they face when working with men."[139] Mastering details is one way to command respect.[140] Former CEO Carol Barz advises women, "Don't be half anywhere. Wherever you are, be there."[141] The CEO of a leading advertising agency agrees: "Don't ever be in a job or a place where you're not all in. When you're there, you're all in."[142] Of course, perpetual perfection is impossible. Women need to use "good enough strategically— and still be excellent when it really counts."[143] They also should be sure that their outstanding performance gets noticed. In one Catalyst study, the career advancement strategy that made the most difference in terms of promotions and professional satisfaction was drawing attention to successes.[144] To avoid self-promotion that can be off-putting, women benefit from sponsors or other colleagues who can draw attention to their contributions.

Women also need to be proactive in pursuing positions and assignments that will showcase their talents. In *Think Like a Leader, Act Like a Leader*, professor Herminia Ibarra notes that people "become leaders by doing leadership work." They seek new activities and networks that will expand their skills and enhance their reputation and self confidence.[145] "Don't settle for secondary or housekeeping positions," advises Susan Herman, president of the ACLU.[146] Valerie Jarrett, one of Obama's chief advisors, recalls an occasion in her thirties when a client told her that she needed a promotion. Jarrett was doing work in the Chicago mayor's office that her supervisor should be doing. After much prodding, Jarrett finally took the chance and asked her boss for a promotion. He immediately said yes. Years later, she asked why he had never offered her the position without prodding. He told her he'd been busy and just hadn't thought about it.[147]

As Chapter One indicated, women also need a style that couples assertive behavior with warmth and helpfulness.[148] According to Red Cross President Gail McGovern, women who are bosses have to learn how to be "politely bossy."[149] One study that followed business school graduates for eight years found that women who combined male and female qualities were promoted three times as often as purely "masculine" women, and 1.5 times as often as purely "feminine" women.[150] The CEO of a consulting firm noted the importance of her transformation from a "dictatorial maven," ruling with "tight fisted authority," to someone who "wanted to have a company that valued people, nurtured them and fostered their development as human beings."[151] Participatory styles can also be important in making employees feel that they are involved and respected in decision making.[152] A blended style, however, may be less effective in highly masculine settings. There, research suggests that women should lead in an assertive and competent manner, accompanied by more feminine behavior only to the extent that it does not undermine their authority.[153] As one Wall Street executive put it: "You have to be strong and assertive without offending people. So you push a little and then back off, push a little and back off. You're always testing the waters to see how far you can go."[154] Humor can also be useful in helping women fit in. McGovern recalls walking into an all-male meeting and hearing the room go silent. When she asked why, the chair explained that someone had told an off-color joke. She asked how off was the color and was told that the "f-word" was involved. She responded, "What the fuck is the f word?"[155]

Women also need to be strategic in their use of time and not shortchange investment in mentoring and sponsorship. Ilene Lang, former president of Catalyst, advises women to build their reputation "with a focused network of advocates."[156] Kate Wolford, president of the McKnight Foundation, stresses the importance of forming "relationships at all levels of the organization—including senior leadership who . . . [can be] advocates for [your] personal and professional development as a leader.[157] One CEO recalls that early in her career she had made the mistake of thinking that "time spent building relationships was fooling around as opposed to . . . serious business."[158]

This does not mean women must sacrifice their family commitments. Rather, as McGovern advises, aspiring leaders need to "figure out what's important and pick an organization to work where the culture fits their desires."[159] That means purchasing as much domestic labor as feasible, but it may also mean avoiding employers whose primary advice on work-family issues is to "outsource your life."[160] Michelle Obama had a baby-sitter crisis just as she was going for her interview as public liaison for the University of Chicago hospital. At the last minute, she tucked her daughter in the stroller and figured that, since this was partly why she was looking at this job, they needed to know that she put her family first. She took her daughter to the interview and got the job.[161]

Being self-reflective and strategic about goals is also critical. Women need to be careful what they wish for. Carol Robles Roman, president of Legal Momentum, recommends that women "make up [their minds] at the outset" about the leadership positions that interest them and then strategize based on how others have reached those positions.[162] Nan Aron, president of Alliance for Justice, advises women to get some "quick successes under your belt. Think big but start small. . . . Know your strengths and play to them."[163]

Women of color need to exercise special care in choosing where to seek leadership opportunities. Sandra Finley, president of the League of Black Women, advises women of color to "assess a company like you assess a neighborhood. Is it safe? Is it a community where you will be welcome? If you don't see women like you at all levels, the company hasn't figured it out and probably won't on your watch." "If you are hired laterally at a leadership level," Finley suggests, "don't go in alone. Bring a team [of subordinates] who can support you."[164]

Finally, women should do what they can to help level the playing field for other women. Kathleen Westlock, former head of human relations at Cisco, notes that women can be "our best supporters or our own worst enemies. We need to make our voices heard."[165] A CEO of HSBC USA regrets "not having done more to change the status quo." Rather, she kept her head down and focused on her own career. This turned out to be counterproductive because it left her isolated as she attempted to move up the organizational ladder.[166] An executive VP and general counsel at Pfizer similarly advises women to "spend political capital, [and] stand up for something you really believe in, rather than just [deciding to] go with the flow. . . . We're undervaluing the role that we can play in the success of other people and the organization."[167]

Strategies for Organizations

When asked for one piece of advice to organizations interested in advancing women to leadership positions, Jamie Clark, president of Defenders of Wildlife, responded, just "do it."[168] For this to happen, organizations need a commitment to that objective, reflected in organizational policies and priorities. This commitment often appears lacking. In one McKinsey study, although 80 percent of CEO's reported making diversity a priority, only about half of employees from those companies agreed that the CEO was committed to it.[169] In a similar survey, only a third of employees believed that their immediate supervisor or the leadership team at their organization made gender equity a priority.[170] In studies of human resources leaders, only a minority considered their company's gender diversity programs effective or of high quality and well implemented.[171] Ironically enough, some evidence indicates that organizations positioning themselves as highly meritocratic have more gender bias than other organizations. Because leaders in ostensibly meritocratic cultures see themselves as fair, they worry less about how their actions will be perceived, and succumb more easily to bias.[172] For this reason, top management needs to be self-critical. Leaders need to survey women about their experience and create a culture in which candor is possible.[173] Well-designed training programs should sensitize participants to the costs of unconscious bias and strategies that can address it.[174] Ideally, "senior male leaders should be the first to speak up when other men in the organization behave inappropriately, discriminate, or in any way undervalue the contributions of women in the organization."[175]

In short, it is not enough for leaders to proclaim their commitment to equal opportunity; they also need a corresponding commitment to inclusiveness and to the policies and reward structures that will encourage it. To this end, organizations should set goals and targets and hold top management accountable in compensation and advancement.[176]

Leaders can also insist on diverse slates of candidates for any opening.[177] Policies that look good on paper are necessary but not sufficient, and organizations need to monitor the results, through both objective metrics and qualitative surveys. Too few companies take a deep dive into assessments of their performance evaluation, work assignment, and mentoring processes. In one study, 69 percent of companies reported having a mentoring program for women, but only 16 percent of these programs were judged to be well implemented.[178] As earlier discussion indicated, too many women get too much mindless mentoring and too little real sponsorship. By contrast, effective initiatives match high-potential women with high-profile executives who can provide access to opportunities and who are held responsible for their mentees' progress.[179] Well-designed mentoring programs are correlated with modest gains in female representation in managerial positions.[180]

So too, organizations can do more to support women's professional development. One company has developed a program that helps women analyze their strengths and align them with leadership positions, and that matches program participants with senior leaders throughout the organization.[181]

Organizations also need more effective work-family strategies. Half of surveyed women want fewer hours; three-quarters want flexible work options.[182] Yet too many companies seem oblivious to these concerns, and a few have moved in the opposite direction. In one widely publicized example, CEO Marissa Mayer announced she was ending work-at-home hours at Yahoo. Then, in one of the most tone-deaf decisions in recent memory, she had a nursery for her own baby built right next to her office.[183] The needs that Mayer recognized in her own life could have been addressed for others in the company through onsite child care and flexible telecommuting policies.

A growing number of organizations, however, have pioneered programs that are cost-effective for all concerned. The CEO of a startup company allows more than half of its professionals to work fewer than forty hours a week by choice. Her strategy is to design work around discrete projects and to allow people to decide how much to take on.[184] Other companies promote women's leadership by ensuring that those who work part-time or adopt flexible schedules have the same career development

opportunities as those working traditional hours.[185] KPMG accounting offers compressed workweeks, flexible hours, telecommuting, job
sharing, and reduced workloads. Deloitte's Mass Career Customization
allows individuals to work less, work from different places, and shoulder less responsibility if they need to accommodate caretaking commitments.[186] Telstra's "All Roles Flex" permits management-level employees
to determine what arrangement works best for them and the business.
Supervisors can veto the arrangement for business reasons, but then work
with human resources and the employee to find a viable alternative.[187]

Such policies have payoffs for organizations as well as employees.
One study of alternative work schedules found that the majority of flexible workers increased the productivity of their work, in terms of both
quality and quantity. Employees working flexibly were more committed and more satisfied.[188] Accounting, which is a profession scarcely
indifferent to the bottom line, has developed a business model that
more than offsets the costs of work-family accommodation by increasing retention.[189] Although some leadership positions may be hard to
reconcile with substantial family demands, many women could be
ready to cycle into those positions as caregiving obligations decrease.
The challenge lies in creating workplace structures that make it easier
for employees with substantial family responsibilities to remain on a
leadership track, and to ensure that those who temporarily step out of
the workforce or reduce their workload are not permanently derailed
by the decision.

To this end, some organizations have pioneered reentry programs.
One of the most effective has been sponsored by Brenda Barnes, who
quit her job as president and CEO of PepsiCo's North American operation to raise her three children. When they left for college, she became
CEO of Sara Lee. The company has a multitude of flexible work options
and a program called Returnships. It recruits midcareer professionals
who have been out of the workforce for a number of years and offers
them the chance to retool and retrain, with an eye toward a permanent
job.[190] Alpha Company has created an intensive ten-week reentry program for mid- and senior-level women that is designed to build skills,
confidence, and engagement.[191]

Another promising strategy involves organizational outreach in fields where women are particularly underrepresented. So, for example, technology experts recommend creating gender-balanced internship programs for technical positions and building strong ties to conferences, professional organizations, and higher educational institutions where there are substantial proportions of women.[192] Organizations should also take a long view by helping to build a female leadership pipeline in STEM fields by supporting educational initiatives at the elementary, secondary, and collegiate levels.

Finally, self-assessment should be a critical part of all diversity initiatives.[193] Leaders need to know how policies that affect inclusiveness play out in practice. This requires collecting both quantitative and qualitative data on matters such as advancement, retention, assignments, satisfaction, mentoring, and work-family conflicts. As earlier discussion indicated, many organizations have official policies on flexible and reduced schedules that are viewed as unworkable in practice. Surveys, exit interviews, and focus groups can identify problems disproportionately experienced by women.

This is not a modest agenda. But in an increasingly competitive economy, organizations cannot afford to shortchange half the nation's leadership talent. The payoffs from more inclusive workplaces are substantial, and employers as well as women will benefit.

WOMEN IN LAW

One irony of this nation's continuing struggle for diversity and gender equity in employment is that the profession leading the struggle has failed to set an example in its own workplaces.[1] In principle, the bar is deeply committed to equal opportunity and social justice. In practice, it lags behind other occupations in leveling the playing field. Part of the problem lies in lack of consensus on what exactly the problem is. What accounts for gender inequalities in the law? Who is responsible for addressing them? What responses would be most effective? These are not new questions. But recent economic and client pressures have made clear the need for better answers. Many of the obstacles to equity in legal practice are symptomatic of deeper structural problems.

The Gap Between Principle and Practice

Viewed historically, the American legal profession has made substantial progress in the struggle for gender equity. Until the late 1960s, women constituted no more than about 3 percent of the profession and were largely confined to low-prestige practice settings and specialties.[2] Now, close to half of new lawyers are female, and they are fairly evenly distributed across substantive areas.[3] Women also express approximately the same overall level of satisfaction with practice as do men.[4]

Yet significant gender inequalities persist. Women constitute more than a third of the profession but only 18 percent of law firm equity partners and 21 percent of general counsel of Fortune 500 corporations.[5] Just under 3 percent of partners are women of color.[6] Women are less likely than men to make partner even controlling for other factors, including law school grades and time spent out of the workforce or on part-time schedules.[7] Studies find that male lawyers are two to five times more likely to become partner than female lawyers.[8] Even women who never take time out of the labor force and who work long hours have a lower chance of partnership than similarly situated men.[9] The situation is bleakest at the highest levels. Only 12 percent of chairs and managing partners at the one hundred largest firms are female.[10] Women are also underrepresented in leadership positions such as membership on management and compensation committees.[11] According to one recent survey of graduates of differently ranked law schools, the average man, whatever tier school he attended, had roughly twice the chance of becoming a partner in a large firm as the average woman.[12] Gender disparities are similarly apparent in compensation, with women of color at the bottom of the financial pecking order.[13] These disparities persist even after controlling for factors such as productivity and differences in equity-nonequity status.[14]

So too, although female lawyers report about the same overall career satisfaction as their male colleagues, women experience greater dissatisfaction with key dimensions of practice such as level of responsibility, recognition for work, and chances for advancement.[15] Among lawyers in large firms, the ABA's Commission on Women in the Profession found stark differences among racial groups. White men graded their career satisfaction as A, white women and minority men graded theirs as B, and minority women hovered between B minus and C plus.[16]

In attempting to account for why most women lawyers' overall satisfaction is no different from men's, researchers suggest two explanations. The first involves values. Women may attach less significance to aspects of their work environment on which they are disadvantaged, such as compensation and promotion, than to other factors such as intellectual

challenge, which evokes greater satisfaction among female than male attorneys.[17] A second theory is that women have a lower sense of entitlement, in part because their reference group is other women or because
they "have made peace with second best."[18] In either case, female lawyers'
dissatisfaction with key aspects of practice, as well as their underrepresentation in leadership positions, should be cause for concern in a profession committed to equal opportunity and diversity.

Explaining the Gap

In a parody of diversity efforts during a celebrated British television
series, *Yes Minister*, a stodgy white male civil servant explained the folly
of such initiatives. By his logic, if women had the necessary commitment
and capabilities, they would already be well represented in leadership
positions. Since they weren't well represented, they obviously lacked
those qualifications. It should come as no surprise that similar views have
been common among some leaders of the American bar. After all, those
in charge of hiring, promotion, and compensation decisions are those
who have benefited from the current structure, and who have the greatest
stake in believing in its fairness. Although many leaders have been willing
to concede the persistence of bias in society in general, they have been
less likely to see it in their own institutions. Rather, they have attributed
racial, ethnic, and gender differences in lawyers' career paths to differences in capabilities and commitment.[19]

Those traditional views, however, have been subject to increasing
challenge. My own recent survey of managing partners in large firms and
Fortune 100 corporate counsel found that virtually all the participants
mentioned diversity as a high priority in their organization, and many
were dissatisfied with the progress they had made. One managing partner expressed widespread views: ["We're] not nearly successful enough,
no question about it."[20] Some attributed the low representation of lawyers of color to clogs in the pipeline. But others acknowledged unconscious bias and "diversity fatigue."[21] With respect to women generally,
the problem was commonly explained in terms not of credentials but of
commitment and client development. Because women continue to have
disproportionate family responsibilities and are more likely to reduce

their schedules or to take time out of the workplace than men, they are assumed to be less available, less dependable, and less worthy of extensive mentoring.[22] In one survey, although women and men reported working similar hours, more than a quarter of male lawyers thought their female counterparts worked less and a fifth rated the number of hours these women worked as "fair to poor."[23] So too, women are often presumed to be less adept in business development and in the self-promotional abilities that underlie it.[24]

These attitudes may help to explain the relatively rosy assessment that many white male lawyers offer of diversity initiatives. In a survey by Catalyst, only 11 percent of white lawyers felt that diversity efforts were failing to address subtle racial bias, compared with almost half of women of color. Only 15 percent of white men felt that diversity efforts were failing to address subtle gender bias, compared with half of women of color and 40 percent of white women.[25]

The research summarized below, however, suggests that many lawyers underestimate the impact of unconscious bias and overestimate the effectiveness of current responses. Women cannot solve their own problems just by "leaning in," to borrow Sheryl Sandberg's term. In the words of Linda Chanow, executive director of the Center for Women in Law, "Women can 'lean in' as much as they want. . . . But the culture of law firms and their persistent implicit biases can undermine and inhibit women's success."[26] Lawyers who are truly committed to a just and inclusive workplace need a better understanding of what gets in the way. This includes deeper appreciation of how racial, ethnic, and gender stereotypes affect not just evaluations of performance but performance itself, and the relative value attached to specific performance measures.

Gender Bias

Gender stereotypes play a well-documented, often unconscious, role in American culture, and legal workplaces are no exception. These stereotypes subject women to double standards and a double bind. Despite recent progress, women, particularly women of color, often fail to receive the presumption of competence enjoyed by white men.[27] In national surveys, between a third and three-quarters of female lawyers believe that they are held to higher standards than their male colleagues.[28] Studies of performance evaluations support those perceptions; researchers find that similar descriptions of performance result in lower ratings for women than men.[29] Racial and ethnic bias compounds the problem. One recent survey found that senior lawyers rated the writing skills of a junior lawyer much lower if they believed the lawyer was black rather than white.[30] So too, as Chapter One noted, male achievements are more likely to be attributed to capabilities, and female achievements to external factors.[31] In a survey of performance appraisals at a Wall Street law firm, women received more positive comments than the men, but were less than half as likely to be mentioned as potential partner material.[32]

Women, particularly women of color, also receive less latitude for mistakes.[33] As one African American attorney put it, "There is no room for error."[34] This, in turn, may make lawyers reluctant to seek risky "stretch assignments" that would demonstrate outstanding capabilities. Biased assumptions about lawyers' commitment or competence can also affect allocation of work. As Joan Williams and Veta Richardson note, the result is to prevent women and minorities from getting opportunities that would demonstrate or enhance their capabilities, which creates a cycle of self-fulfilling prophecies.[35]

So too, mothers, even those working full-time, are assumed to be less available and committed, an assumption not made about fathers.[36] In one representative study, almost three-quarters of female lawyers reported that their career commitment had been questioned when they gave birth or adopted a child. Only 9 percent of their white male colleagues, and 15 percent of minority male colleagues, had faced similar challenges.[37] Yet women without family relationships sometimes face bias of a different order: they may be viewed as "not quite normal" and thus "not quite leadership material."[38]

Women are also rated lower than men on qualities associated with leadership, such as assertiveness, competiveness, and business development.[39] And as Chapter One noted, when women do display assertiveness, it is often penalized. Female lawyers risk seeming too feminine, or not feminine enough. Either they may appear too "soft" or too "strident— either unable to make tough decisions or too pushy and arrogant to command respect."[40] Women of color are subject to the intersection of race and gender bias. Assertive African American women risk being dismissed as angry blacks; Asian women are often overlooked for leadership roles because they are perceived as insufficiently forceful and outgoing.[41] Even the most accomplished lawyers can encounter such biases. Brooksley Born, now widely acclaimed for her efforts to regulate high-risk derivatives while chair of the Commodity Futures Commission, was dismissed at the time as "abrasive," "strident," and a "lightweight wacko."[42] In commenting on those characterizations, a former aide noted, "She was serious, professional, and she held her ground against those who were not sympathetic to her position. I don't think that the failure to be 'charming' should be translated into a depiction of stridency."[43]

A related set of obstacles involves in-group favoritism. Chapter One documented the preferences that people feel for members of their own sex, race, and ethnicity, and law is no exception.[44] As a consequence, women and minorities face difficulty developing "social capital": access to advice, support, sponsorship, desirable assignments, and new business opportunities.[45] In law firms, racial and ethnic minorities often report isolation and marginalization, while many white women similarly experience exclusion from "old boys" networks.[46] In ABA research, 62 percent of women of color and 60 percent of white women, but only 4 percent of white men, felt excluded from formal and informal networking opportunities; most women and minorities would have liked better mentoring.[47]

Part of the problem lies in numbers. Many organizations lack sufficient women and minorities at the senior level who can assist others on the way up. The problem is typically not absence of commitment. In a Catalyst study, almost three-quarters of women who were actively engaged in mentoring were developing female colleagues, compared with 30 percent of men.[48] But the underrepresentation of women in leadership positions, along with the time pressures for those juggling family responsibilities, leaves an insufficient pool of potential mentors.

Although a growing number of organizations have formal mentoring programs, these do not always supply adequate training, rewards, or oversight to ensure effectiveness.[49] Nor can these formal programs substitute for relationships that develop naturally and that yield not simply advisors but sponsors—individuals who act as advocates and are in positions to open opportunities. As participants in one ABA study noted, female mentors may have "good intentions," but are already pressed with competing work and family obligations or "don't have a lot of power so they can't really help you."[50] Concerns about the appearance of sexual harassment or sexual affairs discourage some men from forming mentoring relationships with junior women. Discomfort concerning issues of race and ethnicity is equally problematic.[51] In cross-racial mentoring relationships, candid dialogue may be particularly difficult. Minority protégés may be reluctant to raise issues of bias for fear of seeming oversensitive. White mentors may hesitate to offer candid feedback to minority associates for fear of seeming racially biased or of encouraging them to leave. The result is that midlevel lawyers of color can find themselves "blindsided by soft evaluations": "Your skills aren't what they are supposed to be, but you didn't know because no one ever told you."[52]

In-group favoritism is also apparent in allocation of work and client development opportunities. Many organizations operate with informal systems that channel seemingly talented junior lawyers (disproportionately white men) to leadership tracks, while relegating others to "workhorse" positions.[53] In the ABA Commission study, 44 percent of women of color, 39 percent of white women, and 25 percent of minority men reported being passed over for desirable assignments; only 2 percent of white men noted similar experiences.[54] Williams and Richardson's research similarly finds that women and minorities are often left out of pitches for client business.[55] What women get instead are a disproportionate share of nonbillable "housekeeping" tasks, such as committee and administrative work.[56]

Lawyers of color are also subject to "race matching"; they receive certain work because of their identity, not their interests, in order to create the right "look" in courtrooms, client presentations, recruiting, and marketing efforts. Although this strategy sometimes opens helpful opportunities, it can also place lawyers in what they describe as "mascot" roles in which they are not developing their own professional skills.[57] Linda Mabry, the first minority partner in a San Francisco firm, recounts an example in which she was asked to join a pitch to a company whose general counsel was African American. "When the firm made the pitch about the firm's relevant expertise, none of which I possessed, it was clear that the only reason I was there was to tout the firm's diversity, which was practically nonexistent. In that moment I wanted to fling myself through the plate-glass window of that well-appointed conference room."[58] Race matching is particularly irritating when lawyers of color are assumed to have skills and affinities that they in fact lack. Examples include a Japanese American who was asked to a meeting to solicit a Korean client, and a Latina who was assigned documents in Spanish even after she explained that she wasn't fluent in the language.[59] "Oh, you'll be fine," she was told. "Look up [anything unfamiliar] in a dictionary."[60]

Workplace Structures and Gender Roles

Escalating workplace demands and inflexible workplace structures pose further obstacles to gender equity. In law, as one director of diversity noted, women are disadvantaged by a "culture that focuses heavily on hours as a metric of contribution."[61] The vast majority of lawyer fees are calculated on an hourly basis, which rewards time rather than efficiency. Hourly demands have risen significantly over the last quarter century, and what hasn't changed are the number of hours in the day. Constant accessibility has become the new norm, with attorneys electronically tethered to their workplaces.

The problem is compounded by the inadequacy of structural responses. Despite some efforts at accommodation, a wide gap persists between formal policies and actual practices concerning work-life conflicts. Although more than 90 percent of American law firms report policies permitting part-time work, only about 6 percent of lawyers actually use them.[62] Many lawyers believe, with good reason, that any reduction in hours or availability will jeopardize their careers.[63] Part-time status and time out of the workforce generally result in long-term losses in earnings as well as lower chances for partnership.[64] In one survey of University of Michigan law school graduates, just a single year out of the workforce correlated with a one-third lower chance of making partner and an earnings reduction of 38 percent.[65] Deborah Epstein Henry, president of Flex-Time Lawyers, notes that many firm leadership tracks are simply too linear and rigid for women with families. Lawyers who temporarily go off the full-time track find that "it's a very unforgiving model that doesn't let you back in."[66]

To avoid such penalties, many women go to extraordinary lengths to demonstrate commitment. All too common are stories of the "faster than a speeding bullet" maternity leave, or women in hospital delivery rooms drafting documents while timing contractions. If you're billing at six-minute intervals, why waste one? Those who opt for a reduced schedule after parental leave often find that it isn't worth the price. Their schedules aren't respected, their hours creep up, the quality of their assignments goes down, their pay is not proportional, and they are stigmatized as "slackers."[67] In a *Working Mother* survey of the "Fifty Best Law Firms for Women, "no lawyer promoted to partner was working a reduced schedule."[68] Even full-time attorneys can experience penalties, as Williams and Dempsey found in *What Works for Women at Work*. A lawyer who missed one meeting to take a child to the emergency room found that for years afterward, that absence figured prominently in assessments of her commitment.[69]

Expectations about commitment can also affect hiring decisions. One lawyer reported that her firm hired a woman with great credentials and spent two years training her, and then she had a baby and left. A second woman did the same. The firm was not large, so the expense of such attrition was significant. One partner responded by stating privately, "You know it's illegal, you're not allowed to say it, but the next time a woman comes through here, don't even bring her into my office. I'm not going to interview her."[70]

Although work-family conflicts are not just "women's issues," women suffer the greatest cost. As Chapter One noted, despite a significant increase in men's domestic work, women continue to shoulder the major burden.[71] It is still women who are most likely to get the "emergency" phone call that federal district judge Nancy Gertner received on her first day on the bench: "Mama, there's no chocolate pudding in my [lunch]."[72] And it was a mother, not her equally busy husband, who heard from her resentful child, "I want to be a client when I grow up." In the American Bar Foundation's survey of young lawyers, women were about seven times more likely than men to be working part-time or to be out of the labor force, primarily due to child care.[73] In a University of Michigan study, only

1 percent of fathers had taken substantial parental leave, compared with 42 percent of women.[74] Part of the reason for those disparities is that the small number of fathers who opt to become full-time caretakers experience particular penalties. Male lawyers suffer even greater financial and promotion consequences than female colleagues who make the same choice.[75]

Although bar leaders generally acknowledge the problem of work-life balance, they often place responsibility for addressing it anywhere and everywhere else. In private practice, clients get part of the blame. Law is a service business, and expectations of instant accessibility reportedly make reduced schedules difficult to accommodate. Resistance from supervisors can compound the problem. In a competitive work environment, they have obvious reasons to prefer junior lawyers to be at their constant beck and call.[76] Many attorneys report working for partners who "don't themselves have work-life balance, and they don't think others should [either]."[77] The message of too many employers' work-life programs is for lawyers to "outsource your life."[78]

In my recent survey of large law firms and corporate counsel offices, many managing partners and general counsel commented on the problem:

> Everyone feels stressed. . . . It's the profession we've chosen.
> We run a 24/7 business. . . . We have a difficult and time-committed job.
> It's a tough environment to be part-time in.
> Clients expect availability twenty-four hours a day.
> It's really difficult in the industry, especially for primary caretakers.
> When you go on a reduced schedule, there are times when you have to work full-time to demonstrate you can do the job. . . . Sometimes people don't recognize that.
> It's a real tough [issue]. We do programs on the subject but I'm not sure people have time to attend.[79]

Yet the problems are not as insurmountable as is often assumed. The evidence available does not indicate substantial resistance among clients to reduced schedules. They care about responsiveness, and part-time lawyers generally appear able to provide it.[80] In one survey of part-time partners, most reported that they did not even inform clients of their status and that their schedules were adapted to fit client needs.[81] Accounting, which is also a service profession, has developed a business model that more than offsets the costs of work-family accommodation by increasing retention.[82] Considerable evidence suggests that law practices could do the same, and reap the benefits in higher morale, lower recruitment and training expenses, and less disruption in client and collegial relationships.[83] Millennial women are particularly eager to see such changes; many reject their predecessors' "gave-it-all at the office approach."[84] Although some leadership positions may be hard to reconcile with substantial family demands, many women could be ready to cycle into those positions as caregiving obligations decrease. The challenge lies in creating workplace structures that make it easier for lawyers of both sexes to have satisfying personal as well as professional lives, and to ensure that those who temporarily step out of the workforce or reduce their workload are not permanently derailed by the decision.

The Case for Gender Equity

The legal profession has a substantial stake in addressing the barriers to women in leadership. A growing number of bar leaders recognize as much. In my recent survey of managing partners and general counsel, participants stressed that diversity was not just the "right thing to do," but was also critical to organizations' economic success. As one put it, "A diverse team is a more effective team: it has a broader base of experience . . . and the client gets a better product." Another agreed: "We're in the human capital business. [Diversity is a way to get] the best people and the best decision making."[85]

The report of one women lawyers' leadership summit, *Manifesto on Women in Law*, elaborated the business case for gender equity. Its core principles state:

> A. The depth and breadth of the talent pool of women lawyers establishes a clear need for the legal profession to recruit, retain, develop and advance an exceptionally rich source of talent.

B. Women increasingly have been attaining roles of influence throughout society; legal employers must achieve gender diversity in their
leadership ranks if they are to cultivate a set of leaders with legitimacy
in the eyes of their clients and members of the profession.

C. Diversity adds value to legal employers in countless ways—from
strengthening the effectiveness of client representation to inserting
diverse perspectives and critical viewpoints in dialogues and decision
making.[86]

Social science research reviewed in Chapter One supports such claims.
Organizations that fail to respond are likely to experience a competitive
disadvantage. As an ABA Presidential Commission on Diversity points
out, increasing numbers of corporate clients are making diversity a priority in allocating work. More than a hundred major companies have signed
the *Call to Action: Diversity in the Legal Profession*, in which they pledge
to "end or limit . . . relationships with firms whose performance consistently evidences a lack of meaningful interest in being diverse."[87] A growing number of clients impose specific requirements, including reports on
diversity within the firm and in the teams working on their matters, as
well as relevant firm policies and initiatives.[88] Wal-Mart, which has been
the most public and detailed in its demands on outside lawyers, specifies
that firms must have flexible time policies and include as candidates for
relationship partner for the company at least one woman and one lawyer
of color. It has also terminated firms that have failed to meet its diversity standards.[89] The Gap inquires into flexible time policies, and sets
out expectations for improvement with firms that fail to meet its goals.[90]
Microsoft provides incentives for firms to hit its diversity targets.[91]

However, the significance of these initiatives should not be overstated.
Almost no research is available to assess the impact of these policies, to
determine how widely they are shared, or to ascertain how often companies that have pledged to reduce or end representation in appropriate
cases have actually done so. Many observers believe that clients are "not
pulling the trigger" when firms fail to deliver diversity.[92] In my recent
study of large firm leaders, only one reported losing business over the
issue, and many were frustrated by clients who asked for detailed information on diversity and then failed to follow up or to reward firms that

had performed well.[93] Still, the direction of client concerns is clear, and in today's competitive climate, the economic and symbolic leverage of prominent corporations should not be discounted.

Nor should organizations overlook the other benefits of diversity initiatives. Some policies, such as those involving work-family accommodations, make business sense. So does fostering diverse perspectives and effectively managing any conflict that results. Many practices that would improve conditions for women serve broader organizational interests. Better mentoring programs, more equitable work assignments, and greater accountability of supervising attorneys are all likely to have long-term payoffs, however difficult to quantify with precision. Skeptics of the business case for diversity often proceed as if the business case for the current model is self-evident. Few experts on law firm management agree.[94] In a world in which the talent pool is half female, it is reasonable to assume that firms will suffer some competitive disadvantage if they cannot effectively retain and advance women.

The question then becomes how organizations can help institutionalize diversity and build cultures of inclusiveness. And equally important, what can women and minorities do to enhance their own career options?

Strategies for Individuals

To improve their chances for success, women and minorities should be clear about their goals, seek challenging assignments, solicit frequent feedback, develop mentoring relationships, build professional contacts, and cultivate a reputation for effectiveness. Succeeding in those tasks also requires attention to unconscious biases and exclusionary networks that can get in the way.

So, for example, aspiring female lawyers need to develop a style that is assertive without seeming abrasive. As Chapter One indicated, some experts suggest being "relentlessly pleasant" without backing down and expressing warmth and concern as well as demonstrating competence.[95] Leadership training and coaching can help in developing such interpersonal styles, as well as other strategic capabilities. One such capability is negotiation on their own behalf. Women do better bargaining for others than for themselves.[96] As one law firm partner put it, "Women tend not to ask at home or at work. They just suck it up!"[97] More women need to acquire the skills and sense of entitlement that would enable them to negotiate for what they need and deserve.

Women can also learn by example. Michele Mayes, one of the nation's most prominent African American general counsels, recalls that after receiving some encouragement from a woman mentor, she approached the chief legal officer at her company and "told him I wanted his job."[98] After the shock wore off, he worked up a list of the skills and experiences that she needed. He also recruited her to follow him to his next general counsel job. She never replaced him, but with his assistance, she prepared for his role in other Fortune 500 companies. Louise Parent, the general counsel of American Express, describes learning to "raise my hand" for challenging assignments and being willing to take steps down and sideways on the status ladder in order to get the experience she needed.[99] Terry McClure, who became the general counsel of United Parcel Service, was told earlier in her career that she needed direct exposure to business operations if she wanted to move up at the company. After accepting a position as district manager, she suddenly found herself as a "lawyer, a black woman, [with] no operations experience walking into a . . . [warehouse] with all the truck drivers."[100] Her success in that role was what helped put her in the candidate pool for general counsel.

Time management is another important leadership skill. For those with substantial family commitments, establishing boundaries and delegating domestic tasks is especially critical. What lawyers should not sacrifice is time spent developing relationships with influential mentors and sponsors.[101] In a Harvard Business School case study of leadership in law, a nationally prominent litigator emphasized the importance of going to informal social events that can help "establish yourself as a player" and can make people feel comfortable with you.[102] So too, an ABA publication aimed at minority women lawyers advised them to "show up" and "speak up" at social gatherings and meetings that could build their networks of support.[103]

In seeking such support, women need to recognize their own responsibility to be effective mentees and to make sure that the relationship is mutually rewarding. Lawyers who step out of the labor force should find ways of keeping professionally active. Volunteer efforts, occasional paying projects, continuing legal education, and reentry programs can all aid the transition back.

Finally, and most importantly, lawyers who want committed relationships need supportive partners. As one law firm leader put it, "If your career is not as important to your partner as it is to you, you don't stand a chance."[104]

Strategies for Organizations

To ensure equal access to leadership opportunities, organizations need a commitment from the top, which is reflected in workplace policies and practices.[105] As one Fortune 500 general counsel noted, diversity must remain "a consistent focus, incorporat[ed] in the way we do business, as opposed to . . . the next flavor of the month."[106] General counsel have a special responsibility to push for diversity not only in their own workplace but also in their outside law firms. This means withdrawing business from firms that fail to place women and minorities in leadership positions.[107]

To build cultures of inclusion, many organizations have found it useful to create task forces or committees with diverse and respected members.[108] Part of the mission of that group should be evaluation. As an ABA Presidential Commission on Diversity recognized, self-assessment must be a critical part of all diversity initiatives.[109] Quantitative and qualitative data are necessary to monitor matters such as advancement, retention, assignments, satisfaction, mentoring, and work-family conflicts. As earlier discussion indicated, many firms have official policies on flexible and reduced schedules that are viewed as unworkable in practice. A key priority should be sharing information about which strategies are most effective. What has helped firms deal with powerful partners who rate poorly on diversity? Are incentives such as mentoring awards and significant bonuses effective in changing organizational culture? More experimentation and pooling of information could help organizations translate shared commitments into workable policies.

Another high priority should be developing effective systems of evaluation, rewards, and allocation of leadership opportunities. Women and minorities need to have a critical mass of representation in key positions such as membership on management committees.[110] Supervisors and heads of practice groups need to be held responsible for their work assignments and their performance on diversity-related issues. That performance should be part of self-assessments and bottom-up evaluation structures.[111] If organizations are serious about enhancing equity in leadership, they need to reward and sanction gatekeepers who can make it possible.[112]

A case study in the kind of tokenism unlikely to succeed comes from a leaked memorandum from a leading Atlanta firm. It proposed ways for attorneys to "become more involved" in diversity efforts. Among the suggestions were to invite "diverse" attorneys to lunch or a weekend social event, or to "take 20 minutes and ask a female attorney and/or a diverse attorney 'where do you want to go from here?'" Lawyers were also reminded to bill the time spent on these collegial interchanges. The memorandum circulated on the Internet under the title, "Is This the Most Offensively Misguided Diversity Memo You've Ever Seen?"[113]

One strategy that requires additional evaluation and research is training. Some surveyed lawyers have been "lukewarm" about the usefulness of diversity education, and some experts who have studied its effectiveness are even less enthusiastic.[114] The large-scale review of diversity initiatives described in Chapter One found that training programs did not significantly increase representation or advancement of targeted groups.[115] Part of the problem is that such programs typically focus only on individual behaviors and not institutional problems; they also provide no incentives to implement recommended practices and sometimes provoke backlash among involuntary participants.[116] Yet findings from my recent survey of managing partners and general counsel offer a more mixed picture. Although some leaders felt that programs were "not solving a problem that we had," many felt they were useful. As one law firm managing partner put it: "Not all men see that there is a need to address women's issues. They see women partners and don't see inhibitions."[117] According to another firm chair, "Most people don't think they need it, but most take from the training the need for understanding the possibility of unconscious bias."[118]

Another common strategy that varies in effectiveness is women's initiatives, or affinity groups, aimed at promoting professional development. A survey by the National Association of Women Lawyers found that virtually all large firms had such initiatives, and many other employers have launched similar efforts.[119] Not all evaluations are positive. The only large-scale study on affinity groups, which was in the corporate rather than legal sector, did not find them effective in career development.[120] Research by the National Association of Women Lawyers notes that not all women's initiatives are well conceived or well funded; and when such an initiative "focuses primarily on female skill development, it unfairly assumes that women themselves are the barrier to their own achievement of parity. Decades of research suggest otherwise."[121] However, many female lawyers feel that these efforts are useful in developing networks and informal mentoring relationships.[122] Well-designed initiatives can also help in identifying effective reform strategies and generating the collective support necessary to achieve them.[123]

Another strategy, one with well-documented benefits, involves mentoring. The most effective programs evaluate and reward mentoring activities and specify some level of contact. Formal programs are not, however, a substitute for informal efforts to encourage not only mentoring but also sponsorship. Women need advocates whose support cannot be mandated.

More attention to work-family issues is also critical. Too many organizations appear resigned to the idea that law is a 24/7 profession and that there is little they can do to address the issue. In my survey of managing partners and general counsel, one commented: "You have to be realistic. It's a demanding profession. . . . I don't claim we've figured it out."[124]

Those attitudes need to change, and so do part-time policies that few lawyers feel willing or able to use. Surveying lawyers and collecting data on reduced-schedule utilization rates and promotion opportunities are critical in educating leaders about whether formal policies work in practice as well as principle. More firms should adopt "new models" of practice, in which lawyers customize their schedules and cut their overhead expenses by working from home or onsite at clients' workplaces.[125] More organizations should follow the example of companies such as Wal-Mart, where in-house lawyers have the option to cut back hours or work from home some number of days per week. In emergencies, all lawyers are expected to be flexible. But that is not common. As the company's executive vice president and chief administrative officer put it, "These days I always tell people we're running a law department, not a fire department."[126]

Of course, in private practice, where lawyers are serving client needs and not calling the shots, there may be more times when part-time attorneys have to work longer hours or adjust their schedules. But in general, firms should provide more opportunities for lawyers to scale back their time commitments or temporarily step out of the workforce without paying a permanent professional price. For example, one Chicago firm allows its associates to choose whether to bill two thousand hours a year and be paid top dollars or to bill eighteen hundred and earn less; more than half of associates choose the reduced schedule.[127] Women with families would also benefit from broader structural reforms that evaluate performance less on billable hours and more on responsiveness, client satisfaction, and quality of work.[128]

Law may be a demanding profession, but too much talent will fall by the wayside if workplaces don't make better adjustments. More support for emergency child care and for lawyers moving on and off reduced schedules is necessary to level the playing field.

Organizations can also help expand the pool of lawyers of color through scholarships and other educational initiatives designed to prepare underrepresented minorities for law schools. The ABA's Pipeline Diversity Directory describes about four hundred such programs throughout the country.[129] For example, a growing number of law firms and corporations have contributed to the Law Preview Scholarship Program, which assists underrepresented low-income students.[130] Some law schools have partnered with donors to create scholarships for disadvantaged students and provide them with support networks for career development.[131] Skadden and Arps committed $10 million for a ten-year program offering law school preparation to students from low-income backgrounds.[132] In commenting on that example, one ABA official noted, "this is the kind of money we need to make a difference. . . . Now we need just 500 other firms to take action."[133]

As someone who has studied gender equity in the legal profession for almost three decades, I find the issues addressed in this chapter frustratingly familiar. But what is encouraging is that these concerns are now widely shared. As one law firm chair observed, "Ten years ago, it wasn't uncomfortable to walk into a room with a non-diverse team. The temperature of the water has changed. It's hard to succeed without a commitment to diversity."[134] The challenge now is to translate that aspirational commitment into daily practices.

WOMEN IN ACADEMIA

"Higher Ed Presidential Pipeline Slow to Change" ran the title of a recent article in *The Higher Education Workplace*. At a time when women constitute more than half of undergraduate, master's degree, and Ph.D. students, they account for less than a quarter of college presidents and a third of chief academic officers at doctoral institutions.[1] Women's share of presidential positions hasn't budged in a decade, and it is lower at the most elite institutions. At top-ranked universities, women hold about 16 percent of provost and president positions.[2] Particularly in the most elite institutions, racial and ethnic minorities still lag far behind. A *Chronicle of Higher Education* headline summed it up: "At the Ivies, It's Still White at the Top."[3] The story reported that only 10 to 20 percent of upper-level administrators were racial or ethnic minorities. Other research similarly finds that women of color are concentrated in less prestigious institutions and on lower rungs of the academic ladder.[4]

To be sure, the academy has done better than other sectors in advancing women. Not all female presidents feel that their "experience has been gendered," as Bates President Clayton Spencer put it. She believed that it has been "relatively easier for women to advance [in the university] than it has been in other areas."[5] The numbers bear this out. But the relatively greater progress that women have made in academia also fosters the perception that the "woman problem" has been solved. In a recent survey at Stanford, virtually all the male participants and about half the female participants believed that leadership positions were equally attainable.[6] Yet the data suggest otherwise. In Stanford as elsewhere, women, particularly women of color, are still underrepresented in leadership roles for much the same reasons as in other occupational fields: unconscious bias, ingroup favoritism, and work-family conflicts.[7] However, one factor unique to academia poses a special challenge. For most female administrators, the path to advancement begins with a tenured position. And the timeline for tenure, the first seven years of an academic appointment, usually coincides with women's peak childbearing years. Women's professional and biological clocks are ticking on the same schedule, and women who sacrifice academic concerns for family interests often take themselves out of the leadership pool. The discussion that follows explores this and other challenges, and the individual and institutional strategies that can best address them.

Unconscious Bias

A major obstacle to women seeking academic leadership positions involves lingering and largely unconscious gender bias. Some male-dominated administrations and boards of trustees doubt women's ability to lead large, complex institutions or balance work and family obligations.[8] Rarely are those doubts explicitly expressed. As Kathleen McCartney, president of Smith College, notes: "Sexism has gone underground. Often you have a gut impression that an experience is gendered, but it's hard to know. We have to make the invisible visible."[9] Empirical research helps. It has consistently found that women still do not enjoy the presumption of competence enjoyed by white men.[10] An illuminating case study of such bias came from Yale researchers. They asked science faculty at six major universities to evaluate an applicant for a lab manager's position. All of the professors received the same description of the applicant, but in half the descriptions the applicant was named John, and in the other half, Jennifer. Professors rated John more competent and more likely to be hired and mentored than Jennifer.[11]

In another study, one involving academic letters of recommendation, letters for women were likely to include "grindstone adjectives" such as "thorough," "hardworking," and "conscientious," while letters for men were likely to include words like "achievement" and "accomplishment."[12] Gender stereotypes may also help account for women's underrepresentation at the leadership level in certain fields. One recent study found fewer women in disciplines where innate raw talent was thought essential for success.[13] In one telling incident, a Stanford scientist who transitioned from being Barbara Barres to Ben Barres reported that after he gave a well-received academic speech, he overheard a member of the audience say, "His work is much better than his sister's."[14]

So too, women in academic leadership frequently report needing to work twice as hard and be twice as good in order to be viewed as equal to men.[15] When they manage to attain upper-level positions, a common assumption is that they gained the slot only because they were women.[16] High-level female administrators often feel that they must do more than their male colleagues to establish their competence.[17] Debora Spar, president of Barnard, recalls questions being raised over "my capability, my clout, and my overall potential to take charge."[18] In one study of female university presidents, participants recounted having their abilities questioned concerning finances, facilities, and athletics.[19] Other common complaints include not being listened to and not being taken as seriously as male colleagues.[20] As one woman put it, "I am still taken aback by the level of ˌ̣ᵢ̣ disrespect female administrators experience, behavior that male colleagues would not direct at male administrators."[21]

Women of color are particularly likely to encounter doubts concerning their competence and credentials.[22] Many are assumed to be beneficiaries of affirmative action and often report marginalization, tokenism, and reservations about their own abilities.[23] The title of a prominent anthology on women of color in the academy summed it up: *Presumed Incompetent*.[24] Many contributors reported experiences along the lines of a black law professor who received a course evaluation stating, "I know we have to have affirmative action but do we have to have her?"[25] A common view, expressed with uncommon candor to another contributor, was, "You only got the position because you are a black female and the department gets to count you twice."[26] The stigma often associated with affirmative action implies that many women of color "cannot possibly be here on [their] own merit."[27] A survey of Latina professors found that half had experienced subtle or overt discrimination, and other studies have found higher percentages of underrepresented minorities reporting a negative campus climate.[28] Women of color are constantly reminded of their different status yet "feel compelled to behave as though this difference did not exist."[29] The result is to add pressure to be overprepared in order to gain credibility.[30] Lesbian leaders report dealing with "stereotypes, discomfort, or morbid fascination."[31]

So too, women, particularly women of color, find that peers and superiors are often intolerant of their mistakes. This can be costly in a leadership position; one serious misstep in an unforgiving environment can waylay a career.[32] Women who worry that they will be judged more harshly than their male counterparts may avoid risks that could provide substantial professional development. As Chapter One indicated, many women also internalize prevailing stereotypes and discount their own leadership potential. Lack of confidence can keep women from even aspiring to top positions or proactively shaping their careers to lead there. In Susan Madsen's study of women university presidents, none had a career path targeted at a presidency.[33] Other research similarly finds that many female administrators simply "fell into positions."[34] In my own survey, even some of the most accomplished women, including Drew Faust, president of Harvard, did not actively seek leadership positions.[35] Because women often report that they are not recruited into upper-level administrative ranks as frequently as men, too much talent falls by the wayside.[36]

A related problem, as Smith President McCartney pointed out, is that "qualities we value in a leader we don't like in a woman."[37] As in other fields described in this book, many traits traditionally associated with leadership in academia are masculine. Women thus confront a double bind and a double standard.[38] They can appear too assertive or not assertive enough, and what is assertive in a man can be seen as "overbearing" in a woman.[39] Either way, women do not seem sufficiently "presidential."[40] Upper-level female administrators report being perceived as too "weak" or too "pushy and aggressive."[41] As one president put it, "I think the problem that women have is that everyone wants you to be sweetness and light, and if you are sweetness and light then you're too soft to make tough decisions."[42] By contrast, female academics who fall on the other end of the sweetness spectrum risk being criticized as "cold," "unfeeling," "insensitive," "hard-nosed," "nasty," and "ironfisted."[43] In describing the president at the University of Nevada at Las Vegas, one regent noted, "If she were a man, she would be regarded as an aggressive and strong leader, but as a woman, to many people she is a bitch."[44] At a Harvard Education School program for aspiring women leaders, participants were asked how many of them had been described as "bossy." Every hand in the room went up.[45] Fear of being labeled pushy or problematic also silences women who feel that they have not received equal treatment.[46] The fears are not unfounded.[47]

A further problem involves in-group favoritism. Research reviewed in Chapter One documents the preferences that individuals feel for members of their own groups. These members are likely to experience more loyalty and career opportunities than similarly qualified outsiders. Academia is no exception, as a recent *New York Times* article reported under the title "Professors Are Prejudiced, Too."[48] What some experts label "the cloning effect" results in subtle, often unintentional, marginalization of women. As one female participant in a leadership study put it, men are "not actively excluding anybody," but they aren't actively including them either.[49] Another female faculty member agreed: "I don't think it's a conscious thing, but it has consequences in the end."[50] Women in upper-level academic administration often remain out of the loop of support and sponsorship available to their male colleagues.[51] And because the numbers of women in academic leadership lag behind those of men, there are fewer female mentors for aspiring colleagues.[52] Again, this shortage is particularly pronounced for women of color; their isolation can be especially acute.[53] Women are similarly underrepresented on the governance boards that select presidents, and male members of those boards may be more comfortable with male leaders.[54]

Women also end up with disproportionate academic housekeeping tasks—the grunt work of low-level committee and administrative assignments—both because women are more likely than men to be asked and because they are less likely to say no.[55] For example, in one survey of about fourteen hundred political science professors, women

advised more undergraduate students and participated on more committees than their male colleagues.[56] In other surveys, female faculty
spent more than four more hours per week on university service committees and were twice as likely as male colleagues to volunteer to be
on a committee.[57] These assignments take time away from other, more
highly valued tasks involving research and teaching. One woman who
was recruited to be a principal investigator because a campus center
needed a female PI on a large grant responded that she would do it, but
expressed the hope that "there's not a swimsuit and eveningwear competition with this also."[58]

In fields where women are particularly underrepresented, the burdens are particularly great. As one computer scientist put it, "I know
in my case, if it's got the word 'computer' in it, I don't care what it is,
I'm on that panel. I get stuck on [that] committee."[59] Women of color
are especially vulnerable. They are often expected to be the "face of
diversity," as well as to mentor minority students who also have disproportionate problems fitting in.[60] One participant in a leadership
study noted that "we've got a Native American on our faculty, and boy
is she spread thin."[61] Her account was confirmed in another study of
Native American women, which reported that for many participants,
service work was a "full-time job by itself."[62] All too often, such service
is unrewarded or unrewarding. Many female academics report experiences similar to those of Barnard President Spar, who "can't count the
number of times I've been the token women on a committee, panel or
council . . . I can't help but feel I'm sometimes selected for the wrong
reasons—chosen for my biology rather than my brains, bearing the
brunt of the sheer distance between the appearance of equality and
true appreciation of women leaders."[63]

Work-Family Conflicts

A final barrier to women in academic leadership involves work-family
conflicts. Colleges and universities are what sociologists label "greedy
institutions."[64] The time demands of running complex organizations,
coupled with evening and weekend events, pose challenges for anyone
with significant caretaking commitments. When asked about one

piece of advice she would give to women interested in leadership positions, Debora Spar responded:

> Think very very hard about how you envision the other aspects of your future—those outside your corner office with a view. Do you want children? Do you want to eat dinner with them every night? Every other night? Or will you be happy with the nanny feeding them, feeling their foreheads for fevers and chaperoning field trips in your stead? Sixty-plus-hour work weeks are often the norm.[65]

So too, as Chapter One documented, despite men's increasing assumption of family responsibilities, women continue to assume a disproportionate burden in the home. "When push comes to shove," said Bates President Spencer, "if forced to choose between the best interest of their children or their job," more women than men will choose their children."[66] Other research similarly finds that most women chief academic officers do not wish to become president, partly because of the time demands and heavy social obligations.[67] When, as is often the case, administrative positions are understaffed and underfunded, they are unattractive to those with substantial caretaking commitments.[68] Women's unequal family responsibilities make it harder for them than for their male colleagues to achieve tenure, to assume academic leadership roles, and to compile performance records that would equip them for such administrative positions.[69]

Because women's peak childbearing years coincide with the time when academic career foundations are laid, aspiring female leaders face challenges that colleges and universities must do more to address. Too often women simply assume that leadership positions are incompatible with their personal commitments, without asking whether the positions themselves could be restructured or better supported. As one woman who had stepped down from a demanding role put it, "I consider this a great failure on my part."[70] And when women do ask for accommodations, they are too often stigmatized or viewed as insufficiently committed. One participant in a leadership study recalled a discussion over scheduling a meeting in which she had said, "That's fine, but I need to be able to leave at five o'clock." To which a male faculty member responded,

"Yeah, it's always the women who have to leave at five o'clock."[71] Shirley Tilghman, former president of Princeton, noted that "we haven't figured out how to make it possible for women to think about work and family as complementary. Until we figure this out, I think we're always going to be sort of running uphill."[72]

A related problem is that, as University of California President Janet Napolitano points out, in upper levels of academia, "people move around where jobs become available. And it's harder for women to do that. . . . They are less portable."[73] But this gender disadvantage is not an intractable feature of academic life. It is culture, not biology, that assigns women the role of trailing spouse. And the culture can and should change to grant wives' careers equal priority with those of their husbands.

Strategies for Individuals

What enables women to overcome these obstacles and rise to positions of authority, and what makes them effective once they get there? Do women lead differently from men? A growing body of research on women who reach positions of academic leadership speaks to these issues.

As Chapter One reported, women leaders tend to have a more democratic decision-making approach than men.[74] Academics are no exception; female leaders in higher education gravitate toward participatory, consultative leadership styles.[75] Part of the reason, one president observed, is that women "have been socialized to be concerned about relationships."[76] This concern lends itself to a collaborative approach that is well suited to academic environments, which value nonhierarchical, process-oriented leadership.[77] However, this style is not without its difficulties. To some audiences, a participatory approach can seem weak and indecisive.[78] Women have often responded by adopting a more authoritative style, or an "androgynous" approach that combines traditionally masculine and feminine traits.[79] For many women, the goal is to appear assertive but not abrasive.[80] As Harvard President Drew Faust points out, "Women are read as much more aggressive. I think you just have to be aware of that. You have to be firm, you have to be clear, you have to not be angry. And if someone says you're angry, you just have to live with that."[81] Nannerl Keohane,

former president of Wellesley and Duke, described her style as com-
bining both "forcefulness and sensitivity." She would "work for collaboration, try to bring in partners, and look for a win-win where lots of
people can get credit."[82] In the phrase quoted earlier from University
of Michigan President Mary Sue Coleman, women benefit from being
"relentlessly pleasant."[83]

However, as many female academics have recognized, there is "no
one model of successful leadership that fits all circumstances."[84] Women
need to adapt to what the situation demands.[85] As one explained, their
approach must

> grow out of the needs of the times. If the house is on fire, you'd better be
> very directive. If you are going to revise the promotion and tenure guide-
> lines, you had better be very participatory. If you have a style and some-
> body can say, "you're always going to do this," you're going to be a disaster
> because you don't have enough sense to read the situation and know what's
> required.[86]

A substantial body of research finds that leaders who are most successful
have a repertoire of styles that can fit diverse contexts.[87]

In addition to that mix of styles, certain other qualities appear critical
to academic leaders' success. High ethical standards are at the top of the
list.[88] Academic women leaders speak of not losing sight of core values,
needing to be open and honest, and serving as a model of integrity. A
related quality is a willingness to put the institution's interests first.[89]
Successful presidents recognize that it is "not about you."[90] Obvious
though this seems in principle, it can prove challenging in practice.
Individuals often rise to a position of leadership because they have high
needs for personal achievement. But once they are in such a position,
especially in higher education, they must subordinate those needs. This
will often require using their power to empower others.[91]

Another critical leadership quality is a capacity for lifelong learning.
Female presidents emphasize a willingness to do their homework, hear
criticism, acknowledge mistakes, and reflect on failures.[92] Self-knowledge
and commitment to continuous personal development are essential to
success. James Kouzes and Barry Posner find that "the best leaders . . .

are the best learners."[93] To facilitate learning, women should get outside their comfort zone and look for leadership opportunities that build a broad skill set.[94]

Aspiring leaders should also seek mentors and sponsors and cultivate the ability to connect with others. Formal and informal networks of women can be helpful in building bridges at all stages of an academic career. Advice and support from individuals who have held academic leadership positions is often necessary for professional development.[95] Many women presidents report such assistance, even mock job interviews.[96] By the same token, mentoring and sponsoring the next generation of leaders is part of their own professional responsibilities.[97]

Other key leadership traits are judgment and conflict management. Effective leaders pick their battles wisely. They are not always presiding over a "peaceable kingdom," and some have encountered situations where the faculty was "split on almost everything."[98] Often high-level administrators face an initial period of intense scrutiny, which former University of Miami President Donna Shalala labeled the "gotcha phase."[99] During this period, they need to tread especially carefully and consult broadly before embarking on significant change. Academic administrators may also need advice or training in mediating disputes, since these are skills that are not central to successful faculty careers. Commonly advised strategies involve expressing concern for all parties, helping them identify shared values and objectives, focusing on underlying needs, and creating structures for ongoing problem solving.[100]

In making their way across academic minefields, leaders need to set clear priorities. Sometimes they have to keep their head above the fray. One woman earned the label "get it done Dunn" because of her ability to remain task-oriented.[101] As another woman put it, "You can't fight for every issue. It's demanding and exhausting and may distract you from issues that matter more. . . . Women [should] choose their battles deliberately, cautiously, and carefully."[102] Among the factors to consider are timing, the odds of winning, the price of losing, and the values at issue. In "Lessons from the Experiences of Women of Color Working in Academia," Yolanda Niemann advised, "Focus on what is in your power to challenge, change, or address."[103] Some presidents have warned against seeking too much too soon. "Don't try to change things until you are in a position of strength," one leader advised.[104] Women need to give others "the time to become accustomed to your ideas . . . You are in this for the long haul; be strategic with your influence and your energy."[105] Extensive consultation is often essential to legitimate change.[106] Presidential power must be earned, not assumed, and is a resource not to be squandered prematurely.[107]

A case history in the value of incremental change is the failed campus coup at the University of Virginia. In 2012, the board of trustees summarily forced the resignation of Teresa Sullivan on the grounds that she lacked "bold and proactive leadership" on controversial issues such as budgetary cuts and online education.[108] But when the campus erupted in protest, the board was forced to retreat and reinstate Sullivan. What she had recognized and the trustees had not was that, as she explained to a *New York Times* reporter, "This was an institution steeped in tradition. People love the tradition, and they would not react well to sudden change."[109] Clearly the trustees had also not reckoned with all the stakeholders that now influence what happens in higher education. Academic institutions rarely tolerate dictatorial decision making, whether by boards or by presidents.

Exercising good judgment also requires good listening. As one president put it, "Being able to just sit and listen is more than half of communicating. It is the hardest thing we do. It's much more tiring than talking."[110] Another similarly commented on the importance of strategic silence. Leaders need to understand stakeholders' concerns, and "you can only do that if you are quiet enough to listen to what they are saying."[111] Good listening skills are also the foundation of other key leadership abilities such as forming alliances, facilitating teamwork, and building consensus.[112]

Finally, a striking number of female leaders mentioned a quality that seldom figures in leadership texts. Donna Shalala, who has held three academic presidencies, as well as a cabinet position, put it bluntly: "You have to have a good sense of humor."[113] Other leaders agreed; humor can go a long way in relieving tension and stress.[114] It can also communicate difficult truths.[115] The ability to laugh at oneself is especially critical.[116] Of course in higher education, as in every other context, leaders need cultural sensitivity. They should be aware of the power dynamics of a situation, and avoid using humor in ways that might alienate potential supporters.[117]

Finally, and most importantly, women need to be self-reflective and proactive in shaping their career paths. This sometimes requires saying no to tasks that do not lead to advancement, which women find more difficult to do than men.[118] Women of color should be especially careful not to become the "all-purpose 'woman minority'" member of committees, task forces, panels, and so forth.[119] As a past president of the American Association for Higher Education put it, women of color need to be "selective" and "selfish" about their time commitments: "Institutions do not hug back! You have to be the keeper of your career trajectory."[120]

Women also should let upper-level administrators know that they are interested in leadership opportunities.[121] Keohane advises, "Take time to think carefully about your significant priorities in life, and engage in a realistic assessment of your strengths and weaknesses, your preferences and aversions . . . what you are good at, and what you enjoy. If, after this exercise, you really want this leadership position, Go For It! Develop a strategy, learn a lot about the institution; find allies and hone your arguments for being chosen."[122]

Strategies for Institutions

Significant progress toward gender equity in higher education will require greater commitment to that objective. Diversity in leadership is critical in creating role models and nurturing the aspirations of half the nation's talent pool. The first, and most essential, step is for campus leaders to recognize the underrepresentation of women and minorities as a significant problem and to hold administrators accountable for addressing it. Research reviewed in Chapter One consistently finds that the most important factor in ensuring equal access to leadership opportunities is commitment to that objective, which is reflected in workplace policies and reward structures.[123] Decision makers need to be held responsible for results as well as for practices that influence those results, such as evaluation, career development, mentoring, and work-family accommodation.

In short, campus leaders must make diversity and equity a priority and to assess progress in achieving them. To that end, academic administrations need to monitor results. Campuses should compile information on recruitment, hiring, promotion, and retention, broken down by sex, as well as race and ethnicity. A key recommendation of Stanford's recent Task Force on Leadership was for the university to develop appropriate metrics for assessing the inclusivity of high-level and pipeline positions and to make annual public progress reports.[124] Surveys of current and departing faculty can also provide valuable information on equity, work-family, and quality-of-life issues. Decision makers need to know whether men and women are advancing in equal numbers, whether they feel equally supported in career development, and whether they are performing equal amounts of service work. Campuses should assess their own progress in comparison with similar institutions.

Inclusive search processes are another key strategy. Institutions need to diversify their search committees, and those committees must also diversify their candidate pools.[125] The practice of looking only to academic officers for presidents and provosts not only puts women at a disadvantage, it also preempts access to "new ideas, new viewpoints, and innovative ways of addressing new challenges."[126] One way to encourage more inclusive search processes is to increase their transparency and to actively encourage applications for open positions. Stanford's task force recommended that the university create a website providing information about leadership opportunities and how individuals can express interest in being considered. The task force also recommended that department chairs and other senior administrators explore faculty interest in administration as part of their review and mentoring processes.[127] Another possibility is for search committees to operate with a modified version of the Rooney Rule, developed to identify minority and female candidates for professional football coaching and management positions.[128] Under this approach, committees could agree to include a woman as a finalist for any open leadership position.

Any serious commitment to expand women's leadership opportunities requires a similarly serious commitment to address work-family conflicts. To be sure, most institutions have come a long way since the time that Smith President McCartney couldn't get a maternity leave because it wouldn't be "fair to the men."[129] Best practices and model programs are readily available on matters such as flexible and reduced schedules, tenure-clock-stopping provisions for primary caretakers, telecommuting, leave policies, child-care subsidies, and onsite facilities.[130] Such options are necessary but not sufficient to retain potential leaders. Academics must also feel free to take advantage of them, and some research suggests that a substantial percentage of women attempt to avoid bias by not using family- friendly policies that are available.[131]

For that to change, campuses need to monitor policies for their perceived effectiveness and accessibility. Institutions of higher education must ensure that those who seek temporary accommodations do not pay a permanent price. Individuals on reduced or flexible schedules should not lose opportunities for challenging assignments or eventual promotion. If colleges and universities want the most able and diverse leadership candidates possible, the working environment must do more to support them.

Greater attention should also focus on education and mentoring. Well-designed training programs can help in building awareness of implicit racial and gender bias.[132] Leadership development programs can assist women and minorities in acquiring the skill set necessary for upper-level positions.[133] Most surveyed campuses have yet to institute such programs, and either need to create them or subsidize opportunities that exist offsite.[134] One study found that two-thirds of faculty who became department chairs lacked preparation for their roles.[135] Many women also lack the multiple mentors and sponsors that are critical for advancement. Creating faculty women's forums and minority women's alliances can be helpful in building networks of support. Where informal relationships are lacking, formal mentoring programs can help fill the gap. Of course, relationships that are assigned are seldom as effective as those that are chosen. But at least structured programs can keep talented but unassertive women from falling through the cracks, and remove concerns about appearances of favoritism or sexual impropriety that can inhibit informal mentoring relationships. Well-designed initiatives that evaluate and reward mentoring activities can improve skills, satisfaction, and retention. Adequate feed-back structures can also help ensure that those holding leadership pipe-line positions are getting the advice they need to thrive and advance. Leaders who express commitment to diversity need to persuade others and hold them accountable.[136]

Campuses should also make more efforts to equalize service work and compensate faculty who do more than their fair share. Course relief and additional research assistance could help ensure that women, par-ticularly women of color, are not penalized for disproportionately as-suming responsibilities that meet institutional needs.[137] Efforts to build a more inclusive environment should be affirmatively valued in promotion decisions.[138]

Higher education should also do more to recognize the importance of diversity and gender equity in curricular, programming, and research priorities. These issues should be integrated into relevant courses, and institutions should pay attention to the inclusiveness of conferences, lectures, and other extracurricular programs.[139] So too, professional and MBA programs should increase research support for scholars and con-tinuing education for practitioners on equity and diversity. We need to know much more about what works in the world, and academic institu-tions are uniquely positioned to help fill the gap.

Prominent female presidents offer examples of leadership on gender equity. Drew Faust at Harvard has made it a priority to at-tract more female students and faculty into science, technology, math, engineering, and business. Under her leadership, the number of female faculty has risen from 24 to 40 percent.[140] One of the first acts of former Princeton President Shirley Tilghman was to appoint a woman provost, despite the fact that many viewed one woman at the top of this previously all-male institution as more than suf-ficient. Another important initiative was a Steering Committee on Undergraduate Women's Leadership. It identified an underrepresen-tation of female undergraduates in influential campus positions, and among winners of academic prizes and postgraduate fellowships. As comparative data attested, these patterns were by no means unique to Princeton.[141] And unless academic institutions address problems in the leadership pipeline at its origin, they are unlikely to see different results at its end.

Higher education can and must do better in modeling equal opportunity. College campuses are gatekeepers for positions of leadership in American society, and these institutions ought to reflect the diversity of the society they serve.

WOMEN ON BOARDS

Announcing that he was "shit tired" of the "boys club" dominating Norway corporations, the nation's minister of trade and industry predicted "radical change."[1] That was in 2002, and the change came the following year in the form of a 40 percent quota for women on corporate boards. In subsequent years, the percentage of female representation grew from 6 to 40 percent. Some of those who initially doubted that Norway could find qualified women changed their views, and one quipped that it was business as usual in the boardroom, except for "less dirty talk."[2] Other nations followed suit with mandatory or aspirational quotas specifying a minimum proportion of women on boards; many more have voluntary targets in corporate governance codes.[3]

In the United States, support for gender diversity has grown in principle, but lagged in practice, and controversy has centered on whether and why diversity matters.[4] The stakes in this debate are substantial. Corporate boards affect the lives of millions of employees and consumers, and the policies and practices of the global marketplace.[5] As recent scandals demonstrate, failures in board governance can carry an enormous cost.[6] Who gains access to these boards is therefore an issue of broad social importance.

The Underrepresentation of Women

The last two decades have witnessed substantial progress in appointments of women to corporate boards. No longer do we see companies even in the feminine hygiene or baby food industry with no female members.[7] However, women still hold only 19 percent of the seats on Fortune 500 boards, and women of color, 3 percent.[8] In S&P 1500 companies, the figures are worse: women occupy only 15 percent of seats.[9] Board directors named Robert, William, and James exceeded the total number of women.[10] Female directors are also underrepresented as chairs of compensation, audit, and nominating committees, which are among the most influential board positions.[11] At the current rate of change, it would take almost seventy years before women's representation on corporate boards reached parity with that of men.[12]

Moreover, some of the most encouraging numbers on board diversity may conceal less promising trends. Much of the growth in women directors over the last decade may be attributable to the same individuals sitting on more boards.[13] Many commentators worry that these "trophy directors," who serve on as many as seven boards, are spread too thin to provide adequate oversight.[14] Another concern is that appointment of one or two token female members will lessen pressure for continued diversity efforts.

The Case for Diversity

The growing consensus within the corporate community is that diversity is an important goal. The case for diversity on boards rests on two primary claims. The first is that it provides equal opportunity. The public has a strong interest in "ensuring that opportunities are available to all . . . that women entering the labour market are able to fulfil their potential, and that we make full use of the wealth of talented women" available for board service.[15] The second claim is that diversity will improve organizational processes and performance. This "business case for diversity" tends to dominate debates, because it appeals to a culture steeped in shareholder value as the metric for corporate decision making.[16] This is also the claim that provokes most controversy.

Despite growing acceptance of the business case for diversity, empirical evidence is mixed. Some studies have found positive correlations between board diversity and various measures of financial performance.[17] Others have found the opposite or no significant relationship.[18] A recent meta-analysis of 140 studies covering thirty-five countries found that organizations with more women on their boards had higher accounting returns (measured by returns on assets, and higher returns on equity) and returns on invested capital), but not stronger market performance (measured by stock performance and shareholder returns).[19] What further complicates the issue is that correlations do not demonstrate causation. It could be that better firm performance leads to more board diversity, rather than the reverse.[20] More successful firms may be better positioned to attract the female and minority candidates in high demand for board service.[21] Larger and better-performing organizations may have more resources to devote to pursuing diversity and may face more pressure from the public and large institutional investors to increase diversity on their boards.[22] Finally, some third factor could be causing both improved performance and greater board diversity.[23] Scholars also question whether focusing on short-term accounting measures of financial performance is the best way to measure the impact of diversity. Research is lacking on the relationship between board diversity and long-term stock price performance, which is the "gold standard" measure of shareholder value.[24]

These mixed results may reflect not only differences in research methodology, but also differences in the context in which diversification occurs.[25] The failure to include a critical mass of women may in some cases prevent the potential benefits of diversity.[26] Those benefits may also be reduced by organizations' well-documented tendency to appoint women who are least likely to challenge the status quo, or who are "trophy directors," with too many board positions to provide adequate oversight.[27]

Given the inconclusive evidence of the impact of gender on financial performance, many commentators believe that the "business case for diversity" rests on other grounds, particularly its effects on board decision-making processes, corporate reputation, and governance capacities.

A common argument, which tracks the claims set forth in Chapter One, is that diversity enhances board decision-making and monitoring functions.[28] This assertion draws on social science research on small-group decision making, as well as studies of board processes and members' experiences.[29] The basic premise is that differences in people's knowledge and experience affect how they seek and interpret information.[30] Diversity in board backgrounds may thus inform decision making and lessen the tendency for boards to engage in groupthink—a phenomenon in which members' efforts to achieve consensus override their ability to "realistically appraise alternative courses of action."[31] Diverse boards also make sense because they can tap into the skills of a wider talent pool.[32]

The literature on board decision making reflects several theories about the process by which diversity enhances performance. The first theory is that women and men have differing strengths, and that greater inclusion can ensure representation of valuable capabilities. For instance, some empirical evidence suggests that women tend to be more financially risk-averse than men.[33] For this reason, many commentators have speculated that more female participation in corporate decision making could have helped to curb the tendencies that caused the most recent financial crisis.[34] They cite evidence suggesting that women are "more prudent" and less "ego-driven" than men in financial management contexts.[35] One study found that the presence of at least one woman on a company's board was associated with a reduction of almost 40 percent in the likelihood of a financial restatement.[36] Another study found that banks with female CEOs and board chairs acted more conservatively during the financial crisis.[37] Other research has pointed in similar directions, including studies from researchers at Harvard and Cambridge Universities, which found a correlation between a high level of testosterone and an appetite for risk.[38] Some commentators also rely on evidence indicating that women have more trustworthy and collaborative styles, which can improve board dynamics.[39] As one female director put it, "Women are more cooperative and less competitive in tone and approach. . . . Women often provide a type of leadership that helps boards do their jobs better."[40]

A second theory of how diversity enhances performance is that women have different life experiences from men, which enables the board to consider "a wider range of options and solutions to corporate issues."[41] Compared to male directors, female directors are more likely to hold an advanced degree, to have an interest in philanthropy and community service, and to come from a position other than CEO and COO.[42] One survey of nearly four hundred corporate directors concluded that female directors exhibit a stronger commitment to corporate social responsibility.[43] So too, in a recent Catalyst study, boards with greater gender diversity performed better across four of six measures of corporate social responsibility: environment, consumer relations, contributions to the community, and responsible supply chain management.[44]

Other research also suggests that diversity in experience is productive by generating cognitive conflict: "conflicting opinions, knowledge, and perspectives that result in a more thorough consideration of a wide range of interpretations, alternatives, and consequences."[45] Diversity can enhance the quality of a board's decision-making and monitoring functions because diverse groups are less likely to take extreme positions and more likely to engage in higher-quality analysis.[46] Some scholars have similarly suggested that diverse boards can help prevent corporate corruption and encourage socially responsible behavior because they are "bold enough to ask management the tough questions."[47] In one study, female directors expanded the content of board discussions and were more likely than their male counterparts to raise issues concerning the effects of corporate action on multiple stakeholders.[48] Other research finds that boards with more women tend to be more engaged in monitoring and strategic oversight.[49]

Such claims, however, require significant qualifications. Although research suggests that functionally or occupationally diverse groups may solve problems more quickly and effectively than homogeneous teams, demographic diversity may not improve decision-making processes and outcomes in the same ways.[50] Despite the differences in male and female board member backgrounds noted above, their educational, socioeconomic, and occupational experiences tend to be fairly similar.[51] Accordingly, some commentators have questioned the extent to which demographic diversity brings relevant diversity in perspectives.[52] Even when women and minorities have a different view, if they are represented at only a token level then they may lack sufficient leverage to affect the discussion. Studies on the influence of gender on leadership behavior are mixed, but some suggest that men and women who occupy the same role tend to behave similarly.[53] Moreover, demographic diversity can lead to greater conflict and poorer communication, which can counteract or overshadow the benefit of broader perspectives.[54]

Despite such qualifications, most research suggests that gender diversity can bring some benefits. As Scott Page summarizes the evidence, demographically diverse groups tend to outperform homogeneous groups "when the task is primarily problem solving, when their identities translate into relevant tools, when they have little or no [difference in what they value], and when their members get along with one another."[55] Other researchers find that interacting with individuals who are different forces group members to prepare better, anticipate alternative viewpoints, and think creatively.[56] In a French study, board members believed that the increased presence of women had led to "more methodical, even reasoned deliberation, with . . . less conflict, and more civil behavior."[57]

Additional empirical studies have identified a positive correlation between diversity and measures of good governance. Boards that have a higher representation of women hold more meetings, have a higher attendance rate, experience greater participation in decision making, engage in tougher monitoring, and are more likely to replace a CEO when the stock performs poorly.[58] A study by the Conference Board of Canada found that, on average, organizations whose boards have two or more women adopt a greater number of accountability practices and regularly review more nonfinancial performance measures than organizations with all-male boards.[59] The study further found that boards with more women paid greater attention to audit and risk oversight than all-male boards.[60] In a Scandinavian survey, women prepared better for board meetings and asked more questions than their male counterparts.[61] However, as in many of the preceding studies, correlation does not demonstrate causation, and it could be that well-governed corporate boards are more committed to diversity and seek greater gender parity.[62]

A third theory on how diversity enhances performance is that its very existence sends a positive message to stakeholders and improves corporate governance. Board diversity can imply commitment to equal opportunity, responsiveness to diverse stakeholders, and enlightened leadership, which can enhance the corporation's public image.[63] Catalyst research finds that increasing women's representation on corporate boards is associated with expanded executive opportunities for women.[64] Drawing on signaling theory, some researchers argue that a critical mass of women "conveys a credible [positive] signal to relevant observers of corporate behavior."[65] Conversely, the adverse publicity that Twitter received when it went public with a board of all white men is an illuminating case study. It demonstrates the reputational costs of a leadership structure that fails to reflect the diversity of the community the company serves.[66] As subsequent discussion notes, such case studies suggest the value of making employees, consumers, and the general public more aware of board composition.

In the final analysis, however one evaluates the evidence on gender and financial performance, there are other strong justifications for diversity, including values such as fairness, good governance, and equal opportunity, as well as the symbolic message it sends to corporate stakeholders.[67] Board service offers members valuable leadership experience and credentials, as well as contacts and financial compensation. Women deserve equal access to those benefits. Some evidence also suggests that firms with more women on the board also have more women top executives and are more likely to appoint a woman CEO.[68] This creates a feedback cycle in which the presence of more female executives enlarges the pool of potential female board members, which leads to further growth in the number of female executives.[69]

A diverse board also suggests that women's perspectives are important to the organization, and that the organization is committed to gender equity practice as well as principle.[70] Corporations with such a commitment have access to a wider pool of talent and a broader mix of leadership skills than corporations that lack such a commitment.[71] For all of these reasons, the vast majority of corporate board members support inclusive leadership. Four-fifths of surveyed American directors believe that diversity at least "somewhat" enhances board effectiveness and company performance, and more than a third believe that it does so "very much."[72]

Barriers to Diversity

Given the growing support for diversity on corporate boards, why has it been so difficult to achieve? One obvious explanation is that the

research on performance is too mixed to make diversification a priority. Antonio Perez, former CEO of Kodak, put the point bluntly: "The
real barrier . . . [is that many] corporations don't believe that it is a business imperative."[73] Only about a third of male directors (compared with
almost two-thirds of female directors) believe that gender diversity is
a very important board attribute.[74] Other explanations involve unconscious bias: devaluation of women's competence, in-group favoritism,
and counterproductive effects of tokenism.[75] These factors both directly
impede appointment of qualified female candidates, and prevent others
from gaining the leadership experience that would make them attractive
choices.[76] A third explanation is resistance to "special preferences."[77] As
with other forms of affirmative action, opponents believe that selecting
members on the basis of gender reinforces precisely the kind of sex stereotyping that society should be seeking to eliminate.[78]

One of the most common explanations for the underrepresentation
of women on corporate boards involves the traditional pipeline to board
service.[79] Less than a quarter of surveyed directors "very much" believe
that there is a sufficient number of qualified diverse candidates.[80] Part
of the reason is what has traditionally counted as a qualification. The
primary route to board directorship has long been through experience
as a CEO of a public corporation. One study found that a majority of
male Fortune 500 directors were CEOs or former CEOs, and another
found that nearly half of new appointments hold that status.[81] A National
Association of Corporate Directors survey determined that CEO-level
experience was the most important functional background in the search
for a new director, with 97 percent of respondents considering professional experience "critical" or "important" for board candidates.[82] Given
the low representation of women in top executive positions, their talents
are likely to be underutilized if selection criteria are not broadened. As
Chapter Three reported, women constitute only 4 percent of Fortune
500 CEOs and 15 percent of Fortune 500 executive officer positions.[83]
Even women and minorities who reach upper-level management positions often do so through routes other than profit-and-loss responsibility, which provides crucial experience for board positions.[84] From male
directors' perspective, lack of executive experience is the primary reason
that the percentage of women on boards is not rising.[85]

However, recent developments—including requirements of director independence and financial expertise, restrictions on current CEOs serving on outside boards, and greater attention to age and tenure limits—may encourage boards to revisit traditional criteria for membership and expand the pipeline for women.[86] The number of active CEOs who serve on the boards of other public companies, and the proportion of newly elected independent directors who are CEOs, has decreased significantly during the last decade.[87] There is "no widely accepted" research demonstrating that active CEOs make better board members or ensure better monitoring by the board.[88] In fact, one survey found that 79 percent of corporate directors do not believe that "active-CEO directors [are] better than average directors."[89] As more corporations have positive experiences with board members of varied backgrounds, they may see the value in relying less on chief executives, whose experience may come at a cost because they are "used to running the show" and juggle many competing priorities.[90]

Moreover, considerable evidence suggests that the primary reason for women's underrepresentation on boards is not lack of qualifications. Eighty percent of top female executives at public companies do not serve on any boards, which suggests a large pool of untapped talent.[91] When one large survey asked why corporate boards are so male-dominated, only 30 percent of male members and 7 percent of female members cited a lack of qualified women.[92] A greater barrier, according to most experts, is closed social networks and the "in-group" favoritism that they reflect.[93] Research summarized in Chapter One describes the preferences that individuals feel for those who are like them in important respects.[94] Such favoritism keeps women out of the informal networks of support from which appointments are often made.[95] This form of bias is particularly likely in contexts where selection criteria are highly subjective, as is often true in board selections.[96] When the Government Accountability Office (GAO) asked stakeholders about barriers to diversity, about half identified directors' tendencies to rely on their personal networks to identify new board members.[97] As one interviewee noted, board members want to ensure that new members "fit in," which limits the candidate pool.[98] Female directors see exclusion from such social networks as the most important reason for women's underrepresentation on corporate boards.[99]

In-group favoritism also influences perceptions of competence.[100] Evidence cited in earlier chapters noted how members of in-groups tend to attribute accomplishments of fellow members to intrinsic characteristics, such as intelligence, drive, and commitment.[101] By contrast, the achievements of out-group members are often ascribed to luck or special treatment.[102] As one study concluded, "women's competence has to be widely acknowledged in the public domain or through family connections before boards . . . will be prepared to 'risk' having a woman on the board."[103] Many female directors report they have to be "twice as good as men" to get board appointments.[104] "I have to establish my credentials over and over," noted one board member. "It never stops."[105] Because in-group preferences can disadvantage women at every stage in their careers, they are less likely to have the experience and credentials thought necessary for board appointments.[106] Lack of mentoring and sponsorship of women directors also keeps them from obtaining additional board appointments.[107] Women of color experience particular difficulties of isolation and exclusion.[108]

A final barrier is the lack of turnover in board membership. According to one commentator, "What's holding women back isn't bias. It's the fact that no one ever leaves the boards."[109] Board members are often reluctant to give up positions that provide prestige and a significant salary, especially at the end of their careers.[110] Forty percent of public company directors are age sixty-eight or older.[111] Despite the thousands of board seats within large public companies, relatively few seats turn over in a given year.[112] The GAO study found that only 4 percent of seats in the S&P 1500 open each year.[113] Even if women were to receive the majority of new board appointments, the progress toward gender equity will continue to be slow unless the number of seats becoming available significantly increases.[114]

Gender Bias in the Boardroom

Women's underrepresentation on boards can also impair their performance as members. Rosabeth Moss Kanter's pathbreaking research, confirmed in multiple subsequent studies, found that women in token positions often encounter "social isolation, heightened visibility, . . . and pressure to adopt stereotyped roles. They are likely to do less well in the group, especially if the leader is a member of the dominant category."[115] Thus, underrepresentation may make it more difficult for women and minorities to be heard on an equal basis with other board members.[116] Many women feel marginalized in board deliberations. "I have to yell for them to hear me," one female director told *Harvard Business Review* researchers.[117] Outsiders often have limited opportunities to influence group decisions, particularly in the context of corporate boards where key decision making can take place in unofficial social settings that exclude women.[118] As another female director noted in the *Harvard Business Review* study, "I'm consistently not included in informal gatherings, such as golf games and dinner, by some male board members."[119]

The marginalization that token members experience may also undermine their effectiveness, which discourages further appointment of outsiders. For example, a director may "make herself socially invisible to avoid disrupting perceived group harmony and alleviate discomfort felt by the rest of the (all male) board."[120] As one woman put it, "If you emphasize how different you are, you are considered a troublemaker."[121] The result is that women's strengths may go unrecognized, and their silence may reinforce "antiquated beliefs that a woman brings nothing new to the table."[122] Alternatively, some directors may fall into the role that sociologists identify as the "queen bee" syndrome; they " 'revel in the notoriety of token status,' [enjoy] the perceived advantages of being the only woman in the group, and 'excessively criticiz[e] potential women peers.'"[123] The lesson is that the effectiveness of women on boards may depend on whether they have achieved a critical mass, and avoided the dynamics of tokenism.[124]

Strategies for Change

Strategies to counteract these dynamics and promote board diversity fall into three main categories. The first focuses on increasing women's capacity for service. The second includes legal strategies that might expand the pool of qualified members and level the playing field for their appointment. The third category involves ways to encourage voluntary corporate diversity efforts.

One obvious strategy to increase the number of women on corporate boards is to broaden the pool of qualified applicants. Efforts should begin early because, as one expert notes, "women need to gain [quantitative] skills . . . such as accounting, finance, and mathematics earlier in life, especially because quantitative skills require years of development."[125] Formal mentoring programs, leadership workshops, and diversity advisors or coaches can all help interested applicants enhance their qualifications, expand their networks, and overcome barriers to self-promotion.[126] Providing mentors who themselves have had board experience may be especially critical in bringing qualified candidates to the attention of board nominating committees.[127] Australia has had success in educating potential female directors and then pairing them with mentors who pledge to assist them for a year and, at the close of the relationship, help place them on a corporate board.[128] In the United States, many private groups, in association with advocacy organizations and universities, have established female director networks that provide mentors to aspiring board members.[129]

Law can also play a greater role in reducing the obstacles to women who seek leadership positions, including both board appointments and managerial jobs that make candidates attractive. One common proposal is to require corporations over a certain size to disclose data concerning recruitment, retention, and promotion of women.[130] A number of countries mandate such disclosures, and obligating U.S. companies to supply such information would make it easier for corporations to benchmark their performance relative to other similarly situated organizations, and for stakeholders to hold poor performers accountable.[131] The government could also require transparency surrounding the board search process by requiring companies to disclose whether women and minority candidates were considered or interviewed for open positions.

An even stronger approach would be to require corporations to adopt a version of the "Rooney Rule," developed for professional football. As noted in prior chapters, such a rule would obligate organizations to consider a woman as a finalist for an open leadership position. Securities and Exchange Commissioner Luis Aguilar has suggested that "many corporate boards may need their own Rooney [R]ule."[132]

The strongest measure would be to follow the example of countries that have established gender quotas for board membership.[133] As indicated earlier, Norway led the way. Spain and the Netherlands have followed suit with legislation setting aspirational targets of balanced representation of both sexes.[134] Belgium requires a third of directors to be female, Italy requires a third, Germany requires 30 percent, and Finland requires government bodies and state-owned enterprises to have equal representation of men and women absent "special reasons to the contrary."[135] Effective in 2017, France will impose a 40 percent quota.[136] The United Arab Emirates and India now require certain companies to have women on their boards.[137] The United Kingdom and Sweden have been debating similar legislation.[138]

Critics contend that quotas do not address the problems preventing underrepresented groups from obtaining relevant experience, and that the focus should be on eliminating those obstacles and enhancing the qualifications of women and minorities.[139] Critics further argue that quotas will simply lead to more unqualified directors, either because of an insufficient supply of well-prepared women, or because boards will fill seats with women who won't speak up. For example, in France, "in private, chief executives say they will look for female board members . . . who will look decorative and not rock the boat."[140]

Evidence on the impact of quotas is mixed. Some research suggests that the greater presence of women correlates with slight losses in the company bottom line, which has been linked to women's lower level of top management experience and greater reluctance to support lay-offs.[141] A study by economists in the United States and Norway found that legislative mandates on quotas did not do much in the short run to increase women's representation in executive ranks, decrease the gender pay gap, or produce more family-friendly policies.[142] This has led critics to denounce quota measures as "purely symbolic politics."[143] One other unintended effect of Norway's quota requirements is that because only ASAs (i.e., public limited liability companies) had to comply, many companies simply changed their status.[144] However, the upside is that the presence of more women on boards has reportedly led to more focused and strategic decision making and decreased conflict.[145] Law professor Aaron Dhir's in-depth study found that Norwegian directors generally believed that "quota-induced diversity has positively affected boardroom work and firm governance."[146] They emphasized the "range of perspectives and experience that women bring to the boardroom, as well as the value of women's independence and outsider status to the work of the board. They also stressed women's greater propensity to engage in more rigorous deliberations, risk assessment, and monitoring."[147] Contrary to critics' concerns, Norwegian directors did not believe that quotas had significant adverse effects in stereotyping women as beneficiaries of preferential treatment.[148] As one put it, "you can't stigmatize 40 percent."[149]

A study of the French quota system found that most directors believed that the addition of female members had improved the process but had not changed the substance of board decision making. What had made a greater difference than the sex of the new board members was their outsider status; women were more likely to be foreign, to be expert in a wide range of areas, and to be drawn from nonelite networks than their male counterparts.[150] That outsider perspective reportedly led them to ask different and more difficult questions than their male colleagues.[151]

In the United States, resistance to quotas builds on longstanding concerns about any departure from meritocratic principles.[152] Facebook CEO Mark Zuckerberg typifies this view. When asked in 2011 why his five-member board had no women, he responded, "I'm going to find people who are helpful, and I don't particularly care what gender they are. . . . I'm not filling the board with check boxes."[153] A year later, in anticipation of having the company go public, and in the wake of strong public protests (including a petition signed by fifty-three thousand individuals), Zuckerberg managed to find a qualified woman: his own COO. *Forbes* ran a story under the title, "Sheryl Sandberg Named to Facebook Board, Finally."[154]

However, many corporate leaders still privately share Zuckerberg's view. They worry that preferential treatment will encourage tokenism, result in unqualified appointments, stigmatize beneficiaries, and diminish their credibility.[155] This may be part of the reason why a majority of American female directors oppose quotas, even though they believe that the strategy would increase board diversity.[156] Given this resistance to mandatory quotas, the only U.S. legislation related to board diversity has taken a voluntary approach. For example, in August 2013, the California

State Senate passed a resolution formally urging companies to increase gender diversity on their boards.[157]

A more politically palatable alternative to quotas is a "comply-or-explain" approach.[158] This approach can take several forms. A common proposal is that "companies with a lower proportion [than 30 percent women on their boards] would have to explain [in their annual reports] if they proposed to fill a vacancy with a man."[159] Social science research suggests that requiring individuals to give reasons for particular actions improves decision-making quality, reduces reliance on stereotypes, and helps to level the playing field for underrepresented groups.[160] The UK has its own version of comply-or-explain.[161] The 2010 revision of the country's corporate governance code (applicable to the 350 largest companies) included the principle that companies should conduct searches for board candidates "with due regard for the benefits of diversity on the board, including gender."[162] Companies must comply with that principle or explain their noncompliance.[163]

Australian public corporations are subject to a similar comply-or-explain mandate.[164] It requires that "companies should establish a policy concerning diversity and disclose the policy or a summary of that policy. The policy should include requirements for the board to establish measurable objectives for achieving gender diversity and for the board to assess annually both the objectives and progress in achieving them."[165] Seventeen other nations have comparable comply-or-explain provisions, and the European Council adopted a directive that requires large, publicly traded firms to describe their policy on board diversity and the outcomes that have flowed from it.[166] If companies do not have such a policy, they must provide a "clear and reasoned explanation as to why this is the case."[167]

The United States has adopted a comply-or-explain approach in other corporate governance contexts. For example, under the Sarbanes-Oxley Act of 2002, companies must disclose whether they have adopted a code of ethics for senior financial managers and whether their boards' audit committees have at least one financial expert.[168] If they have not adopted such a code or appointed an expert, the companies must explain why. Also, under the Dodd-Frank Wall Street Reform and Consumer Protection Act, firms must disclose whether they have separated the role of the board chair and chief executive officer, and if they have not done so, they must explain why not.[169]

The Securities and Exchange Commission (SEC) enacted a rule, which went into effect in 2010, pushing companies in the direction of greater disclosure on diversity issues.[170] The rule requires companies to disclose "whether, and if so how, the nominating committee (or the board) considers diversity in identifying nominees for director." In addition, companies whose boards have a diversity policy must explain how the policy is implemented and how the company assesses its effectiveness.[171] The SEC allows companies to define diversity "in ways that they consider appropriate," and acknowledges that some may focus on racial, ethnic, and gender diversity, while others may "conceptualize diversity expansively to include differences of viewpoint, professional experience, education, skill and other individual qualities and attributes that contribute to board heterogeneity."[172]

Dhir's analysis of the first four years of experience under this rule finds that almost all companies (98 percent) claim to consider diversity in making board appointments.[173] Companies can, however, fulfill their reporting obligation by expressly rejecting diversity in the board nomination process. Berkshire Hathaway, for example, stated that in "identifying director nominees, the Governance, Compensation, and Nominating Committee does not seek diversity, however defined."[174] Only 8 percent of corporations reported having a formal diversity policy.[175] When interpreting diversity, most companies focused on experience rather than sociodemographic characteristics. Whether the reporting rule has had significant impact on board diversity remains unclear.[176] In commenting on the effectiveness of the current disclosure rule, SEC Commissioner Luis Aguilar notes that many companies' brief statement failed to identify "any concrete steps taken to give real meaning to its efforts to create a diverse board."[177] Dhir believes that the rule would be stronger if the SEC made clear that diversity includes race, gender, and other demographic characteristics. Identity-related characteristics were what commentators on the rule wanted to see disclosed. SEC Commissioner Mary Jo White recently indicated that a review of the effectiveness of the disclosure rule will be a priority for the commission in the year ahead.[178]

An even more effective approach in securing transparency and accountability would be to require companies to adopt policies with measurable objectives for achieving diversity and to assess progress in achieving them, or to explain why they have not adopted such policies. Comply-or-explain approaches are more politically feasible than mandatory quotas, but their effectiveness remains uncertain.[179] Comparative data on other countries' experience with such rules is lacking.[180] Future research will be necessary to see if these approaches actually produce greater female representation on boards.

If they do not, another option is to require a binding shareholder vote on diversity. Shareholders could decide whether the company should "consider diversity in board appointments, adopt a diversity policy, specify diversity targets, and enforce such targets by internal mechanisms."[181]

A final set of strategies involves voluntary organizational efforts to diversify boards, to promote inclusiveness in boardroom culture, and to build the pipeline of qualified women.[182] One possibility is for boards to set their own goals or requirements for new appointments in order to ensure a critical mass of women and minorities.[183] Such approaches often involve a "structured search" that starts with an analysis of the board's functional needs and then identifies female and minority candidates who could fill them.[184] Whatever the process, companies need to establish appropriate criteria and an inclusive nominating committee that is committed to diversity.[185] Ilene Lang, former president of Catalyst, recalls a board search where the position was described in "unintentionally gender-stereotyped language" even though she had been on the committee that wrote the description.[186]

Boards also need to expand their searches beyond the traditional pool of CEOs, and to consider other corporate executives, nonprofit directors and officers, university presidents, and academic experts.[187] Professional consultants, who now conduct approximately half of board searches, can help identify promising candidates from outside the board's network and from less traditional backgrounds.[188] At least sixteen organizations and initiatives have also formed to assist companies diversify their boards.[189] These and other efforts to demonstrate a commitment to diversity could help boards make service seem more attractive to well-qualified members of underrepresented groups.[190]

Other diversity strategies are for companies to institute age limits and term restrictions, which open up seats for women and minorities, and to reduce the influence of CEOs in the membership selection process.[191] Some commentators argue that the interests of top corporate executives may be skewed by their desire to maintain control and high personal compensation.[192] Such considerations may lead them to prefer candidates who share their interests—socially similar, fellow CEOs.[193] Simply giving the board more power over the appointment process could expand the pool of potential candidates.

Nonprofit organizations should also focus on making board diversity (or its absence) more visible and enlisting pressure from stakeholder groups to push for change. Some empirical research has found a significant increase in women and minority directors when companies include pictures of the board in annual reports.[194] Disclosure not only prompts stakeholders to press for diversity, it may also encourage institutional reflection and reform.[195]

Some prominent companies in Silicon Valley, including Hewlett-Packard, Intel, Google, Yahoo, Facebook, and LinkedIn, have released information about the diversity of their employees and leaders.[196] The workforces of these technology companies tend to be 60 to 70 percent male and approximately 90 percent white and Asian.[197] Many of the companies released the numbers through official blog posts pledging to increase diversity and transparency.[198] Such voluntary disclosure efforts can help bring more attention to the issue and may ultimately enlarge the pool of candidates qualified for board service.

Large institutional investors could also demand such disclosure and use their leverage to advance diversity among companies in which they hold significant shares.[199] The Thirty Percent Coalition is a group composed of leading women's organizations, institutional investors, executives, elected officials, and activists who joined together in 2011 to achieve 30 percent representation of women on public company boards.[200] The coalition has reported some success in using letter-writing campaigns and shareholder resolutions to target companies with no women serving on their boards.[201] In the United Kingdom, the group has helped increase women's representation to 23 percent, up from 12.5 percent when the organization started.[202]

Activists can also bring more attention to the performance of particular companies by publishing report cards and rankings on board diversity. Such ratings are a form of "soft power" that is often effective in securing change.[203] One organization, 2020 Women on Boards, releases an annual Gender Diversity Index of Fortune 1000 Companies.[204] U.S. stock exchanges, such as NASDAQ and NYSE, could follow the example of exchanges in Australia and New Zealand that require listing companies to provide greater disclosure regarding board composition and search processes.[205]

Investors can also act, individually and collectively, to make board diversity a higher priority in investment decisions. For example, in 2009, the Women's Leadership Fund was created to invest up to $2 billion in publicly listed companies with a high percentage of women in senior positions, including board members; the fund also pushes for change in companies lacking such gender representation.[206] One strategy for exerting pressure is through diversity-related proxy proposals. Such proposals have been underutilized.[207] A study of one year's proxy submissions found that shareholders in U.S. companies filed only twelve diversity proposals—and retracted ten of these subsequent to negotiation.[208] One of the proposals that shareholders did not withdraw targeted Urban Outfitters, which had never had a female director. The corporation opposed the proposal but eventually announced that it was appointing a female director—the CEO's spouse.[209] Another strategy that has had partial success is for shareholders to initiate informal contact with companies concerning gender and racial inclusion.[210] More investors should pursue such strategies to reward and reform companies on the basis of their diversity records.[211]

A related approach is for organizations that publish indexes for socially responsible investing and corporate social responsibility to include measures of diversity in leadership.[212] Only a few publications now compile information along these lines, despite evidence that many investors are interested in receiving it.[213] If diversity on boards becomes part of the standard criteria for measuring corporate social responsibility, then investors, consumers, and public-interest organizations can more readily hold corporations accountable.

Finally, professional organizations can urge public companies to do more to diversify their boards. For example, the American Bar

Association is considering a resolution that would call on these companies to ensure that their boards more closely reflect the diversity of the workforce; it would also urge governmental bodies and investors to call on public companies to adopt and publicly disclose diversity policies and practices.[214]

As recent initiatives make clear, board membership remains a significant issue in the struggle for more equitable leadership structures. As sites of institutional power, boards need to become more inclusive. To that end, it matters to get the arguments right, and to make a case for diversity that is based on compelling arguments about equal opportunity and board governance, rather than on more contested claims about financial performance. The gains in diversity that corporate America has made over the last quarter century demonstrate its capacity for progressive change. But the distance we remain from truly inclusive corporate boards reminds us of the progress yet to be made.

CONCLUSION

At Seneca Falls, New York, a national park commemorates the adoption of the 1848 Declaration of Sentiments, the nation's first statement of women's rights. The park includes an interactive exhibit that invites visitors to envision what the world would look like if men and women were truly equal. When last I visited, suggestions included:

- Homophobia would be unnecessary
- Revlon would go bankrupt
- Things would be pretty much the same, only women would be equally responsible

This book offers a different vision, one in which women's full inclusion improves the quality of leadership and promotes fundamental values of merit and fairness.

This chapter concludes the discussion by reviewing the major themes of the book, and considering what women want from leadership and what constitutes success in that role.

Leveling the Playing Field

For women who aspire to positions of influence, this is a time of transition. The last half century has witnessed a transformation in gender roles, but expectations of equality outrun experience. Women remain underrepresented at the top and overrepresented at the bottom of political and occupational hierarchies. Women are 25 percent of college presidents, 19 percent of Congress, 19 percent of corporate boards, 18 percent of law firm equity partners, 12 percent of governors, and 4 percent of Fortune 500 CEOs. At current rates of change, it would take more than a century to reach gender equity in leadership.

Women's choices account for only part of the gender gap in positions of greatest status and power. Women are less likely to run for political office than men, and more likely to reduce their workforce participation or take extended leaves. But those individual choices are made in a context of gender inequalities. Women do not believe that they have the same political and occupational opportunities as men, and they receive less encouragement, mentoring, and support for leadership aspirations. Women also assume disproportionate responsibilities in the home, which limits their options in the world outside it. Although young women report comparable ambitions as men, they encounter more bumps along the road to achieving their goals.

Some of the obstacles involve gender bias. Women, particularly women of color, are more likely to have their competence and credentials questioned. Women's mistakes are less tolerated, and more readily recalled than those of white male colleagues. In-group favoritism and inadequate mentoring compound the problem. Motherhood is penalized in ways that fatherhood is not. Moreover, such gender bias often becomes self-perpetuating. It prevents women from getting assignments and opportunities that might prove their capabilities. Women also suffer from the disconnect between qualities associated with leadership and those associated with femininity. The line between too assertive and not assertive enough is difficult to navigate, particularly because what seems assertive in a man can seem abrasive in a woman.

Other obstacles stem from women's disproportionate assumption of family responsibilities. The extended hours and constant availability that characterize most leadership positions are often difficult to reconcile with those responsibilities. When asked at a Stanford talk how women can solve the work-family conflict, Gloria Steinem once responded, "Women can't until men are asking that question too."

The good news is that more men are doing just that. In a Pew survey, half of fathers say they find it very or somewhat difficult to balance work and family, and 46 percent say they are not spending enough time with their children.[1] Not only are more men expressing a desire for more family time, examples of leaders who insist on it are increasingly visible, including at the highest levels. While president, Bill Clinton put off an important trip to Japan so he could help his daughter, then a high school junior, prepare for her midterms.[2] So too, a *New York Times* article titled, "He Breaks for Band Recitals," reported that Barack Obama was willing to leave key meetings in order to "get home for dinner by six" or attend one of his daughters' school functions. According to a senior advisor, certain functions "are sacrosanct on his schedule—kid's recitals, soccer games . . ."[3] However, the true test of leadership on work-family issues is when the leaders not only model caretaking commitments in their own lives, but also extend that same opportunity to subordinates.

More good news is that a growing number of male leaders are recognizing the case for gender equity. Organizations with a commitment to diversity in leadership have access to a broader pool of talent and better mix of skills and perspectives than organizations lacking such a commitment. In an ever-more-competitive workplace, the inability to attract and retain the most qualified women carries obvious costs. Women outperform men on most of the capabilities related to leadership.[4] More diverse groups are better at problem solving and avoiding groupthink.

Ensuring women's access to leadership positions also advances fundamental principles of equal rights and increases the likelihood that women's interests will be reflected in decision making. Just as female politicians are more likely than their male colleagues to make women's issues a priority, there is reason to hope that many female CEOs and university presidents will be particularly sensitive to women's concerns. A larger number of women in leadership positions will also mean more mentors and role models for those who are aspiring to such positions.

What then can be done to enhance women's leadership opportunities? At the organizational level, the first priority should be a commitment to gender equity that is reflected in organizational policies, priorities, and reward structures. The tone at the top is critical. Leaders need to set goals, hold individuals accountable, and resist "diversity fatigue."[5] They should also develop initiatives that can level the playing field. Examples include monitoring hiring decisions and performance evaluations for subtle evidence of bias; establishing mentorship and sponsorship programs; and addressing work-family conflicts through effective part-time and flexible schedule options, telecommuting, child-care assistance, and related policies. Self-evaluation is equally important. Organizations need to know how gender equity principles play out in practice. Greater transparency regarding organizational performance can assist stakeholders in holding leadership accountable.

At the societal level, we should push for more effective work-family policies, what Anne-Marie Slaughter calls a "care infrastructure."[6] In *What Women Want,* I have described such policies in some detail.[7] They include access to quality, affordable child care, paid parental and medical leave, and a right to request part-time or flexible work schedules. We also need more specific initiatives targeted at increasing women's representation in politics such as training and mentoring for female politicians. And to achieve more inclusive board memberships, we should require publicly traded companies to consider demographic diversity when selecting members, or explain why they do not do so. The media and grassroots organizations can also pressure employers, boards, universities, and political parties to include more women at leadership levels. For example, the Gender Avengers is a group devoted to increasing diversity by publicizing its absence in conferences and public dialogue.

At the individual level, women should be more proactive in seeking leadership positions, demanding gender equity policies, and supporting politicians and organizational leaders who make those policies a priority. Women should be clear about their goals and look for opportunities to develop skills and mentoring relationships. Setting priorities, managing time, taking risks, and finding a style that blends warmth and assertiveness are critical to professional development. So is striking a sustainable balance between work and family, and having a partner who will enable it. Women who succeed in reaching leadership positions should also reflect on what it is they are leading for, and how they can support opportunities for other women.

Leadership for What

"What is the purpose behind what I'm doing? What purpose will link me to my ideal of excellence? Of a good person? Of a good society?"[8] Those are the questions posed by Laura Nash and Howard Stevenson of the Harvard Business School, who studied the careers of successful leaders. They found that those who are most fulfilled do not lose sight of such questions. Nor do they settle for answers that center on the external rewards of leadership. Individuals who are motivated by intrinsic goals, such as personal growth and assisting others, tend to be more satisfied than those motivated primarily by extrinsic goals, such as wealth or fame.[9] Part of the reason is that material desires tend to grow as rapidly as they are satisfied. If self-worth is confused with net worth, leaders can become trapped on a "hedonic treadmill": the more they have, the more they need to have.[10] Money and status are positional goods; individuals' satisfaction depends on how they compare relative to others, and increases in wealth or position are readily offset by changes in reference groups.[11] Leaders who look hard enough can always find someone getting more.

How then can women with high needs for achievement and recognition find greatest fulfillment? A wide variety of research suggests that professional satisfaction depends on feeling effective, exercising strengths and virtues, and contributing to socially valued ends that bring meaning and purpose.[12] As one British leader put it, "You make a living by what you get; you make a life by what you give."[13] Nash and Stevenson found

> four irreducible components of enduring success: happiness (feelings of pleasure and contentment); achievement (accomplishments that compare favorably against similar goals others have strived for); significance (the sense that you've made a positive impact on people you care about);

and legacy (a way to establish your values or accomplishments so as to help others find future success).[14]

Leaders must strike a balance among all four domains. This, in turn, requires being clear about what matters most. When asked for one piece of advice that she would give to aspiring women, Carolyn Miles, president of Save the Children, responded, "Decide [the] values that are important to you and stick with them."[15]

What constitutes "legacy" is often the hardest measure of accomplishment to assess. The philosopher William James insisted that the greatest use of life is to spend it on something that outlasts it. Contemporary research on happiness similarly finds that goals transcending the self have the greatest impact on individuals' sense of fulfillment.[16] It is, however, important not to confuse fame with legacy.[17] A focus on ensuring recognition of one's legacy can get in the way of achieving it; leaders can be tempted to hoard power, status, and credit. Leadership experts underscore the distinction between "making a difference" and "making 'my' difference and making sure everyone knows it."[18] Thinking about legacy is helpful only if it directs attention to ultimate goals and values, not if it diverts energy into quests for personal glory.

In a tongue-in-cheek list of the advantages of being a woman artist, the Guerrilla Girls put first, "working without the pressure of success." Although that needs to change, women need to pursue their own definition of success and not assume that external rewards are an adequate measure of a well-lived life. Part of that life should include doing for other women what was done for them. To make significant progress on women's leadership, those who reach positions of influence need to assume some responsibility for using their time and talents on behalf of other women.

For some women, this will require a shift in perspective; they may have achieved leadership positions by ignoring the significance of gender. When asked about instances of gender bias in her career, Patricia Harrison, president of the Corporation for Public Broadcasting, reported that "I never focused on gender bias. . . . I just pushed through until I reached my goal and then I delivered."[19] When asked for one piece of advice for women interested in leadership positions, Ingrid Newkirk, president of PETA, advised, "Don't concentrate on being a woman."[20] But to get to a world in which gender doesn't matter in leadership opportunities, women who become leaders cannot afford to ignore its influence. We don't yet live in that world, and we are unlikely to reach it unless women take the lead in challenging barriers to gender equity. Of course, in addressing those barriers, women need to pick their battles wisely. As former secretary of state Condoleezza Rice points out, women faced with bias based on sex or race sometimes do best by ignoring or overcoming it, but there are also times when the stakes justify confronting the problems directly.[21] Madeleine Albright famously claimed that "there's a special place in hell for women who don't help other women."[22] Of course, reminding women of that responsibility can be counterproductive in some contexts, as it was in the 2016 Clinton presidential campaign.[23] However, Albright's point is one that those who care about gender equity can ill afford to ignore. There are special rewards for female leaders whose legacy includes helping those who might follow them. A feminist bumper sticker reminds us that "well-behaved women do not make history." Those who reach positions of leadership have a unique ability to ruffle a few feathers in pursuit of equal opportunity for others.

Those efforts will benefit not only women. An early slogan of the feminist movement asserted that "women's liberation is men's liberation too," and better work-family policies will help everyone with significant caretaking responsibilities. So too, increasing the number of leaders who have a participatory collaborative style may serve organizational interests. Enlisting men as allies on these issues should be a critical priority. A frequently reprinted *Punch* cartoon pictures a meeting with a group of men seated around the table and one woman. The chair looks out at the woman and says, "That's an excellent suggestion, Miss Trigg. Perhaps one of the men here would like to make it." The humor works on two levels. It not only captures the familiar experience of female employees in having their insights reattributed to male colleagues. It also points up the value in having men take responsibility for issues related to women's advancement. When men speak out on these issues, their voices carry special force because their commitment cannot be attributed to self-interest.

We should, of course, be careful not to overestimate the difference that women's different leadership approaches and priorities will bring. Early feminists were bitterly disappointed when gaining the vote did not, as predicted, "purify politics," end poverty, or secure for women "all the opportunities and advantages of life."[24] Putting more women in positions of power is not an all-purpose prescription for empowering all women. But it will bring us closer to a meritocracy that is fair to individual women and that takes full advantage of their talents. Our nation can afford to do no less.

ACKNOWLEDGMENTS

I am deeply grateful to David McBride at Oxford University Press, whose insights and editorial comments were critical throughout the publication process. Lucy Ricca, executive director of Stanford Law School's Center on the Legal Profession, gave generously of her time and talent in helping with the survey that is reflected in this book. Aaron Dhir and Amanda Packel offered helpful comments. The staff of the Stanford Law library provided invaluable reference assistance: Sean Kaneshiro, Marion Miller, Sonia Moss, Rachael Samberg, Sergio Stone, Beth Williams, and George Wilson. My assistant, Eun Sze, provided superb work in preparing the manuscript for publication. My greatest debt is to my husband, Ralph Cavanagh, whose support and guidance made this book possible.

The book is dedicated to Barbara Kellerman, the James MacGregor Burns lecturer in public leadership at Harvard University's Kennedy School of Government and the former executive director of the Kennedy School's Center for Public Leadership. Her contributions to this field are in part responsible for my own interest, and her scholarship and friendship have meant more than I can adequately express.

NOTES

CHAPTER 1

1. Frank Bruni, "If Trump Changed Genders," *New York Times*, Feb. 28, 2016, SR 3.
2. Karin Klenke, *Women and Leadership: A Contextual Perspective* (New York: Springer, 1996), 27. This chapter draws on Deborah L. Rhode, *What Women Want: An Agenda for the Women's Movement* (New York: Oxford University Press, 2014), and Deborah L. Rhode and Barbara Kellerman, "Women and Leadership," in Barbara Kellerman and Deborah L. Rhode, eds., *Women and Leadership: The State of Play and Strategies for Change* (San Francisco: Jossey-Bass, 2007).
3. Colorado Women's College, *Benchmarking Women's Leadership in the United States* (Denver: Colorado Women's College, 2013).
4. Center for American Women in Politics, "Fact Sheet" (2016), http://www.cawp.rutgers.edu/fast_facts/levels_of_office/documents/cong.pdf.
5. Inter-Parliamentary Union, Women in Parliament (May 2016), http://www.ipu.org/wmn-e/world.htm.
6. Center for Educational Statistics, American Council on Education. Women account for 57 percent of bachelor's degrees and 62 percent of associate degrees): *The American College President 2012* (March 2012), Table 283. Women account for 26.4 percent of college presidents: John W. Curtis, *Persistent Inequity: Gender and Academic Employment* (Washington, DC: American Association of University Professors, 2011).
7. See Chapter 4, note 5.
8. Tiffani Lennon, *Recognizing Women's Leadership: Strategies and Best Practices for Employing Excellence* (New York: Praeger, 2014), 139–40 (organizations with budgets exceeding $25 million).

9. Kristin Bellstrom, "Why 2015 Was a Terrible Year to Be a Female Fortune 500 CEO," *Fortune*, Dec. 23, 2015; Catalyst, "Women CEOs of the S&P 500" (New York: Catalyst, 2016). The figure was down from 5 percent earlier in the year. See Pew Research Center, "Women and Leadership," Jan. 14, 2015, http://www.pewsocialtrends.org/2015/01/14/women-and-leadership/.

10. Nikki Waller and Joann Lublin, "What's Holding Women Back?" *Wall Street Journal,* Sep. 30, 2015, R1.

11. Karin Klenke, *Women in Leadership: Contextual Dynamics and Boundaries* (Bingley, UK: Emerald Group, 2011), 7–8.

12. The survey was conducted by email and telephone between January and March 2015. Women in politics, academe, and the nonprofit sector were targeted because fewer survey data are available about their experience than for women in management. Responses are indicated in the notes with identification of when the telephone interview was conducted or when the email survey was received.

13. Catalyst, "Women in Corporate Leadership" (New York: Catalyst, 2001), 70; Robin J. Ely and David A. Thomas, "Making Differences Matter: A New Paradigm for Managing Diversity," *Harvard Business Review*, September–October 1996, 79.

14. Joan Williams, *Unbending Gender: Why Family and Work Conflict and What to Do About It* (New York: Oxford University Press, 2000), 71–73; *Facing the Grail: Confronting the Cost of Work-Family Imbalance* (Boston: Boston Bar Association, 1999), 39; Catalyst, "A New Approach to Flexibility: Managing the Work/Time Equation" (New York: Catalyst, 1997), 20–21.

15. *Missing Pieces: Women and Minorities on Fortune 500 Boards* (New York: Alliance for Board Diversity, 2012); Ely and Thomas, "Making Differences Matter," 79.

16. Katherine W. Phillips, "How Diversity Works," *Scientific American*, October 2014, 43, 44; Cedric Herring, "Does Diversity Pay? Race, Gender and the Business Case for Diversity," *American Sociological Review* 74 (2009): 208, 220; Elizabeth Mannix and Margaret A. Neale, "What Differences Make a Difference? The Promise and Reality of Diverse Teams in Organizations," *Psychological Science in the Public Interest* 6 (2005): 31, 35; Douglas E. Brayley and Eric S. Nguyen, "Good Business: A Market-Based Argument for Law Firm Diversity," *Journal of the Legal Profession* 34 (2009): 1, 13. Note to reader: throughout this book, discontinuous page numbers in citations of journal articles (e.g., "208, 220" in the Herring cite in this note) refer to (1) the first page of the article in the journal and (2) the page(s) in the source pertaining to the matter under discussion in my chapter.

17. For the way that differing knowledge and experience affect individuals' cognitive frames, see Donald C. Hambrick, "Upper Echelons Theory: An Update," *Academy of Management Review* 32 (2007): 334. See also Anita Williams Woolley, Christopher F. Chabris, Alex Pentland, Nada Hashmi, and Thomas W. Malone, "Evidence for a Collective Intelligence Factor in the Performance of Human Groups," *Science* 330 (2010): 686 (finding that the proportion of females in the group is correlated with higher collective intelligence).

18. Phillips, "How Diversity Works," 45.

19. See Brayley and Nguyen, "Good Business," 13–14; David A. Carter, Betty J. Simkins, and W. Gary Simpson, "Corporate Governance, Board Diversity, and Firm Value," *Financial Review* 38 (2003): 33, 51. For a review of this evidence and its methodological limitations, see Chapter 6.

20. McKinsey Global Institute, "The Power of Parity: Advancing Women's Equality in the United States" (McKinsey Global Institute, 2016), 32; Daniel Victor, "Women in Company Leadership Tied to Stronger Profits, Study Says," *New York Times*, Feb. 9, 2016; Sheryl Sandberg and Adam Grant, "How Men Can Succeed in the Boardroom and the Bedroom," *New York Times*, Mar. 5, 2015, SR 5.

21. Brayley and Nguyen, "Good Business," at 34; Deborah L. Rhode and Amanda K. Packel, "Diversity on Corporate Boards: How Much Difference Does Difference Make?" *Delaware Journal of Corporate Law* 39 (2014); Kathleen A. Farrell and Philip L. Hersch, "Additions to Corporate Boards: The Effect of Gender," *Journal of Corporate Finance* 11 (2005): 85.

22. Lissa Lamkin Broome and Kimberly D. Krawiec, "Signaling Through Board Diversity: Is Anyone Listening?" *University of Cincinnati Law Review* 77 (2008): 431, 446–48.

23. Ray Williams, "Why Leadership Development Fails to Produce Good Leaders," *Psychology Today*, Oct. 26, 2013 (citing the National Leadership Index).

24. Alice H. Eagly and Wendy Wood, "Explaining Sex Differences in Social Behavior: A Meta-Analytic Perspective," *Personality and Social Psychology Bulletin* 17 (1991): 306; Alice H. Eagly and Blair T. Johnson, "Gender and Leadership Style: A Meta-Analysis," *Psychology Bulletin* 108 (1990): 233; Alice H. Eagly, Mona G. Makhijani, and Bruce G. Klonsky, "Gender and the Evaluation of Leaders: A Meta-Analysis," *Psychological Bulletin* 111 (1992): 3; Alice H. Eagly, Steven J. Karau, and Mona G. Makhijani, "Gender and the Effectiveness of Leaders: A Meta-Analysis," *Psychological Bulletin* 117 (1995): 125.

25. Catalyst, "Women 'Take Care', Men 'Take Charge': Stereotyping of U.S. Business Leaders Exposed" (New York: Catalyst, 2005), 9.

26. Crystal L. Hoyt, "Women, Men, and Leadership: Exploring the Gender Gap at the Top," *Social and Personality Psychology Compass* 4 (2010): 488. See also Alice Eagly, "Foreword," in Susan R. Madsen, Faith Wambura Ngunjiri, Karen A. Longman, and Cynthia Cerry, *Women and Leadership Around the World* (Charlotte: Information Age, 2015), 33.

27. Pew Research Center, "Women and Leadership."

28. Ibid.

29. Alice H. Eagly and Linda L. Carli, *Through the Labyrinth: The Truth About How Women Become Leaders* (Boston: Harvard Business School Press, 2007); Hoyt, "Women, Men, and Leadership," at 484, 486; Eagly and Johnson, "Gender and Leadership Style," 233–56; Eagly, Karau, and Makhijani, "Gender and the Effectiveness of Leaders," 125–45; Gary N. Powell, "The Gender and Leadership Wars," *Organizational Dynamics* 40 (2011): 1, 7; Robert L. Kabacoff, "Gender Differences in Organizational Leadership: A Large Sample Study," paper presented at 106th Annual Convention of the American Psychological Association, Washington, DC, 1998.

30. "Do Women Make Better Bosses?" NewYorkTimes.com, Aug. 2, 2009, http://roomfordebate.blogs.nytimes.com/20009/08/02/do-women-make-better-bosses (quoting Alice Eagly).

31. Jamie Rappaport Clark, president, Defenders of Wildlife, telephone interview, Mar. 16, 2015.

32. Debora Spar, email survey, Feb. 20, 2015.

33. For transformational leadership, see James M. Burns, *Leadership* (New York: Plenum, 1978). For women's greater tendency to engage in transformational leadership, see Hoyt, "Women, Men, and Leadership," at 487; Eagly and Carli, *Through the Labyrinth*, 130; Alice H. Eagly, Mary C. Johannesen-Schmidt, and Marloes L. van Engen, "Transformational, Transactional, and Laissez-Faire Leadership Styles: A Meta-Analysis Comparing Women and Men," *Psychological Bulletin* 129 (2003): 569.

34. Eagly and Carli, *Through the Labyrinth*, 125–26; Judith B. Roesner, "Ways Women Lead," *Harvard Business Review*, November–December 1990, 119.

35. Janet Napolitano, telephone interview, Feb. 17, 2015.

36. Eagly and Carli, *Through the Labyrinth*, 131–32.

37. Ibid., 126.

38. Fanny M. Cheung and Diane F. Halpern, "Women at the Top: Powerful Leaders Define Success as Work + Family in a Culture of Gender," *American Psychologist* 65 (2010): 182, 188.

39. Pew Research Center, "Women and Leadership."

40. Hanna Rosin, "Why Doesn't Marissa Mayer Care About Sexism?" *XXfactor* (slate.com), July 16, 2012.

41. Suzanne Nossel and Elizabeth Westfall, *Presumed Equal: What America's Top Women Lawyers Really Think About Their Firms* (Franklin Lakes, NJ: Career Press, 1997), 126, 261, 277.

42. Theresa M. Beiner, "What Will Diversity on the Bench Mean for Justice?" *Michigan Journal of Gender and Law* 6 (1999): 113 (suggesting some differences on civil rights suits); Sue Davis, Susan Haire, and Donald R. Songer, "Voting Behavior and Gender on the U.S. Court of Appeals," *Judicature* 77 (1993): 129 (finding some differences in employment discrimination and search-and-seizure cases but not obscenity cases); Jennifer L. Peresie, "Female Judges Matter: Gender and Collegial Decisionmaking in the Federal Appellate Courts," *Yale Law Journal* 114 (2005): 1759, 1776, 1778 (finding female appellate judges more willing to rule for plaintiffs in sex harassment and sex discrimination cases after controlling for factors such as ideology, race, and prior employment); Elaine Martin and Barry Pyle, "Women of the Courts Symposium: State High Courts and Divorce: The Impact of Judicial Gender," *University of Toledo Law Review* 36 (2005): 923 (finding that women judges were more supportive of women in divorce cases after controlling for party affiliations); Jennifer A. Segal, "Representative Decision Making on the Federal Bench: Clinton's District Court Appointees," *Political Research Quarterly* 53 (2000): 137, 142–46 (finding few gender differences but noting that male judges were somewhat more supportive of women's issues than female judges); But see Donald Songer et al., "A Reappraisal of Diversification in the Federal Courts: Gender Effects in the Court of Appeals," *Journal of Politics* 56 (1994): 425 (finding some gender differences in sex discrimination cases but concluding that most studies find few if any differences in appellate rulings). For overviews of such studies, see Theresa M. Beiner, "Female Judging," *University of Toledo Law Review* 36 (2005): 821, 821–29; Fred O. Smith, Jr., "Gendered Justice: Do Male and Female Judges Rule Differently on Questions of Gay Rights?" *Stanford Law Review* 53 (2005): 2087, 2089–91 (finding difference on gay rights issues).
43. Deborah L. Rhode, *The Difference "Difference" Makes: Women and Leadership* (Stanford: Stanford University Press, 2002), 21.
44. Eagly and Wood, "Explaining Sex Differences in Social Behavior," 306; Eagly and Johnson, "Gender and Leadership Style," 233; Eagly, Makhijani, and Klonsky, "Gender and the Evaluation of Leaders"; Eagly, Karau, and Makhijani, "Gender and the Effectiveness of Leaders."
45. Constance H. Buchanan, *Choosing to Lead* (Boston: Beacon Press, 1996), 213.
46. Deborah L. Rhode and Amanda Packel, *Leadership: Law, Policy and Management* (New York: Wolters Kluwer, 2011), 26–27; Hoyt, "Women, Men, and Leadership," 486; Eagly and Carli, *Through the Labyrinth*.
47. One study found no gender difference in 98 percent of core competencies. Corporate Executive Board Corporate Leadership Council, "Four Imperatives to Increase the Representation of Women in Leadership Positions" (Corporate Executive Board: November 2014), 4. See also

Rochelle Sharpe, "As Leaders, Women Rule: New Studies Find That Female Managers Outshine Their Male Counterparts in Almost Every Measure," *Businessweek*, Nov. 20, 2000, http/www.businessweek.com.

48. Bob Sherwin, "Why Women Are More Effective Leaders Than Men," *Business Insider*, Jan. 24, 2014.

49. Williams, "Why Leadership Development Fails to Produce Good Leaders." See also Alice H. Eagly, "Female Leadership Advantage and Disadvantage: Resolving the Contradictions," *Psychology of Women Quarterly* 31 (2007): 5; Therese Huston, "Are Women Better Decision Makers?" *New York Times*, Oct. 17, 2014.

50. Christine Lagarde, "Women, Power and the Challenge of the Financial Crisis," *New York Times*, May 10, 2010.

51. Eagly, Karau, and Makhijani, "Gender and the Effectiveness of Leaders," 125.

52. Jeanette N. Cleveland, Margaret Stockdale, Kevin R. Murphy, and Barbara A. Gutek, *Women and Men in Organizations: Sex and Gender Issues at Work* (Psychology Press, 2000), 293–99; Barbara Kellerman, *Reinventing Leadership: Making the Connection Between Politics and Business* (Albany: State University of New York Press, 1999), 149. See also Jean Lipman-Blumen, *Connective Leadership: Managing in a Changing World* (New York: Oxford University Press, 2000), 183–201.

53. Catalyst, "Women in Corporate Leadership"; Eagly, "Female Leadership," 5.

54. Sheryl Sandberg with Nell Scovell, *Lean In: Women, Work, and the Will to Lead* (New York: Knopf, 2013).

55. Lisa Belkin, "The Opt-Out Revolution," *New York Times Magazine*, Oct. 26, 2003, 42.

56. Barbara Kellerman, "You've Come a Long Way, Baby—and You've Got Miles to Go," in Deborah L. Rhode, ed., *The Difference "Difference" Makes*, 55.

57. Waller and Lublin, "What's Holding Women Back?" R1.

58. Kristin van Ogtrop, "Why Ambition Isn't Working for Women," *Time*, Sep. 28, 2015, 53.

59. Francesca Gino, Carline Ashley Wilmuth, and Alison Wood Brooks, "Compared to Men, Women View Professional Advancement as Equally Attainable, But Less Desirable," *Proceedings of the National Academy of Sciences*, Early Edition (2015): 1, 5.

60. Sylvia Ann Hewlett and Carolyn Buck Luce, "Off-Ramps and On-Ramps: Keeping Talented Women on the Road to Success," *Harvard Business Review*, March 2005, 43–45.

61. Findings range from 12 to 75 percent. Compare Nachum Sicherman, "Gender Differences in Departures from a Large Firm," *Industrial and Labor Relations Review* 49 (1996): 493, with Monica McGrath, eds., *Back in the Game: Returning to Business After a Hiatus: Experience and*

Recommendations for Women, Employers, and Universities, Executive Summaries (Philadelphia: Wharton Center for Leadership and Change and the Forte Foundation, 2005), 7. However, a consistent finding is that far fewer men opt out.

62. Claudia Wallis, "The Case for Staying Home," *Time*, Mar. 22, 2004, 51, 53.

63. Hewlett and Luce, "Off-Ramps and On-Ramps," 45–47.

64. Claire Cain Miller, "More Than Their Mothers, Young Women Plan Career Pauses," *New York Times*, July 22, 2015.

65. Hoyt, "Women, Men, and Leadership," 486; Catalyst, "Women and Men in U.S. Corporate Leadership: Same Workplace, Different Realities?" (New York: Catalyst, 2004).

66. Sandrine Devillard, Sandra Sancier-Sultan, and Charlotte Werner, "Why Gender Diversity at the Top Remains a Challenge," *McKinsey Quarterly*, 2014, at 23. See McKinsey & Company, *Moving Mind-Sets on Gender Diversity: McKinsey Global Survey Results* (2014).

67. Robin J. Ely, Pamela Stone, and Colleen Ammerman, "Rethink What You 'Know' About High-Achieving Women," *Harvard Business Review*, December 2014, 102.

68. Caryl Rivers and Rosalind Barnett, *The New Soft War on Women: How the Myth of Female Ascendance Is Hurting Women, Men—and Our Economy* (New York: Penguin, 2013), 110.

69. Joann S. Lublin, "Coaching Urged for Women," *Wall Street Journal*, Apr. 4, 2011, http://www.wsj.com/articles/SB10001424052748704530204576 237203974840800.

70. Orit Gadiesh and Julie Coffman, "Companies Drain Women's Ambition After Only 2 Years," *Harvard Business Review*, May 18, 2015.

71. Ely, Stone, and Ammerman, "Rethink What You 'Know' About High-Achieving Women," 107.

72. Ibid., 105–6.

73. Laura Colby, "Why Wall Street's Women Are Stuck in the Middle," *Bloomberg Business*, June 25, 2015.

74. Ely, Stone, and Ammerman, "Rethink What You 'Know' About High-Achieving Women," 105.

75. Ibid.

76. Anne-Marie Slaughter, *Unfinished Business: Women, Men, Work, Family* (New York: Random House, 2015), 14–15.

77. Laura Liswood, *The Loudest Duck: Moving Beyond Diversity While Embracing Differences to Achieve Success at Work* (Hoboken: Wiley, 2009).

78. Alice H. Eagly and Steven J. Karau, "Role Congruity Theory of Prejudice Toward Female Leaders," *Psychological Review* 109 (2002): 573; Whitney Botsford Morgan, Veronica L. Gilrane, Tracy C. McCausland, and Eden B. King, "Social Stigma Faced by Female Leaders in the Workplace," in

Michele A. Paludi and Breena E. Coates, eds., *Women as Transformational Leaders, Volume 1* (Santa Barbara: Praeger, 2011), 30–31.

79. Ann M. Koenig, Alice H. Eagly, Abigail A. Mitchell, and Tiina Ristikari, "Are Leader Stereotypes Masculine? A Meta-Analysis of Three Research Paradigms," *Psychological Bulletin* 137 (2011): 616, 617; Rhode and Kellerman, "Women and Leadership," 7; Hoyt, "Women, Men, and Leadership," 490.

80. Therese Huston, *How Women Decide: What's True, What's Not, and What Strategies Spark the Best Choices* (Boston: Houghton Mifflin Harcourt, 2016), 74, 80–81.

81. For evidence that stereotypes are weakening, see Eagly, "Female Leadership," 1; Emily E. Duehr and Joyce E. Bono, "Men, Women, and Managers: Are Stereotypes Finally Changing?" *Personnel Psychology* 59 (2006): 846. For ratings of men higher on leadership, see Laurie A. Rudman and Stephen E. Kilianski, "Implicit and Explicit Attitudes Toward Female Authority," *Personality and Social Psychology Bulletin*, 26 (2000): 1315. Catalyst, "Women 'Take Care', Men 'Take Charge'"; Linda L. Carli and Alice H. Eagly, "Overcoming Resistance to Women Leaders: The Importance of Leadership Style," in Kellerman and Rhode, *Women and Leadership*, 127.

82. Virginia Valian, "The Cognitive Bases of Gender Bias," *Brooklyn Law Review* 65 (1999): 1048–49.

83. Powell, "The Gender and Leadership Wars," 1–2; Eagly and Carly, *Through the Labyrinth*, 97.

84. Felice Batlan, "'If You Become His Second Wife, You Are a Fool': Shifting Paradigms of the Roles, Perceptions, and Working Conditions of Legal Secretaries in Large Law Firms," *Studies in Law, Politics and Society* 52 (2010): 169, 200.

85. Herminia Ibarra, Robin J. Ely, and Deborah Kolb, "Women Rising: The Unseen Barriers," *Harvard Business Review*, September 2013, 65; Powell, "The Gender and Leadership Wars," 3.

86. Huston, *How Women Decide*, 179.

87. See research reviewed in Peter Glick and Susan T. Fiske, "Sex Discrimination: The Psychological Approach," in Faye J. Crosby, Margaret S. Stockdale, and Ann S. Ropp, eds., *Sex Discrimination in the Workplace: Multidisciplinary Perspectives* (Malden: Blackwell, 2007), 170; Rhode and Kellerman, "Women and Leadership," 7; Ibarra, Ely, and Kolb, "Women Rising," 65; Madeline E. Heilman, Aaron S. Wallen, Daniella Fuchs, and Melinda M. Tamkins, "Penalties for Success: Reactions to Women Who Succeed at Male Gendered–Typed Tasks," *Journal of Applied Psychology* 89 (2004): 416.

88. Catalyst, "The Double-Bind Dilemma for Women in Leadership: Damned If You Do, Doomed If You Don't" (New York: Catalyst, 2007), 6.

89. D. Anthony Butterfield and James P. Grinnell, "'Re-Viewing' Gender, Leadership, and Managerial Behavior: Do Three Decades of Research Tell Us Anything?" in Gary N. Powell (ed.), *Handbook of Gender and Work* (Thousand Oaks, CA: Sage, 1998), 223, 235; Eagly, Makhijani, and Klonsky, "Gender and the Evaluation of Leaders," 17; Cleveland et al., *Women and Men in Organizations*, 106–7; Sharpe, "As Leaders, Women Rule."

90. Tyler G. Okimoto and Victoria L. Brescoll, "The Price of Power: Power Seeking and Backlash Against Female Politicians," *Personality and Social Psychology Bulletin* 36 (2010): 923; Huston, *How Women Decide*, 86.

91. Glick and Fiske, "Sex Discrimination," 155, 173.

92. Heilman et al., "Penalties for Success," 426.

93. "Visible Invisibility," ABA Commission on Women in the Profession (Chicago: ABA, 2012), 25.

94. Claire Cain Miller, "In Silicon Valley Suit, More Subtle Questions About Sex Bias," *New York Times*, Mar. 7, 2015, at B3.

95. Eric Newcomer and Sarah Frier, "The Trial That Makes Silicon Valley Shudder," *Bloomberg Business*, Mar. 17, 2015, http://www.bloomberg .com/news/articles/2015-03-17/the-trial-that-makes-silicon-valley-shudder (quoting Pao).

96. Eagly and Karau, "Role Congruity Theory of Prejudice Toward Female Leaders," 111; Todd L. Pittinsky, Laura M. Bacon, and Brian Welle, "The Great Women Theory of Leadership: Perils of Positive Stereotypes and Precarious Pedestals," in Kellerman and Rhode, *Women and Leadership*, 101.

97. Crystal L. Hoyt, "Women, Men, and Leadership," 484, 486; Huston, *How Women Decide*, 196–97.

98. Rivers and Barnett, *The New Soft War on Women*, 77.

99. Hannah Riley Bowles, Linda Babcock, and Lei Lai, "Social Incentives for Gender Differences in the Propensity to Initiate Negotiations: Sometimes It Does Hurt to Ask," *Organizational Behavior and Human Decision Processes* 103 (2007): 84.

100. Hoyt, "Women, Men, and Leadership," 486.

101. Catalyst, "The Double-Bind Dilemma for Women in Leadership," 19; Hoyt, "Women, Men, and Leadership," 491; Heilman et al., "Penalties for Success," 416; Madeline E. Heilman, "Description and Prescription: How Gender Stereotypes Prevent Women's Ascent up the Organizational Ladder," *Journal of Social Issues* 57 (2001): 657, 667.

102. Linda Babcock and Sara Laschever, *Women Don't Ask: Negotiation and the Gender Divide* (Princeton: Princeton University Press, 2003), 88; Carol Hymowitz, "Women to Watch (A Special Report); Through the Glass Ceiling: How These 50 Women Got Where They Are—And Why They Bear Watching," *Wall Street Journal*, Nov. 8, 2004, R1. The point is widely

acknowledged in trade publications featuring advice for aspiring women leaders. See Donna Brooks and Lynn Brooks, *Seven Secrets of Successful Women: Successful Strategies of the Women Who Have Made It—And How You Can Follow Their Lead* (New York: McGraw-Hill, 1997), 63–65, 147–53; Gail Evans, *Play Like a Man, Win Like a Woman: What Men Know About Success That Women Need to Learn* (New York: Broadway Books, 2000), 68–87.

103. Babcock and Laschever, *Women Don't Ask*, 1.

104. Hannah Riley Bowles and Kathleen L. McGinn, "Gender in Job Negotiations: A Two-Level Game," *Negotiation Journal* 24 (2008): 393, 399 (citing studies).

105. Babcock and Laschever, *Women Don't Ask*, 1–11, 41–44.

106. Crystal L. Hoyt and Susan E. Murphy, "Managing to Clear the Air: Stereotype Threat, Women, and Leadership," *Leadership Quarterly*, 2015 (available online January 2016) http://dx.doi.org/10.1016/j.leaqua.2015.11.002; Gregory M. Walton, Mary C. Murphy, and Ann Marie Ryan, "Stereotype Threat in Organizations: Implications for Equity and Performance," *Annual Review of Organizational Psychology and Organizational Behavior* 2 (2015): 523.

107. Eli Wald, "Glass Ceilings and Dead Ends: Professional Ideologies, Gender Stereotypes, and the Future of Women Lawyers at Large Law Firms," *Fordham Law Review* 78 (2010): 2245, 2256; Cecilia L. Ridgeway and Paula England, "Sociological Approaches to Sex Discrimination in Employment," in Crosby, Stockdale, and Ropp, eds., *Sex Discrimination in the Workplace*, 189, 195. In national surveys, half to three-quarters of female lawyers believe that they are held to higher standards than their male colleagues. Deborah L. Rhode and Joan C. Williams, "Legal Perspectives on Employment Discrimination," in Crosby, Stockdale, and Ropp, eds., *Sex Discrimination in the Workplace*, at 235, 245. Even in experimental situations where male and female performance is objectively equal, women are held to higher standards, and their competence is rated lower. Martha Foschi, "Double Standards in the Evaluation of Men and Women," *Social Psychology Quarterly* 59 (1996): 237.

108. Gallup Poll, Aug. 2, 2005, http://www.gallup.com/poll/17614/gender-differences-views-job-opportunity.aspx; Pew Research Center, "Women and Leadership," Jan. 14, 2015, http://www.pewsocialtrends.org/2015/01/14/women-and-leadership.

109. Clark, telephone interview.

110. Heather K. Davison and Michael J. Burke, "Sex Discrimination in Simulated Employment Contexts: A Meta-Analytic Investigation," *Journal of Vocational Behavior* 56 (2000): 225.

111. Claudia Goldin and Cecilia Rouse, "Orchestrating Impartiality: The Impact of 'Blind' Auditions on Female Musicians," *American Economic Review* 90 (2007): 715.

112. Eagly and Karau, "Role Congruity Theory of Prejudice Toward Female Leaders," 573; Catalyst, "The Double-Bind Dilemma for Women in Leadership," 16.

113. Michael I. Norton, Joseph A. Vandello, and John M. Darley, "Casuistry and Social Category Bias," *Journal of Personality and Social Psychology* 87 (2004): 817.

114. Eagly and Carli, *Through the Labyrinth*, 115.

115. Janet K. Swim and Lawrence J. Sanna, "He's Skilled, She's Lucky: A Meta-Analysis of Observers' Attributions for Women and Men's Successes and Failures," *Personality & Social Psychology Bulletin* 22 (1996): 507; Jeffrey H. Greenhaus and Saroj Parasuraman, "Job Performance Attributions and Career Advancement Prospects: An Examination of Gender and Race Effects," *Organizational Behavior & Human Decision Processes* 55 (1993): 273, 276, 290; Jennifer Crocker, Brenda Major, and Claude Steele, "Social Stigma," in Daniel T. Gilbert, Susan T. Fiske, and Gardner Lindzey, eds., *Handbook of Social Psychology* (New York: McGraw Hill, 1998), 504–53; John F. Dovidio and Samuel L. Gaertner, "Stereotypes and Evaluative Intergroup Bias," in Diane M. Mackie and David L. Hamilton, eds., *Affect, Cognition, and Stereotyping: Interactive Processes in Group Perception* (San Diego: Academic Press, 1993), 167–93; Martha Foschi, "Double Standards for Competence: Theory and Research," *Annual Review of Sociology* 26 (2000): 21–42; Linda Krieger, "The Content of Our Categories: A Cognitive Bias Approach to Discrimination and Equal Employment Opportunity," *Stanford Law Review* 47 (1995): 1161–1248; Cecilia L. Ridgeway, "Interaction and the Conservation of Gender Inequality: Considering Employment," *American Sociological Review* 62 (1997): 218.

116. Rebecca J. Rosen, "In the *New York Times*, Sheryl Sandberg Is Lucky, Men Are Good," *The Atlantic*, Feb. 7, 2012.

117. Virginia Valian, *Why So Slow? The Advancement of Women* (Cambridge: MIT Press, 1998), 39–40; Galen V. Bodenhausen, C. Neil Macrae, and Jennifer Garst, "Stereotypes in Thought and Deed: Social-Cognitive Origins of Intergroup Discrimination," in Constantine Sedikides, John Schopler, and Chester A. Insko, eds., *Intergroup Cognition and Intergroup Behavior* (Mahwah, NJ: Erlbaum, 1998); Robin J. Ely, "The Power in Demography: Women's Social Constructions of Gender Identity at Work," *Academy of Management Journal* 38 (1995): 589–634.

118. See sources cited in Joan C. Williams, *Reshaping the Work-Family Debate: Why Men and Class Matter* (Cambridge: Harvard University Press, 2012), 94.

119. Huston, *How Women Decide*, 131; Charlotte Alter, "10 Questions with Sheryl Sandberg," *Time*, Sep. 11, 2014.

120. Catalyst, "Advancing African-American Women in the Workplace: What Managers Need to Know" (New York: Catalyst, 2004); Marilyn Y. Byrd, "Telling Our Stories of Leadership: If We Don't Tell Them They Won't Be Told," *Advances in Developing Human Resources* 11 (2009): 582, 587, 598.

121. Catalyst, "Advancing African-American Women in the Workplace," 12.

122. Ibid.

123. Marianne Bertrand and Sendhil Mullainathan, "Are Emily and Greg More Employable than Lakisha and Jamal? A Field Experiment on Labor Market Discrimination," *American Economic Review* 94 (2004): 991.

124. Ibid.

125. Ashleigh Shelby Rosette, Geoffrey J. Leonardelli, and Katherine W. Phillips, "The White Standard: Racial Bias in Leader Categorization," *Journal of Applied Psychology* 93 (2008): 758.

126. A third of African American women believe that white colleagues perceive them as underqualified. Catalyst, "Advancing African-American Women in the Workplace," 14.

127. Ashleigh Shelby Rosette and Robert W. Livingston, "Failure Is Not an Option for Black Women: Effects of Organizational Performance on Leaders with Single Versus Dual-Subordinate Identities," *Journal of Experimental Psychology* 48 (2012): 1162.

128. Debra M. Kawahara, Edna M. Esnil, and Jeanette Hsu, "Asian American Women Leaders: The Intersection of Race, Gender and Leadership," in Jean Lau Chin, Bernice Lott, Joy K. Rice, and Janice Sanchez-Hucles (eds.), *Women and Leadership: Transforming Visions and Diverse Voices* (Malden: Blackwell, 2007), 309.

129. Janis Sanchez-Hucles and Penny Sanchez, "Introduction," in Chin et al., *Women and Leadership*, 220.

130. Joan C. Williams and Rachel Dempsey, *What Works for Women at Work: Four Patterns Working Women Need to Know* (New York: New York University Press, 2014), 238–40.

131. Kevin L. Nadal, "Preventing Microaggressions: Recommendations for Promoting Positive Mental Health," in *Prevention in Counseling Psychology: Theory, Research, Practice and Training* 2(1), publication of Prevention Section in Division 17 of APA (2008): 22–23; Kevin L. Nadal, Katie E. Griffin, and Yinglee Wong, "Gender, Racial and Sexual

Orientation Microaggressions," in Paludi and Coates, eds., *Women as Transformational Leaders*, 4.

132. Maria Chavez, *Everyday Injustice: Latino Professionals and Racism* (Lanham, MD: Roman and Littlefield, 2011), 83.

133. Napolitano, telephone interview.

134. Amy J. C. Cuddy, Susan T. Fiske, and Peter Glick, "When Professionals Become Mothers, Warmth Doesn't Cut the Ice," *Journal of Social Issues* 60 (2004): 701.

135. Shelley J. Correll, Stephen Benard, and In Paik, "Getting a Job: Is There a Motherhood Penalty?" *American Journal of Sociology* 112 (2007): 1297.

136. Ibid.

137. "Women in the Workplace: A Research Roundup," *Harvard Business Review*, September 2013, 88.

138. For motherhood, see Cuddy et al., "When Professionals Become Mothers," 701, 709; Kathleen Fuegen, Monica Biernat, Elizabeth Haines, and Kay Deaux, "Mothers and Fathers in the Workplace: How Gender and Parental Status Influence Judgments of Job-Related Competence," *Journal of Social Issues* 60 (2004): 737, 745; Claire Etaugh and Denise Folger, "Perceptions of Parents Whose Work and Parenting Behaviors Deviate from Role Expectations," *Sex Roles* 39 (1998): 215. For pregnancy, see Glick and Fiske, "Sex Discrimination," 171.

139. Cecilia L. Ridgeway, "Gender as an Organizing Force in Social Relations: Implications for the Future of Inequality," in Francine D. Blau, Mary C. Brinton, and David Grusky, eds., *The Declining Significance of Gender* (New York: Russell Sage Foundation, 2006), at 279; David L. Hamilton and Jeffrey W. Sherman, "Stereotypes," in Robert S. Wyer, Jr., and Thomas K. Srull, eds., *Handbook of Social Cognition* 2 (Hillsdale, NJ: Erlbaum, 1994), 1–68; Galen V. Bodenhausen and Robert S. Wyer, Jr., "Effects of Stereotypes on Decision Making and Information-Processing Strategies," *Journal of Personality and Social Psychology* 48 (1985): 267, 281–82.

140. Melvin J. Lerner, *The Belief in a Just World: A Fundamental Delusion* (New York: Plenum Press, 1980), vii–viii; Valian, "The Cognitive Bases of Gender Bias," 1037.

141. Deborah L. Rhode, *Balanced Lives: Changing the Culture of Legal Practice* (Chicago: American Bar Association Commission on Women in the Profession, 2002), 16; Krieger, "The Content of Our Categories," 34.

142. Marilyn B. Brewer and Rupert J. Brown, "Intergroup Relations," in Daniel T. Gilbert, Susan T. Fiske, and Gardner Lindzey, eds., *The Handbook of Social Psychology* (New York: McGraw-Hill, 1998), 554–94; Susan T. Fiske, "Stereotyping, Prejudice and Discrimination," in Gilbert et al., 357–414; Barbara Reskin, "Rethinking Employment Discrimination

and Its Remedies," in Mauro F. Guillén, Randall Collins, Paula England, and Marshall Meyer, eds., *The New Economic Sociology: Developments in an Emerging Field* (New York: Russell Sage Foundation, 2002), 218–44; Katharine T. Bartlett, "Making Good on Good Intentions: The Critical Role of Motivation in Reducing Implicit Workplace Discrimination," *Virginia Law Review* 95 (2009): 1893, 1913 (reviewing studies).

143. Hoyt, "Women, Men, and Leadership," 489; Herminia Ibarra, Nancy M. Carter, and Christine Silva, "Why Men Still Get More Promotions Than Women," *Harvard Business Review*, September 2010; Ida O. Abbott, *The Lawyer's Guide to Mentoring* (Washington, DC: National Association for Law Placement [NALP], 2000); Belle Rose Ragins, "Gender and Mentoring Relationships: A Review and Research Agenda for the Next Decade," in Powell, *Handbook of Gender and Work*, 347, 350–62; "Women in Corporate Leadership: Progress and Prospects" (New York: Catalyst, 1996); Timothy L. O'Brien, "Up the Down Staircase," *New York Times*, Mar. 19, 2006, A4.

144. Marlene G. Fine, "Women, Collaboration and Social Change: An Ethics-Based Model of Leadership," in Chin et al., *Women and Leadership*, 183.

145. Orit Gadiesh and Julie Coffman, "Companies Drain Women's Ambition After Only 2 Years," *Harvard Business Review*, May 2015.

146. Catalyst, "Advancing African-American Women," 12.

147. A Kleiner Perkins partner denied having made the statement. Elizabeth Weise, "Pao Case Presents Dueling Views of Opportunity," *USA Today*, Feb. 25, 2015.

148. Newcomer and Frier, "The Trial That Makes Silicon Valley Shudder."

149. Sandberg with Scovell, *Lean In*.

150. The term comes from Pierre Bourdieu, "The Forms of Capital," in John G. Richardson, ed., *Handbook of Theory and Research for the Sociology of Education* (New York: Greenwood Press, 1986), 241, 248. See Sylvia Ann Hewlett, with Kerrie Peraino, Laura Sherbin, and Karen Sumberg, "The Sponsor Effect: Breaking Through the Last Glass Ceiling," *Harvard Business Review* Research Report, December 2010, 8; Cindy A. Schipani, Terry M. Dworkin, Angel Kwolek-Folland, and Virginia G. Maurer, "Pathways for Women to Obtain Positions of Organizational Leadership: The Significance of Mentoring and Networking," *Duke Journal of Gender Law & Policy* 16 (2009): 89.

151. David R. Hekman and Maw-Der Foo, "Does Valuing Diversity Result in Worse Performance Ratings for Minority and Female Leaders?" (paper presented at the Academy of Management 2014 meeting), discussed in Rachel Feintzeig, "Women Penalized for Promoting Women, Study Finds," *Wall Street Journal*, July 21, 2014, at D3.

152. Catherine J. Taylor, "Occupational Sex Composition and the Gendered Availability of Workplace Support," *Gender and Society* 24 (2010): 189.
153. Alison Cook and Christy Glass, "Women and Top Leadership Positions: Towards an Institutional Analysis," *Gender, Work and Organization* 21 (2014): 91, 101.
154. Huston, *How Women Decide*, 141.
155. See Karen L. Proudford, "Isn't She Delightful? Creating Relationships That Get Women to the Top (and Keep Them There)," in Kellerman and Rhode, *Women and Leadership*, 431; Ragins, "Gender and Mentoring Relationships," 361–63; Diane F. Halpern and Fanny M. Cheung, *Women at the Top: Powerful Leaders Tell Us How to Combine Work and Family* (West Sussex: Wiley Blackwell, 2008), 39.
156. Mirembe Birigwa and Karen Sumberg, "Lack of Sponsorship Keeps Women from Breaking Through the Glass Ceiling," *Harvard Business Review* Research Report, January 2011.
157. Ella L. J. Edmondson Bell and Stella M. Nkomo, *Our Separate Ways: Black and White Women and the Struggle for Professional Identity* (Cambridge, MA: Harvard Business School Press, 2001), 123–32; Bernardo M. Ferdman, "The Color and Culture of Gender in Organizations: Attending to Race and Ethnicity," in Powell, *Handbook of Gender and Work*, 17, 18–26; Catalyst, "Women of Color in Corporate Management: Dynamics of Career Advancement" (New York: Catalyst, 1998), 15; David B. Wilkins and G. Mitu Gulati, "Why Are There So Few Black Lawyers in Corporate Law Firms? An Institutional Analysis," *California Law Review* 84 (1996): 493; Deborah L. Rhode, *The Unfinished Agenda: Women and the Legal Profession* (Chicago: ABA Commission on Women and the Profession, 2001), 16.
158. Martin N. Davidson, *The End of Diversity As We Know It: Why Diversity Efforts Fail and How Leveraging Difference Can Succeed* (San Francisco: Berrett-Koehler, 2011), 26.
159. Minority Corporate Counsel Association, "Mentoring Across Differences," http://www.mcca.com/index.cfm?fuseaction=page.viewpage&pageid= 666; Leigh Jones, "Mentoring Plans Failing Associates," *National Law Journal*, Sep. 15, 2006, 1, http://www.nationallawjournal.com/id=90000 5462642?slreturn=20150804172809.
160. MCCA, "Mentoring Across Differences."
161. Davidson, *The End of Diversity*, 35–36.
162. Jessica Grose, "The Great Yahoo! Baby Debate," *Bloomberg Businessweek*, Oct. 22–26, 2012.
163. Eagly and Carli, *Through the Labyrinth*, 176.
164. Rivers and Barnett, *The New Soft War on Women*, 200–201.
165. Rhea Suh, telephone interview, Apr. 7, 2015.

166. Charlotte J. Patterson, Erin L. Sutfin, and Megan Fulcher, "Division of Labor Among Lesbian and Heterosexual Parenting Couples: Correlates of Specialized Versus Shared Patterns," *Journal of Adult Development* 11 (2004): 179.

167. "American Time Use Survey" (Washington, DC: Bureau of Labor Statistics, 2015); http://www.bls.gov/TUS?CHARTS?HOUSEHOLD.HTM; Bureau of Labor Statistics, "Care of Household Children" (2015), http://www.bls.gov/tus/charts/childcare.htm (describing time spent on physical care).

168. Richard W. Johnson and Joshua M. Weiner, "A Profile of Frail Older Americans and Their Caregivers" (Washington, DC: Urban Institute Occasional Paper No. 8, 2006), http://www.urban.org/sites/default/files/alfresco/publication-pdfs/311284-A-Profile-of-Frail-Older-Americans-and-Their-Caregivers.pdf.

169. See research cited in Sandberg, *Lean In*, 106.

170. Claire Cain Miller, "Millennial Men Aren't the Dads They Thought They'd Be," *New York Times*, July 30, 2015 (noting that only 8 percent of men shouldered most of the families' child-care responsibilities).

171. Pamela Stone and Meg Lovejoy, "Fast-Track Women and the 'Choice' to Stay Home," *Annals of the American Academy of Political and Social Science* 596 (2004): 62, 66.

172. Jonathan Vespa, Jamie M. Lewis, and Rose M. Kreider, "America's Families and Living Arrangements: 2012," U.S. Census Bureau (August 2013), 26, https://www.census.gov/prod/2013pubs/p20-570.pdf.

173. PEW Research Center, "Growing Number of Dads Home with the Kids" (2014), 8, 12 (finding that about a million fathers are staying home with at least one child under eighteen but only 21 percent report the reason as caring for the family; 35 percent are ill or disabled, 23 percent can't find work, 9 percent are retired, and 8 percent are in school).

174. Ann Weisberg, "The Workplace Culture That Flying Nannies Won't Fix," *New York Times*, Aug. 24, 2015 (citing Pew survey).

175. "What Moms Choose," Working Mother Research Institute, 2011, 11; Pamela Stone and Lisa Ackerly Hernandez, "The Rhetoric and Reality of 'Opting Out': Toward a Better Understanding of Professional Women's Decisions to Head Home," in Bernie D. Jones, *Women Who Opt Out: The Debate over Working Mothers and Work-Family Balance* (New York: New York University Press, 2012), 48–50.

176. Pamela Stone, *Opting Out? Why Women Really Quit Careers and Head Home* (Berkeley: University of California Press, 2007), 62.

177. Stone and Hernandez, " 'Opting Out,' " 61.

178. Ibid., 73.

179. Ibid., 69.

180. Williams, *Unbending Gender,* 71.

181. Weisberg, "Workplace Culture."

182. Sylvia Ann Hewlett, Carolyn Buck Luce, and Cornel West, "Leadership in Your Midst: Tapping the Hidden Strengths of Minority Executives," *Harvard Business Review,* November 2005, 74, 79.

183. Cameron Stracher, "All Aboard the Mommy Track," *American Lawyer,* March 1999, 126; Meredith K. Wadman, "Family and Work," *Washington Lawyer,* November–December 1998, 33; Abbie F. Willard and Paula A. Patton, *Perceptions of Partnership: The Allure and Accessibility of the Brass Ring* (Washington, DC: NALP, 1999); Cynthia Fuchs Epstein, Robert Sauté, Bonnie Oglensky, and Martha Gever, "Glass Ceilings and Open Doors: Women's Advancement in the Legal Profession," *Fordham Law Review* 64 (1995): 391–99.

184. Sheila Wellington and Catalyst with Betty Spence, *Be Your Own Mentor: Strategies from Top Women on the Secrets of Success* (New York: Random House, 2001), 110.

185. Juliet B. Schor, *The Overworked American: The Unexpected Decline of Leisure* (New York: Basic Books, 1993), 1–5, 79–82.

186. Wallis, "The Case for Staying Home," 52; Williams, *Unbending Gender,* 71; Arlie Russell Hochschild, *The Time Bind: When Work Becomes Home and Home Becomes Work* (New York: Holt, 1997), 70.

187. Betsy Morris, "Executive Women Confront Midlife Crisis," *Fortune,* Sep. 18, 1995; Rhode, *The Difference "Difference" Makes,* 15.

188. Hewlett, Luce, and West, "Leadership in Your Midst," 77.

189. Ann Crittenden, *The Price of Motherhood: Why the Most Important Job in the World Is Still the Least Valued* (New York: Metropolitan Books, 2001), 96; see also Cynthia Fuchs Epstein, Carroll Seron, Bonnie Oglensky, and Robert Sauté, *The Part-Time Paradox: Time Norms, Professional Life, Family and Gender* (New York: Routledge, 1998).

190. Hewlett and Luce, "Off-Ramps and On-Ramps," 45; Pamela Kephart and Lillian Schumacher, "Has the 'Glass Ceiling' Cracked? An Exploration of Women Entrepreneurship," *Journal of Leadership and Organizational Studies* 12 (2005): 10; Jenny Anderson, "The Fork in the Road: Can Women and Wall Street Work Together? *New York Times,* Aug. 6, 2006, Section 3, 1.

191. Hewlett and Luce, "Off-Ramps and On-Ramps," 45; Kephart and Schumacher, "Has the 'Glass Ceiling' Cracked?" 10.

192. Jody Heymann with Kristen McNeill, *Children's Chances: How Countries Can Move from Surviving to Thriving* (Cambridge: Harvard University Press, 2013), 136.

193. See Rhode, *What Women Want,* 62–64.

194. Ibid., 57–59.

195. 42 U.S.C. Section 2000 (2012).
196. Minna J. Kotkin, "Outing Outcomes: An Empirical Study of Confidential Employment Discrimination Settlements," *Washington & Lee Law Review* 64 (2007): 11, 115 (citing studies). See Laura Beth Nielsen, Robert L. Nelson, and Ryan Lancaster, "Individual Justice or Collective Legal Mobilization? Employment Discrimination Litigation in the Post Civil Rights United States," *Journal of Empirical Legal Studies* 7 (2010): 175, 187, 195–96 (noting that only about 2 percent of plaintiffs win in court); Kevin M. Clermont and Stewart J. Schwab, "Employment Discrimination Plaintiffs in Federal Court: From Bad to Worse?" *Harvard Law & Policy Review* 3 (2009): 3, 13, 35 (noting that compared to other plaintiffs, employment discrimination complainants win a lower proportion of trials and appeals); Kevin M. Clermont and Stewart J. Schwab, "How Employment Discrimination Plaintiffs Fare in Federal Court," *Journal of Empirical Legal Studies* 1 (2004): 429 (finding low success rates for employment discrimination plaintiffs in federal court).
197. "Enforcement and Litigation Statistics from the U.S. Equal Employment Opportunity Commission, FY 1997 through 2012," http://www.eeoc.gov/eeoc/statistics/enforcement/.
198. Kotkin, "Outing Outcomes," 111 (noting mean recovery of $54,651); Nielson, Nelson, and Lancaster, "Individual Justice," 187.
199. Clermont and Schwab, "Employment Discrimination Plaintiffs," 35.
200. Rhode and Williams, "Legal Perspectives on Employment Discrimination," in Crosby et al., *Sex Discrimination in the Workplace*, 243; *Riordan v. Kempiners*, 831 F.2d 690, 697 (7th Cir. 1987); Elizabeth Schneider and Hon. Nancy Gertner, " 'Only Procedural': Thoughts on the Substantive Law Dimensions of Preliminary Procedural Decisions in Employment Discrimination Cases," *New York Law School Law Review* 57 (2013): 767, 775.
201. *Hopkins v. Price Waterhouse*, 618 F. Supp. 1109 (D.D.C. 185), aff'd in part and rev'd in part, 825 F.2d 458 (D.C. Cir. 1987), aff'd in part and rev'd in part, 490 U.S. 228 (1989); Ann Branigar Hopkins, *So Ordered: Making Partner the Hard Way* (Amherst: University of Massachusetts Press, 1996), 172.
202. *Hopkins v. Price Waterhouse*, 618 F. Supp. at 1117.
203. Hopkins, *So Ordered*, 235.
204. *Hopkins v. Price Waterhouse*, 618 F. Supp. at 1115, 1117.
205. *Ezold v. Wolf, Block, Schorr and Solis-Cohen*, 751 F. Supp. 1175 (E.D. Pa. 1990), reversed, 983 F.2d 509 (3d Cir. 1992), cert. denied, 510 U.S. 826 (1993).
206. Ibid., at 1184–86.
207. Weise, "Pao Case Presents Dueling Views."

208. Heather Somerville, "Kleiner Perkins Is Run by Sexists, Lawyer Argues," *San Jose Mercury News*, Mar. 25, 2015 (quoting Alan Exelrod).

209. K. A. Dixon, Duke Storen, and Carl E. Van Horn, *A Workplace Divided: How Americans View Discrimination and Race on the Job* (New Brunswick: John J. Heldrich Center for Workforce Development, 2002), 15.

210. Laura Beth Nielsen and Robert L. Nelson, "Rights Realized? An Empirical Analysis of Employment Discrimination Litigation as a Claiming System," *Wisconsin Law Review* (2005): 663.

211. Susan Bisom-Rapp, Margaret S. Stockdale, and Faye J. Crosby, "A Critical Look at Organizational Responses to and Remedies for Sex Discrimination," in Crosby, Stockdale, and Ropp, *Sex Discrimination in the Workplace*, 274–75; Faye Crosby, "The Denial of Personal Discrimination," *American Behavioral Scientist* 27 (1984): 380–81.

212. Cheryl R. Kaiser and Brenda Major, "A Social Psychological Perspective on Perceiving and Reporting Discrimination," *Law and Social Inquiry* 31 (2006): 801, 808; Crosby, "The Denial of Personal Discrimination," 381; see studies cited in Deborah L. Brake and Joanna L. Grossman, "The Failure of Title VII as a Rights-Claiming System," *North Carolina Law Review* 86 (2008): 860, 887–88, 890; and Deborah L. Rhode, *Speaking of Sex: The Denial of Gender Inequality* (Cambridge: Harvard University Press, 1997), 9.

213. Rhode and Williams, "Legal Perspectives on Employment Discrimination," 244.

214. Hopkins, *So Ordered*, at 384 (noting fees of $500,000 in 1991 dollars). For the conversion to today's dollars, see the U.S. Department of Labor Inflation Calculator, http://146.142.4.24/cgi-bin/cpicalc.pl.

215. For Ezold's expenses, see Deborah L. Rhode, "What's Sex Got to Do with It? Diversity in the Legal Profession," in Deborah L. Rhode and David Luban, eds., *Legal Ethics: Law Stories* (New York: Foundation Press, 2006), 246 ($150,000 in 1993 dollars). For the conversion to today's dollars, see the U.S. Department of Labor Inflation Calculator, http://www.bls.gov/data/inflation_calculator.htm. For Pao's expenses, see Heather Sommerville, "Judge Rules Ellen Pao Must Pay $276,000 to Kleiner Perkins," *San Jose Mercury News*, June 17, 2015.

216. Hopkins, *So Ordered*, 197.

217. Fred Strebeigh, *Equal: Women Reshape American Law* (New York: Norton, 2009), 193 (discussing litigation against Sullivan and Cromwell).

218. Loren Feldman, "What's Sex Got to Do with It: Partnership on Trial," *American Lawyer*, November 1990, 56 (quoting Charles Kopp).

219. ABA Commission on Women in the Profession, "Visible Invisibility," 20 (aggressive, bitch); Joan C. Williams and Veta T. Richardson, "New Millennium, Same Glass Ceiling? The Impact of Law Firm Compensation Systems on Women," *Hastings Law Journal* 62 (2010–11): 630 (confrontational);

Nancy J. Reichman and Joyce S. Sterling, "Sticky Floors, Broken Steps, and Concrete Ceilings in Legal Careers," *Texas Journal of Women and the Law* 14 (Fall 2004): 47, 65 (bitch); Jill L. Cruz and Melinda S. Molina, "Hispanic National Bar Association, National Study on the Status of Latinas in the Legal Profession, Few and Far Between: The Reality of Latina Lawyers," *Pepperdine Law Review* 37 (2010): 971, 1019 (rock the boat); Rhode, *The Unfinished Agenda*, 21 (troublemaker, oversensitive). For reputational concerns generally, see Elizabeth H. Dodd, Traci A. Giuliano, Jori M. Boutell, and Brooke E. Moran, "Respected or Rejected: Perceptions of Women Who Confront Sexist Remarks," *Sex Roles* 45 (2001): 567.

220. For the advice, see Robert Kolker, "The Gay Flannel Suit," *New York Magazine*, Oct. 24, 2007, http://nymag.com/news/features/28515/; ABA Commission on Women in the Profession, "Visible Invisibility," 21. For negative consequences following complaints about compensation, see Williams and Richardson, "New Millennium," 639.

221. Rhode, *Speaking of Sex*, 162. See Susan Antilla, "After Boom-Boom Room, Fresh Tactics to Fight Bias," *New York Times*, Apr. 1, 2013, A1 (noting reluctance of women to sue because of career repercussions). The problem is true of employment discrimination litigation generally. See Nielsen and Nelson, "Rights Realized?" 663; Linda Krieger, "The Watched Variable Improves," in Crosby, Stockdale, and Ropp, *Sex Discrimination in the Workplace*, 296, 309–10.

222. Brake and Grossman, "The Failure of Title VII," 859, 903.

223. Paul M. Barrett, *The Good Black: A True Story of Race in America* (New York: Plume, 1998), 59 (quoting George Galland).

224. Hopkins, *So Ordered*, 166.

225. *Stopka v. Alliance of American Insurers*, 141 F.3d 681, 686 (7th Cir. 1998).

226. *Georgen-Saad v. Texas Mutual Insurance Co.*, 195 F. Supp. 2d 853 (W.D. Tex. 2002).

227. Rhode, *Speaking of Sex*, 160; Krieger, "The Content of Our Categories," 34.

228. Susan P. Sturm, "Second Generation Employment Discrimination: A Structural Approach," *Columbia Law Review* 101 (2001): 458, 460. See also Samuel R. Bagenstos, "The Structural Turn and Limits of Antidiscrimination Law," *California Law Review* 94 (2006): 5.

229. *Heim v. State of Utah*, 8 F.3d 1541, 1546 (10th Cir. 1993).

230. *Bullington v. United Airlines, Inc.*, 186 F.3d 1301, 1319 (10th Cir. 1999); *Deines v. Texas Department of Protective and Regulatory Services*, 164 F.3d 277, 280 (5th Cir. 1999). For other cases, see Tristin K. Green, "Discrimination in Workplace Dynamics: Toward a Structural Account of Disparate Treatment Theory," *Harvard Civil Rights–Civil Liberties Law Review* 38 (2003): 118.

231. Sturm, "Second Generation."
232. Kate White, *Why Good Girls Don't Get Ahead But Gutsy Girls Do: Nine Secrets Every Woman Must Know* (New York: Grand Central, 1995).
233. Lois P. Frankel, *Nice Girls Don't Get the Corner Office: 101 Unconscious Mistakes Women Make That Sabotage Their Careers* (New York: Warner Business Books, 2010).
234. Karen Salmansohn, *How to Succeed in Business Without a Penis: Secrets and Strategies for the Working Woman* (New York: Three Rivers Press, 1996), 161.
235. Christy Whitman and Rebecca Grado, *Taming Your Alpha Bitch: How to Be Fierce and Feminine (and Get Everything You Want!)* (Dallas: BenBella Books, 2012), 196; Jean Hollands, *Same Game, Different Rules: How to Get Ahead Without Being a Bully Broad, Ice Queen, or "Ms. Understood"* (New York: McGraw-Hill, 2002), 65.
236. Catalyst, "The Double-Bind Dilemma for Women in Leadership," 26.
237. Joanna Barsh and Lareina Yee, *Unlocking the Full Potential of Women at Work* (New York: McKinsey & Company, 2012), 9.
238. Marsha Blackburn, email survey, Apr. 30, 2015.
239. Rivers and Barnett, *The New Soft War on Women*, 164.
240. Katty Kay and Claire Shipman, *The Confidence Code: The Science and Art of Self-Assurance—What Women Should Know* (New York: HarperCollins, 2014), 12.
241. Claire Shipman and Katty Kay, *Womenomics: Write Your Own Rules for Success* (New York: HarperCollins, 2009), 145.
242. L. Vesterland, L. Babcock, and L. Weingart, "Breaking the Glass Ceiling with 'No': Gender Differences in Declining Requests for Non-Promotable Tasks," cited in Judith D. Singer, *Fostering the Advancement of Women in Academic Statistics*, in Amanda L. Golbeck, Ingram Olkin, and Yulia R. Gel, *Leadership and Women in Statistics* (Boca Raton, FL: CRC Press, 2016), 425.
243. Joanna Barsh, Susie Cranston, and Geoffrey Lewis, *How Remarkable Women Lead: The Breakthrough Model for Work and Life* (New York: Crown, 2009), 231; Hoyt, "Women, Men, and Leadership," 492.
244. Napolitano, telephone interview.
245. Catalyst, "Women in Corporate Leadership."
246. Linda Babcock and Sara Laschever, *Ask for It: How Women Can Use the Power of Negotiation to Get What They Really Want* (New York: Bantam, 2008), 252; Halpern and Cheung, *Women at the Top*, 227.
247. Babcock and Laschever, *Ask for It*, at 252–62. See also Maria Konnikova, "Lean Out: The Dangers for Women Who Negotiate," *New Yorker*, June 10, 2014.

248. Joan Biskupic, *Sandra Day O'Connor: How the First Woman on the Supreme Court Became Its Most Influential Justice* (New York: HarperCollins, 2009), 56 (quoting Benie Wynn).

249. Cecilia Ridgeway, "Gender, Status, and Leadership," *Journal of Social Issues* 57 (2001); Kathryn Heath, Jill Flynn, and Mary Davis Holt, "Women, Find Your Voice," *Harvard Business Review*, June 2014; Napolitano, telephone interview.

250. Ridgeway, "Gender, Status, and Leadership," 645.

251. Kay and Shipman, *The Confidence Code*, xviii.

252. Daniel Goleman, "Leadership That Gets Results," *Harvard Business Review*, March–April 2000, 78.

253. Robin J. Ely, Herminia Ibarra, and Deborah Kolb, *Taking Gender into Account: Theory and Design for Women's Leadership Development Program*, Harvard Business School, September 2011; Erin White, "Female Training Classes Flourish: Executive-Education Tactic Aims to Bolster the Ranks of Women in Management," *Wall Street Journal*, Sep. 25, 2006, B3. The Leadership Council on Legal Diversity also offers a fellowship program for minorities on the leadership track.

254. Sue Shellenbarger, "The XX Factor: What's Holding Women Back?" *Wall Street Journal*, May 7, 2012, B10.

255. Megan McArdle, *The Up Side of Down: Why Failing Well Is the Key to Success* (New York: Penguin, 2014); Melanne Verveer and Kim K. Azzarelli, *Fast Forward: How Women Can Achieve Power and Purpose* (New York: Houghton Mifflin Harcourt, 2015), 184.

256. Shellenbarger, "The XX Factor," S10; Susan A. Berson, "The Rules (for Women): Steps May Be Unspoken But They Are Necessary, Successful Partners Say," *ABA Journal*, Jan. 1, 2012, at 28; Linda Bray Chanow and Lauren Stiller Rikleen, *Power in Law: Lessons from the 2011 Women's Power Summit on Law and Leadership* (Austin, TX: Center for Women in Law, 2012), at 15; Barsh, Cranston, and Lewis, *How Remarkable Women Lead*, 162.

257. Sylvia Ann Hewlett, *Forget a Mentor, Find a Sponsor: The New Way to Fast Track Your Career* (Boston: Harvard Business Review Press, 2013).

258. Deborah Gillis, personal correspondence, Apr. 9, 2015.

259. Ingrid Newkirk, email survey, Feb. 3, 2014.

260. Williams and Dempsey, *What Works for Women at Work*, 102, 106.

261. Marie Wilson, email survey, Aug. 6, 2015.

262. Carol S. Dweck, *Mindset: The New Psychology of Success* (New York: Ballantine Books, 2007), 7, 110; Barsh and Yee, *Unlocking the Full Potential of Women at Work*, 9; Adam Bryant, "Susan Story of American Water: The Job Description Is Just the Start," *New York Times*, Sep. 13, 2014, at B2 (quoting Story on the need for honest feedback).

263. Barsh and Yee, *Unlocking the Full Potential of Women at Work*, 9.

264. Angela Duckworth, *Grit: The Power of Passion and Perseverance* (New York: Scribner, 2016).

265. Valerie Young, *The Secret Thoughts of Successful Women: Why Capable People Suffer from the Impostor Syndrome and How to Thrive in Spite of It* (New York: Crown Business, 2011), 245.

266. Suh, telephone interview.

267. Gay Gaddis, "Linda Addison Delivers Advice to All with a 'Lawyer's Dozen,'" *Forbes*, Apr. 25, 2014, http://www.forbes.com/sites/gaygaddis/2014/04/25/linda-addison-delivers-advice-to-all-with-a-lawyers-dozen/ (quoting Xerox CEO Ursula Burns).

268. Slaughter, *Unfinished Business*, 162.

269. Shipman and Kay, *Womenomics*, 177.

270. Ibid., 186.

271. Ibid., 188.

272. Sharon Meers and Joanna Strober, *Getting to 50/50: How Working Couples Can Have It All* (New York: Bantam, 2009), 4.

273. Cheung and Halpern, "Women at the Top," 182, 187; Halpern and Cheung, *Women at the Top*, 89.

274. Jennifer Granholm, email survey, Jan. 21, 2015.

275. Herminia Ibarra, Robin Ely, and Deborah Kolb, "Women Rising."

276. Patricia Harrison, email survey, Feb. 4, 2015.

277. Condoleezza Rice, Leadership Presentation, Stanford University, May 9, 2016.

278. Ilene Lang, email survey, Apr. 20, 2015.

279. Jennifer A. Chatman and Jessica A. Kennedy, "Psychological Perspectives on Leadership," in Nitin Nohria and Rakesh Khurana, eds. *Handbook of Leadership Theory and Practice* (Boston: Harvard Business Press, 2010), 169, 174.

280. *The Wisdom of Laotse*, translated and edited by Lin Yutang (New York: Modern Library, 1948), 114.

281. Frank Dobbin, Alexandra Kalev, and Erin Kelly, "Diversity Management in Corporate America," *Context* 6 (2007): 21; Catalyst, *Advancing Women in Business: The Catalyst Guide: Best Practices from the Corporate Leaders* (Hoboken: Jossey-Bass, 1998), 6, 12–13; Catalyst, "Women of Color in Corporate Management," 69.

282. Deepali Bagati, "Women of Color in U.S. Law Firms" (New York: Catalyst, 2009), 49; Rhode and Kellerman, "Women and Leadership," 27; Cecilia Ridgeway and Paula England, "Sociological Approaches to Sex Discrimination in the Workplace," in Crosby, Stockdale, and Rapp, *Sex Discrimination in the Workplace*, 202; Ely, Ibarra, and Kolb, *Taking Gender into Account*, 481; Barsh and Yee, *Unlocking the Full Potential of Women at Work*, 11.

283. Frank Dobbin and Alexandra Kalev, "The Architecture of Inclusion: Evidence from Corporate Diversity Programs," *Harvard Journal of Law and Gender* 30 (2007): 279, 293–94; Dobbin, Kalev, and Kelly, "Diversity Management," 23–24.

284. Shellenbarger, "The XX Factor," B9.

285. Dobbin and Kalev, "The Architecture of Inclusion," 283; Jeanine Prime, Marissa Agin, and Heather Foust-Cummings, "Strategy Matters: Evaluating Company Approaches for Creating Inclusive Workplaces" (Catalyst, 2010); Theresa M. Beiner, "Not All Lawyers Are Equal: Difficulties That Plague Women and Women of Color," *Syracuse Law Review* 58 (2008): 333; Alexandra Kalev, Frank Dobbin, and Erin Kelly, "Best Practices or Best Guesses? Assessing the Efficacy of Corporate Diversity Policies," *American Sociological Review* 71 (2006): 589–617.

286. "Diversity in the Legal Profession: The Next Steps," ABA Presidential Initiative Commission on Diversity (2010).

287. Julie Coffman and Bill Neuenfeldt, "Everyday Moments of Truth: Front Line Managers Are Key to Women's Career Aspirations," Bain & Company (2014), 14.

288. Inclusion, Deloitte, http://www2.deloitte.com/us/en/pages/about-deloitte/articles/deloitte-inclusion.html.

289. Emilio J. Castilla, "Gender, Race, and Meritocracy in Organizational Careers," *American Journal of Sociology* 113 (2008): 1479, 1485; Stephen Benard, In Paik, and Shelley J. Correll, "Cognitive Bias and the Motherhood Penalty," *Hastings Law Review* 59 (2008): 1359, 1381.

290. Spar, email survey.

291. Margaret Hopkins, Deborah O'Neil, Angela Passarelli, and Diana Bilimoria, "Women's Leadership Development: Strategic Practices for Women and Organizations," *Consulting Psychology Journal: Practice and Research* 60 (2008): 358.

292. Jake Simpson, "Firms Eyeing Gender Equality Should Adopt Corporate Culture," *Law360*, Apr. 22, 2014, http://www.law360.com/articles/530686/firms-eyeing-gender-equality-should-adopt-corporate-culture.

293. Rosabeth Moss Kanter, *Men and Women of the Corporation: New Edition* (New York: Basic Books, 1977); Eagly and Carli, *Through the Labyrinth*, 157.

294. Tiffany N. Darden, "The Law Firm Caste System: Constructing a Bridge Between Workplace Equity Theory and the Institutional Analyses of Bias in Corporate Law Firms," *Berkeley Journal of Employment and Labor Law* 30 (2009): 85, 100. For the limited research and mixed or negative findings on effectiveness, see Deborah L. Rhode, "Social Research and Social Change: Meeting the Challenge of Gender Inequality and Sexual Abuse," *Harvard Journal of Law and Gender* 30 (2007): 11, 13–14. Elizabeth Levy

Paluck, "Diversity Training and Intergroup Contact: A Call to Action Research," *Journal of Social Issues* 62 (2006): 577, 583, 591.

295. Pierre Gurdjian, Thomas Halbeisen, and Kevin Lane, "Why Leadership-Development Programs Fail," *McKinsey Quarterly* (January 2014).

296. Iris Bohnet, *What Works: Gender Equality by Design* (Cambridge, MA: Harvard University Press, 2016), 99.

297. Ibid.; Harrison Monarth, "Evaluate Your Leadership Development Program," *Harvard Business Review* (January 2015); Gurdjian, Halveisen, and Lane, "Why Leadership Development Programs Fail."

298. Alexandra Kalev and Frank Dobbin, "Try and Make Me! Why Corporate Diversity Training Fails" (unpublished paper, 2015).

299. Elizabeth Paluck and Donald Green, "Prejudice Reduction: What Works? A Review and Assessment of Research and Practice," *Annual Review of Psychology* 60 (2009): 339.

300. Dobbin and Kalev, "The Architecture of Inclusion," 293–95; Dobbin, Kalev, and Kelly, "Diversity Management," 23–25.

301. Darden, "The Law Firm Caste System," 117; Diane Vaughan, "Rational Choice, Situated Action, and the Social Control of Organizations," *Law and Society Review* 32 (1998): 23, 34; Kalev and Dobbin, "Try and Make Me!"

302. Iris Bohnet, *What Works*, 50. See Adam D. Galinsky and Gordon B. Moskowitz, "Perspective Taking: Decreasing Stereotype Expression, Stereotype Accessibility, and In-Group Favoritism," *Journal of Personality and Social Psychology* 78 (2000):708; Michelle M. Duguid and Melissa C. Thomas-Hunt, "Condoning Stereotyping? How Awareness of Stereotyping Prevalence Impacts Expression of Stereotypes," *Journal of Applied Psychology* 100 (2015): 343 (finding that telling subjects about the widespread prevalence of stereotyping increases stereotyping).

303. Deborah L. Rhode and Lucy B. Ricca, "Diversity in the Legal Profession: Perspectives from Managing Partners and General Counsel," *Fordham Law Review* 83 (2015): 2483, 2495 (quoting Larren Nashelsky and anonymous participant).

304. Walton, Murphy, and Ryan, "Stereotype Threat," 541. See also Huston, *How Women Decide*, 112 (noting that training can reduce vulnerability to stereotype threat).

305. Schipani et al., "Pathways for Women," 131; Kalev, Dobbin, and Kelley, "Best Practices or Best Guesses?"; Rhode and Kellerman, "Women and Leadership," 30.

306. Bob Yates, "Law Firms Address Retention of Women and Minorities," *Chicago Lawyer*, March 2007.

307. Dobbin, Kalev, and Kelly, "Diversity Management," 25.

308. Kalev, Dobbin, and Kelly, "Best Practices or Best Guesses?" 594; Rhode and Kellerman, "Women and Leadership," 30; Schipani et al., "Pathways for Women," 89, 100–101; Abbott, *The Lawyer's Guide to Mentoring*, 25, 32–33.

309. "Diversity and Gender Equity in the Legal Profession: Best Practices Guide," Minnesota State Bar Association, Diversity Implementation Task Force, June 2008, http://c.ymcdn.com/sites/ncbp.org/resource/collection/009B4863-0F53-424D-BC57-45E6489126D1/Diversity_and_Gender_Equity_in_the_Legal_Profession_Best_Practices_Guide.pdf.

310. Ibid.

311. "Mentoring Across Differences: A Guide to Cross-Gender and Cross-Race Mentoring," Minority Corporate Counsel Association, http://www.mcca.com/index.cfm?fuseaction=page.viewpage&pageide=666/; Jones, "Mentoring Plans Failing Associates."

312. Jones, "Mentoring Plans," 1.

313. Janet Napolitano, telephone interview.

314. "Pipeline's Broken Promise," part of The Promise of Future Leadership: A Research Program on Highly Talented Employees in the Pipeline (New York: Catalyst, 2010), 5; Coffman and Neuenfeldt, "Everyday Moments of Truth."

315. Rivers and Barnett, *The New Soft War on Women*, 27–28.

316. Shellenbarger, "The XX Factor."

317. *Generation and Gender in the Workplace* (New York: Families and Work Institute, 2004).

318. Coffman and Neuenfeldt, "Everyday Moments of Truth," 11; Verveer and Azzarell, *Fast Forward*, 68, 120.

319. Deloitte pioneered the program. Slaughter, *Unfinished Business*, 214.

320. George F. Dreher, "Breaking the Glass Ceiling: The Effects of Sex Ratios and Work Life Programs on Female Leadership at the Top," *Human Relations* 56 (2003): 541.

321. Slaughter, *Unfinished Business*, 16.

322. Frederick A. Miller and Judith H. Katz, *The Inclusion Breakthrough: Unleashing the Real Power of Diversity* (San Francisco: Berrett-Koehler, 2002), 37–38.

CHAPTER 2

1. Karen Middleton, "Get Women out of Binders and into the Halls of Power," *San Francisco Chronicle*, Oct. 22, 2012, A8. This chapter draws on Deborah L. Rhode, *What Women Want: An Agenda for the Women's Movement* (New York: Oxford University Press, 2014): 150–59.

2. Deborah L. Rhode, "Perspectives on Professional Women," *Stanford Law Review* 40 (1988): 1163, 1173.

3. Kira Sanbonmatsu, "Reaching Executive Office: The Presidency and the Office of the Governor," Political Parity (2015), 2, https://www.politicalparity.org/wp-content-uploads/2015/08/Parity-Research-women-and-excutiveoffice.pdf.

4. Liza Mundy, "100 Women in Congress? So What," Politico, Nov. 6, 2014, http://www.politico.com/magazine/story/2014/11/100-women-in-congress-so-what-112663.

5. Ibid.

6. Jennifer L. Lawless and Richard L. Fox, Men Rule: The Continued Under-Representation of Women in U.S. Politics (Washington, DC: Women and Politics Institute, 2012).

7. Farida Jalalzai and Manon Tremblay, "North America," in Gretchen Bauer and Manon Tremblay, eds., Women in Executive Power (New York: Routledge, 2011): 122–23.

8. Gail Collins, "Hillary in History," New York Times, Nov. 8, 2015 (twenty-five out of sixty women were widows).

9. Nicholas Kristof, "Trump Plays the Man's Card," New York Times, May 1, 2016, SR 9 (quoting Nixon).

10. Roberto Suro, "The 1990 Elections: Governor-Texas; Fierce Election for Governor Is Narrowly Won by Richards," New York Times, Nov. 7, 1990, at 2.

11. Kathleen Dolan, When Does Gender Matter? Women Candidates and Gender Stereotypes in American Elections (New York: Oxford University Press, 2014), 187 (quoting Schroeder).

12. Larry Rohter, "Woman in the News: Clinton Picks Miami Woman, Veteran State Prosecutor, to Be His Attorney General: Tough 'Front-Line Warrior' Janet Reno," New York Times, Feb. 12, 1993, A22. See Kathleen Hall Jamieson, Beyond the Double Bind: Women and Leadership (New York: Oxford University Press, 1995), 169–71.

13. Jamieson, Beyond the Double Bind, 169–70.

14. Torild Skard, Women of Power: Half a Century of Female Presidents and Prime Ministers Worldwide (Chicago: Policy Press, 2015), 486, 403.

15. Christina Wolbrecht, "Introduction: What We Saw at the Revolution: Women in American Politics and Political Science," in Christina Wolbrecht, Karen Beckwith, and Lisa Baldez, eds., Political Women and American Democracy (New York: Cambridge University Press, 2008), 7.

16. Sanbonmatsu, "Reaching Executive Office," 2.

17. Pew Research Center, "Women and Leadership," Jan. 14, 2015, http://www.pewsocialtrends.org/2015/01/14/women-and-leadership/.

18. Dolan, When Does Gender Matter? 54 (58 percent think there should be more women); NBC News/Wall Street Journal Survey, April 2013

(two-thirds of Americans believe the country would be better off with more women in office).

19. Dolan, *When Does Gender Matter?* 123 (quoting Clinton).

20. Center for American Women in Politics, "Fact Sheet" (2016), http://www.cawp.rutgers.edu/fast_facts/levels_of_office/documents/cong.pdf; Sanbonmatsu, "Reaching Executive Office."

21. Center for American Women in Politics, "Women of Color in Elective Office Fact Sheet," 2016, http://www.cawp.rutgers.edu/fast_facts/levels_of_office/documents/cong.pdf. See also Kira Sanbonmatsu, "Women of Color in American Politics," Political Parity (2015), https://www.politicalparity.org/wp-content/uploads/215/08/Parity-Research-women-of-color.pdf.

22. Susan J. Carroll, "Women in State Government: Stalled Progress," in *The Book of the States* (Council of State Governments, 2014), 410–18; Jay Newton-Small, "The Last Politicians," *Time*, Oct. 28, 2013, 27.

23. "Voices. Votes. Leadership. The Status of Black Women in American Politics," report for the Higher Heights Leadership Fund (Center for American Women and Politics, 2015), ii; Sanbonmatsu, "Women of Color in American Politics."

24. Jalalzai and Tremblay, "North America," 136.

25. Joan C. Williams, "The End of Men? Gender Flux in the Face of Precarious Masculinity," *Boston University Law Review* 93 (2013): 699–700.

26. Inter-Parliamentary Union, "Women in Parliament" (May 2016), http://www.ipu.org/wmn-e/classif-arc.htm.

27. Adam Nagourney, "In Los Angeles, Women Yield Top Seats to Men When Politics Is Arena," *New York Times*, Aug. 5, 2013, A1.

28. Center for American Women and Politics, "Fact Sheet." For other statistics on underrepresentation of Republican women, see Jay Newton-Small, *Broad Influence: How Women Are Changing the Way America Works* (New York: Time Books, 2016), 165.

29. Derek Willis, "G.O.P. Women in Congress: Why So Few?" *New York Times*, June 1, 2015.

30. Gail Collins, "Twenty and Counting," *New York Times*, Dec. 8, 2012, A21.

31. Kira Sanbonmatsu, "Women Candidates and Their Campaigns," Political Parity (2015), https://www.politicalparity.org/wp-content/uploads/2015/08/Parity-Research-women-andcampaigns.pdf; Dolan, *When Does Gender Matter?* 149; Jennifer L. Lawless, "Female Candidates and Legislators," *Annual Review of Political Science* 18 (2015): 349, 352 (summarizing studies); Kira Sanbonmatsu, "Money and Women Candidates," Political Parity (2015, summarizing studies); Lawless and Fox, *Men Rule*, ii.

32. Dolan, *When Does Gender Matter?* 11; Lawless, "Female Candidates and Legislators," 357; Molly Ball, "Why Both the Dems and the GOP Now

Think Voters Prefer Female Candidates: A Women's Edge?" *Atlantic*, May 2013, 16–17.

33. Richard Kim and Betsy Reed, eds., "Introduction," in *Going Rogue: Sarah Palin: An American Nightmare* (New York: OR Books, 2009), 171.

34. Lawless, "Female Candidates and Legislators," 352; Gary C. Jacobson, *The Politics of Congressional Elections*, 8th ed. (New York: Pearson, 2012).

35. Jennifer L. Lawless and Kathryn Pearson, "The Primary Reason for Women's Underrepresentation? Reevaluating the Conventional Wisdom," *Journal of Politics* 70 (2008): 67.

36. Kristin Rowe-Finkbeiner, *The F Word: Feminism in Jeopardy: Women, Politics, and the Future* (Emeryville, CA: Seal Press, 2004), 222–23.

37. Christopher F. Karpowitz and Tali Mendelberg, *The Silent Sex: Gender Deliberation and Institutions* (Princeton: Princeton University Press, 2014), 353; Center for American Women and Politics, "Voices. Votes. Leadership." ii.

38. Katie Fisher Ziegler, "The Glass Dome," *State Legislatures* (July/August 2015), 23.

39. Lawless and Fox, *Men Rule*, ii.

40. Lawless, "Female Candidates and Legislators," 352–53; Jean Sinzdak and Kathy Kleeman, *A National Call to Action: Teaching Young People About Women's Public Leadership and Promoting Public Leadership for Girls* (Rutgers, NJ: Center for American Women and Politics, 2015), 4.

41. Lawless, "Female Candidates and Legislators," 355; Melody Crowder-Meyer, "Gendered Recruitment Without Trying: How Local Party Recruiters Affect Women's Representation," *Politics and Gender* 9 (2013): 390.

42. Lawless and Fox, *Men Rule*, 7.

43. Ziegler, "Glass Dome," 24.

44. Pew Research Center, "Women and Leadership" (38 percent think it is a major reason and 24 percent think it is a minor reason).

45. Michele L. Swers, *Women in the Club: Gender and Policy Making in the Senate* (Chicago: University of Chicago Press, 2013), 238; Virginia Foxx, telephone interview. Apr. 24, 2015.

46. Foxx, telephone interview.

47. Newton-Small, "The Last Politicians," 27; Newton-Small, *Broad Influence*, 31–32.

48. Mary Hawkesworth, "Congressional Enactments of Race-Gender: Toward a Theory of Race-Gendered Institutions," *American Political Science Review* 97 (2003): 529.

49. Dittmar, *Navigating Gendered Terrain: Stereotypes and Strategy in Political Campaigns* (Philadelphia: Temple University Press, 2015), 100. See also Laura Liswood, secretary general of Council of Women World Leaders, telephone interview, Apr. 16, 2015.

50. Kira Sanbonmatsu, "Women Candidates and Their Campaigns," 1; Lawless, "Female Candidates and Legislators," 356; Sarah Fulton, "Running Backwards and in High Heels: The Gendered Quality Gap and Incumbent Electoral Success," *Political Research Quarterly* 65 (2012): 303; "Chronic Challenges: Double Standards Are Alive and Well," Barbara Lee Foundation, 2015, http://www.barbaraleefoundation.org/chapter/chronic-challenges-double-standards-are-alive-and-well. For recent research finding similar qualifications in candidates, see Dolan, *When Does Gender Matter?* 146, 191.

51. Foxx, telephone interview; Elizabeth Kolbert, "The Tyranny of High Expectations," in Susan Morrison, *Thirty Ways of Looking at Hillary* (New York: HarperCollins, 2008), 13. For similar views, see Dittmar, *Navigating Gendered Terrain*, 101.

52. Karpowitz and Mendelberg, *The Silent Sex*, 53; Kristen C. Kling, Janet Hyde, Caroline Showers, and Brenda Buswell, "Gender Differences in Self-Esteem: A Meta Analysis," *Psychological Bulletin* 125 (1999): 470.

53. Lawless and Fox, *Men Rule*, 9.

54. Ibid., 10.

55. Ibid., 12.

56. Ibid., 11. Sarah Mimms, "Republicans Confront Lady Problems in Congress," *Atlantic,* Aug. 6, 2013.

57. Jennifer Granholm, telephone interview, Feb. 5, 2015.

58. Janet Napolitano, telephone interview, Feb. 17, 2015.

59. Swers, *Women in the Club*, 15; Dittmar, *Navigating Gendered Terrain*, 23–25. For belief that stereotypes transcend party, see Kira Sanbonmatsu and Kathleen Dolan, "Do Gender Stereotypes Transcend Party?" *Political Research Quarterly* 62 (2009): 485. For evidence that party overwhelms gender-based stereotypes, see Danny Hayes, "When Gender and Party Collide: Stereotyping in Candidate Trait Attribution," *Politics and Gender* 7 (2011): 133.

60. Jennifer L. Lawless, "Sexism and Gender Bias in Election 2008: A More Complex Path for Women in Politics," *Politics and Gender* 5 (2009): 137.

61. Dolan, *When Does Gender Matter?* 32, 80, 85, 187.

62. Ibid., 184.

63. Ibid., 187.

64. Skard, *Women of Power*, 78.

65. Eleanor Clift and Tom Brazaitis, *Madam President: Shattering the Last Glass Ceiling* (New York: Scribner, 2000), 128.

66. Jodi Kantor and Kate Taylor, "In Quinn's Loss, Questions About Role of Gender and Sexuality," *New York Times,* Sep. 12, 2013, http://www.nytimes.com/2013/09/12/nyregion/in-quinns-loss-questions-about-role-of-gender-and-sexuality.html.

67. For examples, see Newton-Small, *Broad Influence*, 69, 71.

68. Ann E. Kornblut, *Notes from the Cracked Ceiling* (New York: Broadway, 2011), 50; Elizabeth Kolbert, "The Tyranny of High Expectations," in Morrison, *Thirty Ways of Looking at Hillary*, 11–12. See also Dittmar, *Navigating Gendered Terrain*, 21 (quoting Chris Paretta about "fine line" women have to walk between appearing tough but not "bitchy").

69. Dittmar, *Navigating Gendered Terrain*, 32.

70. Ibid., 48.

71. Karin Klenke, *Women in Leadership: A Contextual Perspective* (New York: Springer, 1996), 61.

72. Dolan, *When Does Gender Matter?* 2.

73. Elizabeth Kolbert, "The Student," *New Yorker*, Oct. 13, 2003, http://www.newyorker.com/magazine/2003/10/13/the-student.

74. Dittmar, *Navigating Gendered Terrain*, 149.

75. Amy Chozick and Trip Gabriel, "Democrats See Gains as Trump Targets a Wife," *New York Times,* March 26, 2016.

76. Gail Collins, "Trump Deals the Woman Card," *New York Times*, Apr. 28, 2016.

77. Ibid.

78. Barbara Lee, "What If Bernie Sanders Were a Woman?" *Boston Globe*, Feb. 13, 2016.

79. Emily Cahn, "Hillary Clinton: Women Running for Office Bear a 'Much Greater Burden,'" *Mashable*, Feb. 6, 2016, http://mashable.com/2016/02/06/hillary-clinton-women-politics-double-standard/#E9Y_7Atznuqj.

80. Catherine Rampall, "Be Pretty But Not Too Pretty: Why Women Just Can't Win," *Washington Post*, Jan. 21, 2016 (quoting Clinton).

81. Newton-Small, *Broad Influence*, 77; Jay Newton-Small, "Exclusive: Hillary Clinton on Running and Governing as a Woman," *Time*, Jan. 7, 2016.

82. Lawless and Fox, *Men Rule*, 14.

83. Julie Dolan, Melissa Deckman, and Michele L. Swers, *Women and Politics: Paths to Power and Political Influence*, 2nd ed. (New York: Longman, 2011), 138.

84. Patricia Schroeder, *24 Years of House Work . . . and the Place Is Still a Mess* (Kansas City: Andrews McMeel, 1998), 24.

85. Dolan, *When Does Gender Matter?* 2; Julia Prodis Sulek, "The #Womancard," *Mercury News*, Apr. 28, 2016, P1.

86. Diana B. Carlin and Kelly L. Winfrey, "Have You Come a Long Way, Baby? Hillary Clinton, Sarah Palin, and Sexism in 2008 Campaign Coverage," *Communication Studies* 60 (2009): 326, 333–34.

87. Dittmar, *Navigating Gendered Terrain*, 116.

88. Ibid., 118.

89. Susan R. Madsen, *Developing Leadership: Learning from the Experience of Women Governors* (Lanham, MD: University Press of America, 2009).

90. Elizabeth Kolbert, "The Tyranny of High Expectations," in Susan Morrison, ed., *Thirty Ways of Looking at Hillary* (New York: Harper Collins, 2008), 11–12.

91. Torben Iversen and Frances Rosenbluth, *Women, Work, and Politics: The Political Economy of Gender Inequality* (New Haven: Yale University Press, 2010), xiv. For proportional representation, see Skard, *Women of Power*, 74; and Jalalzai and Tremblay, "North America," 182; Farida Jalalzai, *Shattered, Cracked, or Firmly Intact: Women and the Executive Glass Ceiling Worldwide* (New York: Oxford University Press, 2013), 24.

92. Iversen and Rosenbluth, *Women, Work, and Politics*, 9, 135, 165; Lawless and Fox, *Men Rule*, 11.

93. Lawless and Pearson, "The Primary Reason for Women's Underrepresentation," 75–78.

94. Kelly Dittmar, "Encouragement Is Not Enough: Addressing Social and Structural Barriers to Female Recruitment," *Politics and Gender* 11 (2015): 759, 761.

95. Carlin and Winfrey, "Have You Come a Long Way, Baby?" 327 (quoting Palin).

96. David A. Graham, "50 Shades of Terrible: Here's What an Awful Debate Question Looks Like," *Atlantic*, Oct. 18, 2012, http://www.theatlantic.com/politics/archive/2012/10/50-shades-of-terrible-heres-what-an-awful-debate-question-looks-like/263808.

97. Caryl Rivers and Rosalind C. Barnett, *The New Soft War on Women: How the Myth of Female Ascendance Is Hurting Women, Men—and Our Economy* (New York: Penguin, 2013).

98. Susan J. Carroll, "Reflections on Gender and Hillary Clinton's Presidential Campaign: The Good, the Bad and the Misogynic," *Politics and Gender* 5 (2009): 1, 13. Katha Pollitt, "Hillary Rotten," in Morrison, *Thirty Ways of Looking at Hillary*, 16–18.

99. Richard L. Fox and Zoe M. Oxley, "Why No Madame President: Gender and Presidential Politics in the United States," in Michael A. Genovese and Janie S. Steckenrider, eds., *Women as Political Leaders: Studies in Gender and Governing* (New York: Routledge, 2013), 350.

100. Kornblut, *Notes from the Cracked Ceiling*, 70.

101. Women's Media Center, "Campaign Update: Sexism Sells, But We're Not Buying It," July 25, 2008, http://www.womensmediacenter.com/blog/entry/campaign-update-sexism-sells-but-were-not-buying-it.

102. Anna Quindlen, "Still Stuck in Second," *Newsweek*, Mar. 17, 2008, 70.

103. Julia Baird et al., "From Seneca Falls to Sarah Palin?" *Newsweek*, Sep. 22, 2008.

104. Robin Givhan, "Hillary Clinton's Tentative Dip into New Neckline Territory," *Washington Post*, July 20, 2007, http://www.washingtonpost

.com/wp-dyn/content/article/2007/07/19/AR2007071902668.html; Irin Carmon, "Tim Gunn: Hillary Clinton Dresses Like 'She's Confused About Her Gender'," *Jezebel*, July 27, 2011, http://jezebel.com/5825314/tim-gunn-hillary-clinton-dresses-like-shes-confused-about-her-gender.

105. Amanda Fortini, "The Feminist Reawakening: Hillary Clinton and the Fourth Wave," *New York Magazine*, Apr. 13, 2008.

106. Gail Sheehy, *Hillary's Choice* (New York: Random House, 1999), 331.

107. Elizabeth Frock, "Hillary Clinton's Long-Time Hairstylist Shares Secrets Behind the Diplomat's Ever Changing Hair," *U.S. News and World Report*, Nov. 27, 2012.

108. Todd Van Luling, "Hey Politicians, It's the 21st Century. Time to Stop Being Sexist Idiots," *Huffington Post*, Oct. 8, 2013, http://www.huffingtonpost.com/2013/10/08/sexist-politician-quotes_n_4038199.html.

109. Jessica Misener, "Michele Bachmann Wears Tons of Makeup for CNN Debate," *Huffington Post*, Nov. 23, 2011, http://www.huffingtonpost.com/2011/11/23/michele-bachmann-makeup_n_1109553.html.

110. "Krystal Ball on Sexy Photos Scandal: 'It Was Devastating'," *Huffington Post*, Nov. 29, 2012, http://www.huffingtonpost.com/2012/11/29/krystal-ball-photos_n_2212963.html.

111. http://radioboston.wbur.org/2012/09/13/payne-warren; Rivers and Barnett, *The New Soft War on Women*, 36.

112. Rachel Weiner, "Obama Calls Kamal Harris 'the Best Looking Attorney General'," *Washington Post*, Apr. 4, 2013.

113. Nicholas Kristof, "Clinton, Trump and Sexism," *New York Times*, Jan. 24, 2016 (quoting Trump).

114. David Martosko and Wills Robinson, "Donald's New Woman Trouble," *Daily Mail*, Sep. 9, 2015.

115. Patrick Healy and Michael Luo, "$150,000 Wardrobe for Palin May Alter Tailor-Made Image," *New York Times*, Oct. 22, 2008.

116. Michael Luo, "Top Salary in McCain Campaign? Palin's Makeup Stylist," *New York Times*, Oct. 24, 2008.

117. "Name It. Change It: An Examination of the Impact of Media Coverage of Women Candidates' Appearance," Women's Media Center, 2013, http://wmc.3cdn.net/63fa94f234fe3bb7eb_g4m6ibsyr.pdf.

118. Karrin Anderson, "Girls Gone Mad: The Wild-Eyed Lunacy of Bachmann, Palin, Pelosi, Clinton … Etc.," *Bagnews*, July 16, 2011, http://www.bagnewsnotes.com/2011/07/the-wild-eyed-lunacy-of-bachmann-palin-pelosi-clinton-etc. Maya Dusenbery, "Bachmann Sexism Watch: 'Crazy-Eyed Queen of Rage' Edition," *Feministing*, Aug. 9, 2011, http://feministing.com/2011/08/09/bachmann-sexism-watch-crazy-eyed-queen-of-rage-edition/; Kornblut, *Notes from the Cracked Ceiling*, 102–3, 182; Pollitt, "Hillary Rotten," 18.

119. Newton-Small, *Broad Influence*, 72.

120. Liswood, telephone interview (quoting woman head of state).

121. Theda Skocpol, *Protecting Soldiers and Mothers: The Political Origins of Social Policy in the United States* (Cambridge: Harvard University Press, 1992), 332 (quoting Dorr).

122. Jane Addams, "The Modern City and the Municipal Franchise for Women," in Susan B. Anthony and Ida Husted Harper, eds., *History of Woman Suffrage* (Indianapolis: Hollenbeck Press, 1902), iv, 178; Deborah L. Rhode, *Justice and Gender: Sex Discrimination and the Law* (Cambridge: Harvard University Press, 1989), 14.

123. Michele L. Swers, *The Difference Women Make: The Policy Impact of Women in Congress* (Chicago: University of Chicago Press, 2002), 1 (quoting Lincoln).

124. Karpowitz and Mendelberg, *The Silent Sex*, 49; David E. Campbell and Christine Wolbrecht, "See Jane Run: Women Politicians as Role Models for Adolescents," *Journal of Politics* 68 (2006): 233; Laurel E. Elder, "Why Women Don't Run: Explaining Women's Underrepresentation in America's Political Institutions," *Women and Politics* 26 (2004): 27.

125. Beth Reingold, *Representing Women: Sex, Gender, and Legislative Behavior in Arizona and California* (Chapel Hill: University of North Carolina Press, 2000), 3.

126. Barbara Boxer, Susan Collins, Diane Feinstein, et al., *Nine and Counting: The Women of the Senate* (New York: Harper Perennial, 2001), 102 (quoting Boxer).

127. Reingold, *Representing Women*, 3, 219.

128. See Rhode, *What Women Want*.

129. Pamela Paxton and Melanie M. Hughes, *Women, Politics and Power: A Global Perspective* (Thousand Oaks, CA: 2007), 2, 193. For Congress, see Jessica C. Gerrity, Tracy Osborn, and Jeanette Morehouse Mendez, "Women and Representation: A Different View of the District?" *Politics and Gender* 3 (2007): 179; Swers, *Women in the Club*, 38, 62, 93–94, 100; Christina Wolbrecht, *The Politics of Women's Rights: Parties, Positions and Change* (Princeton: Princeton University Press, 2000). For state legislatures, see Tracy L. Osborn, *How Women Represent Women: Political Parties, Gender, and Representation in the State Legislatures* (New York: Oxford University Press, 2012), 12; Swers, *The Difference Women Make*, 8, 72; Reingold, *Representing Women*, 243; Osborn, *How Women Represent Women*, 118; Kathleen A. Bratton, "Critical Mass Theory Revisited: The Behavior and Success of Token Women in State Legislatures," *Politics and Gender* 1 (2005): 97.

130. Amy Caiazza, "Does Women's Representation in Elected Office Lead to Women-Friendly Policy? Analysis of State-Level Data," *Women & Politics*, 26 (2004): 35.

131. Kira Sanbonmatsu, "Why Women? The Impact of Women in Elective Office," Political Parity (2015), https://www.politicalparity.org/wp-content/uploads/2015/08/Parity-Research-women-impact.pdf.

132. Ibid.

133. Debra L. Dodson, "Representing Women's Interests in the U.S. House of Representatives," in Sue Thomas and Clyde Wilcox, eds. *Women and Elective Office* (New York: Oxford University Press, 1998), 130.

134. Skard, *Women of Power*, 111, 114. See also Sarah L. Henderson, "Gro Harlem Brundtland of Norway," in Genovese and Steckenrider, *Women as Political Leaders*, 68–70.

135. Linda S. Stevenson, "The Bachelet Effect on Gender-Equity Policies," *Latin American Perspectives* 39 (2012): 129, 132–37; Alexei Barrionuevo, "Chilean Leader's Legacy Is Upended Traditions and Balanced Books," *New York Times*, Oct. 29, 2009, A6.

136. Skard, *Women of Power*, 402.

137. Reingold, *Representing Women* (finding no evidence that Arizona women were better represented than California's, though Arizona had a higher proportion of women legislators); Kimberly Cowell-Meyers and Laura Langbein, "Linking Women's Descriptive and Substantive Representation in the United States," *Politics & Gender* 5 (2009): 491, 512 (women's legislative representation predicted the presence of only five out of thirty-four women-friendly policies in the states and nonadoption of three); Iversen and Rosenbluth, *Women, Work, and Politics*, xiii, 8 (the percentage of women in national legislatures has little relation to other measures of gender equality). See generally Beth Reingold, "Women as Office Holders," in Wolbrecht et al., *Political Women and American Democracy*, 131.

138. Osborn, *How Women Represent Women*, 7; Swers, *The Difference Women Make*, 124; Julie Dolan, "Support for Women's Interests in the 103rd Congress: The Distinct Impact of Congressional Women," *Women & Politics* 18 (1997): 81; Michele Swers and Amy Caiazza, "Transforming the Political Agenda? Gender Differences in Bill Sponsorship on Women's Issues," Institute for Women's Policy Research, Research-in-Brief (October 2000); Susan Gluck Mezey, "Increasing the Number of Women in Office: Does It Matter?" in Elizabeth Adell Cook, Sue Thomas, and Clyde Wilcox, eds., *The Year of the Woman: Myths and Realities* (Boulder: Westview Press, 1996), 255–70; Karen L. Tamerius, "Sex, Gender, and Leadership in the Representation of Women," in Georgia Duerst-Lahti and Rita Mae Kelly, eds., *Gender Power, Leadership, and Governance* (Ann Arbor: University of Michigan Press, 1996), 93, 107.

139. Sarah Childs and Mona Lena Krook, "Critical Mass Theory and Women's Political Representation," *Political Studies* 56 (2008): 725–28.

140. Madeleine M. Kunin, *The New Feminist Agenda: Defining the Next Revolution for Women, Work, and Family* (White River Junction, VT: Chelsea Green, 2012), 155–56 (quoting DeLauro).

141. Collins, "Twenty and Counting," A21, http://www.nytimes.com/2012/ 12/08/opinion/collins-twenty-and-counting.html.

142. Kira Sanbonmatsu, "Representation by Gender and Parties," in Wolbrecht et al., *Political Women and American Democracy*, 108; Reingold, "Women as Office Holders," 144; Swers, *Women in the Club*, 98.

143. "Carly Fiorina on Abortion," On the Issues (2016), http://www.onthe issues.org/2016/Carly_Fiorina_Abortion.htm.

144. Swers, *Women in the Club*, 239.

145. Ibid., 239–40.

146. Ibid., 240.

147. For Trump's charges, see Collins, "Trump Deals the Woman Card"; Newton-Small, *Broad Influence*, 159. For other charges against Clinton, see Erika Falk, "Clinton and the Playing-the-Gender-Card Metaphor in Campaign News," *Feminist Media Studies* 13 (2013): 192, 202. For Fiorina's claim, see Kenneth T. Walsh, "Playing the Gender Card," *U.S. News & World Report*, Oct. 23, 2015 ; Abby Johnston, "Carly Fiorina Used the Gender Card in the Fifth GOP Debate, Something She Said She'd Never Do," *Bustle*, Dec. 15, 2015, http://www.bustle.com/articles/ 130146-carly-fiorina-used-the-gender-card-in-the-fifth-gop-debate-something-she-said-shed-never.

148. Jill Filipovic, "Hillary's Office Politics," *New York Times*, Feb. 21, 2016 (quoting Sanders).

149. Curtis Houck, "PBS's Ifill to Sanders: Would You Be 'The Instrument of Thwarting History' If You Beat Hillary?" NewsBusters, Feb. 11, 2016, http://www.newsbusters.org/blogs/nb/curtis-houck/2016/02/11/pbss-if.

150. Jose A. Delreal and Anne Gearan, "Trump: If Clinton 'Were a man, I don't think she'd get 5 percent of the vote,' " *Washington Post*, April 27, 2016.

151. Jay Newton-Small, "Hillary and Women: Can Gender Be a Force Multiplier?" *Time*, Jan. 18, 2016, 28.

152. Beth Reingold, "Women as Office Holders," 133.

153. For claims that women are more conciliatory and collaborative, see Karpowitz and Mendelberg, *The Silent Sex*, 21, 64. Raymond Hernandez, "A Gillibrand Campaign: More Women in Politics," *New York Times*, July 4, 2011, http://www.nytimes.com/2011/07/05/nyregion/gillibrand-wants-women-involved-in-politics.html?_r=0. For women's self-description as collaborative, see Madsen, *Developing Leadership*, 299; Sue Tooeson Rinehart, "Do Women Leaders Make a Difference? Substance, Style and Perceptions," in Debra Dodson, ed., *Gender and Policy Making* (New Brunswick, NJ: Center for American Women and Politics, 1991).

154. Chris Ogden, *Maggie: An Intimate Portrait of a Woman in Power* (New York: Simon and Schuster, 1990), 250; Anthony King, *The British Prime Minister* (London: Macmillan, 1986), 117.

155. Peter Jenkins, *Mrs. Thatcher's Revolution: The Ending of the Socialist Era* (Cambridge: Harvard University Press, 1988), 3; Michael A. Genovese, "Margaret Thatcher and the Politics of Conviction Leadership," in Genovese and Steckenrider, *Women as Political Leaders*, 291.

156. Genovese, "Margaret Thatcher," 300 (quoting Melanie Philips).

157. Ibid., 300.

158. Ibid., 298–99.

159. Hugo Young, *The Iron Lady: A Biography of Margaret Thatcher* (New York: Noonday Press, 1990), 304.

160. Jane Everett, "Indira Gandhi and the Exercise of Power," in Genovese and Steckenrider, *Women as Political Leaders*, 167; Blema Steinberg, *Women in Power* (Montreal: McGill-Queens University Press, 2008), 91.

161. Steinberg, *Women in Power*, 152. See also Seth Thompson, "Golda Meir: A Very Public Life," in Genovese and Steckenrider, *Women as Political Leaders*, 176–202.

162. Golda Meir, *My Life* (New York: Putnam, 1975), 113, 115.

163. Jo Freeman, *We Will Be Heard: Women's Struggles for Political Power in the United States* (Lanham, MD: Rowman and Littlefield, 2008), 225.

164. Newton-Small, *Broad Influence*, 27, 18.

165. Barbara Lee Foundation, "Chronic Challenges."

166. Craig Volden, Alan E. Wiseman, and Dana E. Wittmer, *The Legislative Effectiveness of Women in Congress*, Vanderbilt University Center for the Study of Democratic Institutions, Working Paper 04-2010 (2010), 7 (noting value of women's strategies of cooperation and consensus building); Melvin Konner, "A Better World, Run by Women," *Wall Street Journal*, Mar. 7–8, C3 (citing study of mayors and their budget processes), http://www.wsj.com/articles/a-better-world-run-by-women-1425657910.

167. Ziegler, "Glass Dome," 25; Jill Lawrence, "Do Women Make Better Senators Than Men?" *National Journal*, July 11, 2013. See also Newton-Small, *Broad Influence*, 56 (quoting Nancy Pelosi's view of women's strength in forging consensus).

168. Jay Newton-Small, "Women Are the Only Adults Left in Washington," *Time*, Oct. 16, 2013. See also Susan Milligan, "A Woman's Place Is Making Washington Work," *U.S. News & World Report*, Oct. 18, 2013; Siobhan Bennett, "When the U.S. Needed Leaders, Women Saved the Day," *Women's E-News*, Oct. 23, 2013; Ann McFeatters, "Thank Women for Ending Government Shutdown," Scripps Howard News Service, Oct. 24, 2013.

169. Henry Samuel, "Women Make Better Politicians Than Men, Claims French Minister," *Telegraph*, Oct. 11, 2010.

170. Josh Feldman, "Trump Brags About the Size of His Penis in GOP Debate," Mediaite, March 3, 2016, http://www.mediate.com/tv/trump-brags-about-the-size-of-his-penis-at-the-gop-debate/.

171. Debra L. Dodson, *The Impact of Women in Congress* (New York: Oxford University Press, 2006), 255–56.

172. Jalalzai, *Shattered, Cracked or Firmly Intact,* 27.

173. Skard, *Women of Power,* 481; Jalalzai, *Shattered, Cracked, or Firmly Intact,* 25. The number is contested. According to the Global Database of Quotas for Women, seventy-seven countries have quotas by constitutional or statutory decision. Quota Project, Global Database of Quotas for Women, http://www.quotaproject.org/uid/search.cfm.

174. See Pamela Paxton and Melanie M. Hughes, "The Increasing Effectiveness of National Gender Quotas, 1990–2010," *Legislative Studies Quarterly* 40 (2015): 332–35, 354.

175. Rohini Pande and Deanna Ford, "Gender Quotas and Female Leadership: A Review" (Background Paper for the World Development Report on Gender, Apr. 7, 2011), http://scholar.harvard.edu/files/rpande/fil.

176. Skard, *Women of Power,* 74 (noting increase of 10 to 22 percent between 1994 and 2014).

177. Ibid., 74 (noting increase of 6 to 17 percent between 1994 and 2014).

178. Granholm, telephone interview.

179. See for example the Rutgers Center for American Women and Politics' state-by-state resources for women, http://www.cawp.rutgers.edu/education_training.

180. Ziegler, "Glass Dome," 25; Sam Bennett, "Putting Your Money Where Your Mouth Is: Supporting Women Across the Aisle," *Huffington Post,* May 28, 2010, http://www.huffingtonpost.com/sam-bennett/putting-your-money-where_b_593585.html.

181. Kira Sanbonmatsu, "Women of Color in American Politics," Political Parity (2015), https://www.politicalparity.org/wp-content/uploads/2015/08/Parity-Research-women-of-color.pdf.

182. Leslie Bennetts, "Women and the Leadership Gap," *Daily Beast,* Mar. 5, 2012 (describing Emerge America).

183. Elder, "Why Women Don't Run," 27, 38.

184. Katharine Q. Seelye, "School Vote Stirs Debate on Girls as Leaders," *New York Times,* Apr. 11, 2013.

185. Sinzdak and Kleeman, *A National Call to Action,* 9.

186. *Report on Undergraduate Women's Leadership* (Princeton: Princeton University Office of Communications, 2011), 5, 67.

187. Jennifer L. Lawless and Richard L. Fox, *Girls Just Wanna Not Run: The Gender Gap in Young Americans' Political Ambition* (Washington, DC: Women and Politics Institute, 2013), 2.
188. Elder, "Why Women Don't Run," 40–41.
189. Lawless and Fox, *Girls Just Wanna Not Run*, 6–13.
190. Elder, "Why Women Don't Run," 47.
191. Sinzdak and Kleeman, *A National Call to Action*, 16.
192. Center for American Women and Politics, Teach a Girl to Lead, http://www.teachagirltolead.org.
193. Sinzdak and Kleeman, *A National Call to Action*, 17.
194. Bennett, "Putting Your Money Where Your Mouth Is"; Kira Sanbonmatsu, "Women Candidates and Their Campaigns," 4 (citing Dittmar's estimate that only 25 percent of campaign consultants were female).
195. For a history of Emily's List, which began with twenty-five women in a basement and has grown to more than three million supporters, see Ellen R. Malcolm, with Craig Unger, *When Women Win: Emily's List and the Rise of Women in American Politics* (Boston: Houghton Mifflin, 2016), xv.
196. Name It. Change It, http://www.nameitchangeit.org.
197. Dolan, *When Does Gender Matter?* 18; Newton-Small, *Broad Influence*, 29.
198. Newton-Small, *Broad Influence*, 70.
199. Maureen Dowd, "Donald the Dove, Hillary the Hawk," *New York Times*, May 1, 2016, SR 9.
200. Dylan Stabelford, "Hillary Clinton Addresses Sexism after Madeleine Albright and Gloria Steinem Scold Young Women for Backing Bernie," Yahoo, Feb. 7, 2016, https://www.yahoo.com/news/hillary-clinton-addresses-sexism-after-madeleine-210913805.html.
201. Jalalzai and Tremblay, "North America," 185.
202. S. Laurel Weldon, "Beyond Bodies: Institutional Sources of Representation of Women in Democratic Policymaking," *Journal of Politics* 64 (2002): 1153, 1169.
203. Dara Z. Strolovitch, "Do Interest Groups Represent the Disadvantaged? Advocacy at the Intersections of Race, Class, and Gender," *Journal of Politics* 68 (2006): 894.
204. Dara Z. Strolovitch, *Affirmative Advocacy: Race, Class, and Gender in Interest Group Politics* (Chicago: University of Chicago Press, 2007), 95.
205. Susan Faludi, "Not Their Mother's Candidate," *New York Times*, Feb. 14, 2016; Sheryl Gay Stolberg, "Hillary Clinton's Candidacy Reveals Generational Schism Among Women," *New York Times*, Feb. 16, 2016.
206. Stolberg, "Hillary Clinton's Candidacy Reveals Generational Schism."

CHAPTER 3

1. Garda W. Bowman, N. Beatrice Worthy, and Stephen Greyser, "Are Women Executives People?" *Harvard Business Review* (July–August 1965, 15; Dawn S. Carlson, K. Michele Kacmar, and Dwayne Whitten, "What Men Think They Know About Executive Women," *Harvard Business Review*, September 2006, 23.

2. Beth Milwid, *Working with Men: Professional Women Talk About Power, Sexuality and Ethics* (Hillsboro, OR: Beyond Words, 1990), 13.

3. Katharine Graham, *Personal History* (New York: Knopf, 1997), 343, 346, 418.

4. Ibid., 429.

5. Kristin Bellstrom, "Why 2015 Was a Terrible Year to Be a Female Fortune 500 CEO," *Fortune*, Dec. 23, 2015; Catalyst, "Women CEOs of the S&P 500" (New York: Catalyst, 2016). The figure was down from 5 percent earlier in the year. See Pew Research Center, "Women and Leadership," Jan. 14, 2015, http://www.pewsocialtrends.org/2015/01/14/women-and-leadership/. See Claire Cain Miller, "An Elusive Jackpot," *New York Times*, June 7, 2014.

6. Justin Wolfers, "Fewer Women Run Big Companies Than Men Named John," *New York Times*, March 2, 2015. At latest count, there were 5.3 percent Johns, and 4.1 percent women. "Guys Named John and Gender Inequality," *Ms.*, Spring 2015, 7.

7. "Why Wall Street's Women Are Stuck in the Middle," *Bloomberg Business*, June 25, 2015.

8. Thomas Lee, "Cracks in Glass Ceiling Close Fast," *San Francisco Chronicle*, May 16, 2014, C1.

9. Center for American Progress, "The Women's Leadership Gap" (2015), http://www.americanprogress.org/issues/women/report/2015/08/04/118743/the-womens-leadership-gap.

10. Catalyst, "Catalyst 2013 Census of Fortune 55: Still No Progress After Years of No Progress" (New York: Catalyst, 2013).

11. Joan C. Williams, "The End of Men? Gender Flux in the Face of Precarious Masculinity," *Boston University Law Review* 93 (2013): 699. See Nikki Waller and Joann Lublin, "What's Holding Women Back?" *Wall Street Journal*, Sep. 30, 2015, R1.

12. John Markoff, "Hewlett-Packard Picks Rising Star at Lucent as Its Chief Executive," *New York Times*, July 20, 1999, C1.

13. Carly Fiorina, *Tough Choices: A Memoir* (New York: Penguin, 2006), 173.

14. Nancy Aossey, president of International Medical Corps, telephone interview, March 2015.

15. Pew Research Center, "Women and Leadership."

16. *Everyday Moments of Truth: Frontline Managers Are Key to Women's Career Aspirations* (New York: Bain & Company, 2014), 5.

17. Pew Research Center, "Women and Leadership."
18. Catalyst, "Women 'Take Care,' Men 'Take Charge': Stereotyping of U.S. Business Leaders Exposed" (New York: Catalyst, 2005).
19. Alice H. Eagly, "Female Leadership Advantage and Disadvantage: Resolving the Contradictions," *Psychology of Women Quarterly* 31 (2007): 1, 8; *Benchmarking Women's Leadership in the United States* (Denver: Colorado Women's College, 2013).
20. *Harvard Business Review* Staff, "Women in the Workplace: A Research Roundup," *Harvard Business Review*, September 2013, 88.
21. Bob Sherwin, "Why Women Are More Effective Leaders Than Men," *Business Insider*, Jan. 24, 2014.
22. Catalyst, "Pipeline's Broken Promise" (New York: Catalyst, 2010), 3–4.
23. Jeremy Donovan, "Women Fortune 500 CEOs: Held to Higher Standards" (New York: American Management Association, 2015), http://www .amanet.org/pdf/women-fortune-500-CEOs.
24. Eagly, "Female Leadership Advantage and Disadvantage," 9.
25. "Gender Diversity and Corporate Performance" (Credit Suisse Research Institute, 2012), 28. See also World Economic Forum, Global Agenda Council on Women's Empowerment, "Five Challenges, One Solution: Women" (2013), 11.
26. Virginia Schein, "Women in Management: Reflection and Projections," *Women in Management Review* 22 (2007): 6, 9.
27. Caryl Rivers and Rosalind C. Barnett, *The New Soft War on Women: How The Myth of Female Ascendance Is Hurting Women, Men, and Our Economy* (New York: Penguin, 2013), 18; Madeline Heilman, "Description and Prescription: How Gender Stereotypes Prevent Women's Ascent up the Organizational Ladder," *Journal of Social Issues* 57 (2001): 666.
28. Catalyst, "Women in Corporate Leadership: Progress and Prospects" (New York: Catalyst, 1996), 37. See also Linda Wirth, *Breaking Through the Glass Ceiling: Women in Management* (Geneva: International Labour Office, 2001), 4.
29. Martha Foschi, "Double Standards in the Evaluation of Men and Women," *Social Psychology Quarterly* 59 (1996): 237; Jacqueline Landau, "The Relationship of Race and Gender to Managers' Rating of Promotion Potential," *Journal Organizational Behavior* 16 (1995): 391.
30. Linda Babcock and Sara Laschever, *Women Don't Ask: Negotiation and the Gender Divide* (Princeton: Princeton University Press, 2003), 94; Rhea E. Steinpreis, Katie A. Anders, and Dawn Ritzke, "The Impact of Gender on the Review of the Curricula Vitae of Job Applicants and Tenure Candidates: A National Empirical Study," *Sex Roles* 41 (1999): 509; Joan C. Williams, *Reshaping the Work Family Debate: Why Men and Class Matter* (Cambridge: Harvard University Press, 2010), 93; David Neumark,

Roy J. Bank, and Kyle D. Van Nort, "Sex Discrimination in Restaurant Hiring: An Audit Study," *Quarterly Journal of Economics* 111 (1996): 915 (finding that when male and female job testers with similar resumes approach employers, women's probability of getting hired is 50 percent lower than men's).

31. Emilio J. Castilla and Stephen Benard, "The Paradox of Meritocracy in Organizations," *Administrative Science Quarterly* 55 (2010): 543.

32. Matt O'Brien, "Report: Asian-American Tech Workers Absent from Silicon Valley's Executive Suites," *San Jose Mercury News*, May 6, 2015, B9.

33. Fiorina, *Tough Choices*, 52.

34. Rivers and Barnett, *The New Soft War on Women*, 215.

35. Joan Williams and Rachel Dempsey, *What Works for Women at Work* (New York: New York University Press, 2014), 69.

36. Deborah Gillis, email correspondence, Apr. 9, 2015.

37. Christine Silva, Nancy M. Carter, Anna Beninger, "Good Intentions, Imperfect Execution? Women Get Fewer of the 'Hot Jobs' Needed to Advance" (New York: Catalyst, 2012), 5–7.

38. Sheila Wellington, Marcia Brumit Kropf, and Paulette Gerkovich, "What's Holding Women Back?" *Harvard Business Review* (June 2003): 18. "Breaking Through the Glass Ceiling: Women in Management," update report, International Labour Organization, 2004, 57, http://www.ilo.org/dyn/gender/docs/RES/292/f267981337.

39. Sheryl Sandberg and Adam Grant, "Madam C.E.O., Get Me a Coffee," *New York Times*, Feb. 8, 2015, SR2. See also Linda Babcock, Lise Vesterlund, Maria Recalde, and Laurie Weingart, "Breaking the Glass Ceiling with 'No': Gender Differences in Accepting and Receiving Requests for Non-Promotable Tasks" (University of Pittsburgh, Department of Economics Working Paper Series 15/05, May 2015).

40. Linda Coughlin, "The Time Is Now: A Leaders' Personal Journey," Introduction, in Linda Coughlin, Ellen Wingard, and Keith Hollihan, eds., *Enlightened Power: How Women Are Transforming the Practice of Leadership* (San Francisco: Jossey-Bass, 2005), 1, 8.

41. Rivers and Barnett, *The New Soft War on Women*, 72.

42. Ibid., 59.

43. Ibid., 74.

44. Gail McGovern, telephone interview, Feb. 20, 2015.

45. Claire Shipman and Katty Kay, *Womenomics: Write Your Own Rules for Success* (New York: HarperCollins, 2009), 17.

46. Katty Kay and Claire Shipman, *The Confidence Code: The Science and Art of Self Assurance—and What Women Should Know* (New York: Harper Business, 2014), 21; Hau L. Lee and Corey Billington, "The Evolution of

Supply-Chain-Management Models and Practice at Hewlett–Packard,"
Interfaces 25 (1995): 42.

47. See Chapter One. Because ambition is often disfavored in women, they may
be more reluctant to exhibit it. In a study by the Center for Work-Life Policy,
only a third of women, compared with more than half of men, described
themselves as "extremely" or "very" ambitious. Sylvia Ann Hewlett,
Carolyn Buck Luce, Peggy Shiller, and Sandra Southwell, *The Hidden Brain
Drain: Off-Ramps and On-Ramps in Women's Careers* (New York: Center
for Work Work-Life Policy, 2005), 4. In a survey of senior executives in
multilateral corporations, 19 percent of the men, compared with 9 percent
of women, wanted the CEO position. "Helping Women Get to the Top,"
Economist, July 23, 2004, 11. See also Patricia Sellers, "Power: Do Women
Really Want It?" *Fortune,* Oct. 13, 2003. Other research finds no such differences. Catalyst, "Women and Men in United States Corporations: Same
Workforce, Different Realities" (New York: Catalyst, 2004).

48. Peter Glick and Susan Fiske, "Ambivalent Sexism," in Mark P. Zanna,
ed., *Advances in Experimental Social Psychology* 33 (Thousand Oaks, CA:
Academic Press, 1999), 115–18.

49. Michael Robert Dennis and Adrianne Dennis Kunkel, "Perceptions
of Men, Women, and CEOs: The Effects of Gender Identity," *Social
Behavior and Personality* 32 (2004): 155, 166–68; Alice H. Eagly,
"Achieving Relational Authenticity in Leadership: Does Gender Matter?"
Leadership Quarterly 16 (2005): 459, 469. See also Sabine C. Koch,
Rebecca Luft, and Lenelis Kruse, "Women and Leadership—20 Years
Later: A Semantic Connotation Study," *Social Science Information* 44
(2005): 9 (finding decline in association between men and leadership).

50. Eagly, "Achieving Relational Authenticity," 469; Alice H. Eagly, Mary
C. Johannesen-Schmidt, and Marloes L. van Engen, "Transformational,
Transactional, and Laissez-Faire Leadership Styles: A Meta-Analysis
Comparing Women and Men," *Psychological Bulletin* 129 (2003): 569;
John David Yoder, "Making Leadership Work More Effectively for
Women," *Journal of Social Issues* 57 (2001): 815; Cristina Trinidad and
Anthony H. Normore, "Leadership and Gender: A Dangerous Liaison?"
Leadership and Organization Development Journal 26 (2005): 574, 583.
This point is frequently made in trade publications. Esther Wachs Book,
*Why the Best Man for the Job Is a Woman: The Unique Female Qualities of
Leadership* (New York: Harper Business, 2000).

51. For coworkers' attitudes, see Alice Eagly and Steven Karau, "Role
Congruity Theory of Prejudice Toward Female Leaders," *Psychological
Review* 109 (2002): 574; Donna L. Brooks and Lynn M. Brooks, *Seven
Secrets of Successful Women* (New York: McGraw-Hill, 1997), 195; Eagly,

"Achieving Relational Authenticity," 470; Babcock and Laschever, *Women Don't Ask*, 87–88.

52. Eagly and Karau, "Role Congruity Theory of Prejudice Toward Female Leaders," 574; Brooks and Brooks, *Seven Secrets of Successful Women*, 195; Eagly, "Achieving Relational Authenticity," 470; Babcock and Laschever, *Women Don't Ask*, 87–88.

53. Bryce Covert, "Our Problem with Powerful Women," *New York Times*, June 5, 2015, A23.

54. Neela Banerjee, "The Media Business: Some 'Bullies' Seek Ways to Soften Up; Toughness Has Risks for Women Executives," *New York Times*, Aug. 10, 2001, C1.

55. Fiorina, *Tough Choices*, 173.

56. Carrick Mollenkamp, "Sallie Krawcheck on Taking the Fall—Again," *Marie Claire*, Apr. 17, 2012.

57. Rivers and Barnett, *The New Soft War on Women*, 41.

58. Debra Meyerson and Joyce K. Fletcher, "A Modest Manifesto for Shattering the Glass Ceiling," *Harvard Business Review*, January 2000, 129.

59. Denise T. Cormier, "Retaining Top Women Business Leaders: Strategies for Ending the Exodus," *Business Strategies Series* 8 (2007): 1, 3.

60. Victoria L. Brescoll, "Who Takes the Floor and Why: Gender, Power, and Volubility in Organizations," *Administrative Science Quarterly* 56 (2011): 622.

61. Kieran Snyder, "The Abrasiveness Trap: High-Achieving Men and Women Are Described Differently in Reviews," *Fortune*, Aug. 26, 2014.

62. "Elephant in the Valley" (2015), http://elephantinthevalley.com; Catherine Rampell, "Be Pretty But Not Too Pretty: Why Women Just Can't Win," *Washington Post*, Jan. 21, 2016.

63. Rachel Emma Silverman, "Gender Bias at Work Turns Up in Feedback," *Wall Street Journal*, Sep. 30, 2015.

64. Ibid.

65. Rivers and Barnett, *The New Soft War on Women*, 42.

66. Eagley and Karau, "Role Congruity Theory of Prejudice Toward Female Leaders," 111; Todd L. Pittinsky, Laura M. Bacon, and Brian Welle, "The Great Women Theory of Leadership: The Perils of Positive Stereotypes and Precarious Pedestals," in Barbara Kellerman and Deborah L. Rhode, *Women and Leadership: The State of Play and Strategies for Change* (San Francisco: Jossey-Bass, 2008), 93.

67. Francis J. Flynn, Cameron Anderson, and Sebastian Brion, "Too Tough Too Soon: Familiarity and the Backlash Effect," working paper (2014).

68. Victoria Brescoll, "Who Takes the Floor and Why: Gender, Power, and Volubility in Organizations," Sage Journals, Mar. 26, 2012, http://asq.sagepub.com/content/early/2012/02/28/0001839212439994.

69. Michael Hirsh, *Capital Offense: How Washington's Wise Men Turned America's Future over to Wall Street* (Hoboken, NJ: Wiley, 2010), 1, 12 (quoting Robert Rubin and unnamed staffer).

70. Robin Abcarian, "Is Fired N.Y. Times Editor Jill Abramson the New Lilly Ledbetter?" *Los Angeles Times*, May 15, 2014, http://www.latimes.com/local/abcarian/la-me-ra-new-york-times-fired-jill-abramson-20140515-column.html. Ken Auletta, "Why Jill Abramson Was Fired," *New Yorker*, May 14, 2014, http://www.newyorker.com/business/currency/why-jill-abramson-was-fired.

71. Ravi Somaiya, "After Criticism, Times Publisher Details Decision to Oust Top Editor," *New York Times*, May 18, 2014, A18.

72. Rivers and Barnett, *The New Soft War on Women*, 38.

73. Babcock and Laschever, *Women Don't Ask*, 88; Carol Hymowitz, "Through the Glass Ceiling," *Wall Street Journal*, Nov. 8, 2004, R1. The point is widely acknowledged in trade publications featuring advice for aspiring women leaders. See Brooks and Brooks, *Seven Secrets of Successful Women*, 63–65, 147–53; and Gail Evans, *Play Like a Man, Win Like a Woman* (New York: Broadway, 2000), 68–87.

74. Hannah Riley Bowles, Linda Babcock, and Lei Lai, "Social Incentives for Gender Differences in the Propensity to Initiate Negotiations: Sometimes It Does Hurt to Ask," *Organizational Behavior and Human Decision Processes* 103 (2007): 84.

75. Babcock and Laschever, *Women Don't Ask*, 1–11, 41–44.

76. Virginia Valian, "The Cognitive Bases of Gender Bias," *Brooklyn Law Review* 65 (1999): 1050. Rhode, *The Difference "Difference" Makes*, (Stanford: Stanford University Press, 2003), 9.

77. Susan J. Ashford, "Championing Charged Issues: The Case of Gender Equity Within Organizations," in Roderick M. Kramer and Margaret A. Neale, *Power and Influence in Organizations* (Thousand Oaks: SAGE, 1998), 369–70, 375. See also Suzanne Nossel and Elizabeth Westfall, *Presumed Equal: What America's Top Women Lawyers Really Think About Their Firms* (Franklin Lakes, NJ: Career Press, 1997), 105, 108.

78. Ashford, "Championing Charged Issues," 370, 375. See also Jennifer L. Pierce, *Gender Trials: Emotional Lives in Contemporary Law Firms* (Oakland: University of California Press, 1995), 176–77; Nossel and Westfall, *Presumed Equal*, 50, 59, 105; Peter Glick and Susan T. Fiske, "Hostile and Benevolent Sexism," *Psychology of Women* 21 (1997): 119, 129.

79. Devon Carbado and Mitu Gulati, "Race to the Top of the Corporate Ladder: What Minorities Do When They Get There," *Washington and Lee Law Review* 61 (2004): 1645, 1685.

80. Virginia Valian, *Why So Slow? The Advancement of Women* (Cambridge: MIT Press, 1999), 39–40; Galen V. Bodenhausen, C. Neil Macrae, and Jennifer Garst, "Stereotypes in Thought and Deed: Social Cognitive Origins of Intergroup Discrimination," in Constantine Sedikides, J. Schopler, and C. A. Insko, eds., *Intergroup Cognition and Intergroup Behavior* (Mahwah, NJ: Erlbaum, 1998); Robin Ely, "The Power in Demography: Women's Social Construction of Gender Identity at Work," *Academy of Management Journal* 38 (1995): 589–634.

81. Monica Biernat and Diane Kobrynowicz, "Gender- and Race-Based Standards of Competence: Lower Minimum Standards But Higher Ability Standards for Devalued Groups," *Journal of Personality and Social Psychology* 72 (1997): 555; Heilman, "Description and Prescription"; Madeline Heilman, Richard Martell, and Michael Simon, "The Vagaries of Sex Bias: Conditions Regulating the Undervaluation, Equivaluation and Overvaluation of Female Job Applicants," *Organizational Behavior and Human Decision Processes* 41 (1998): 98–99.

82. Alessandra Stanley, "For Women, To Soar Is Rare, To Fall Is Human," *New York Times*, July 13, 2004, E1. David Carr, "To Reach the Heights, First Be Male," *New York Times*, Jan. 9, 2005, C1. Kephart and Schumacher, "Has the 'Glass Ceiling' Cracked?" 9.

83. Karin Klenke, *Women in Leadership: Contextual Dynamics and Boundaries* (Bradford, UK: Emerald Group, 2011), 96; Jane Margolis and Allan Fisher, *Unlocking the Clubhouse: Women in Computing* (Boston: MIT Press, 2003).

84. Klenke, *Women in Leadership*, 71.

85. Michelle K. Ryan and S. Alexander Haslam, "The Glass Cliff: Exploring the Dynamics Surrounding the Appointment of Women to Precarious Leadership Positions," *Academy of Management Review* 32 (2007): 549; Christy Glass and Alison Cook, "Leading at the Top: Understanding Women's Challenges Above the Glass Ceiling," *Leadership Quarterly* 27 (2016): 51.

86. Glass and Cook, "Leading at the Top," 52; Susanne Bruckmuller and Nyla R. Branscombe, "The Glass Cliff: When and Why Women Are Selected as Leaders in Crisis Contexts," *British Journal of Social Psychology* 49 (2010): 433.

87. Glass and Cook, "Leading at the Top," 53; Catherine J. Taylor, "Occupational Sex Composition and the Gendered Availability of Workplace Support," *Gender and Society* 24 (2010): 189.

88. Compare Alison Cook and Christy Glass, "Women and Top Leadership Positions: Towards an Institutional Analysis," *Gender, Work and Organization* 21 (2014): 91, 93, 100 (research finding no evidence of glass cliff in Fortune 500 companies), with Glass and Cook, "Leading at the Top" (finding evidence of the cliff).

89. Glass and Cook, "Leading at the Top," 56, 59.

90. Belle Rose Ragins, "Gender and Mentoring Relationships: A Review and Research Agenda for the Next Decade," in Gary Powell, *Handbook of Gender and Work* (Thousand Oaks, CA: SAGE, 1999), 347, 350–62; Catalyst, "Women in Corporate Leadership: Progress and Prospects" (New York: Catalyst, 1996); Timothy O'Brien, "Why Do So Few Women Reach the Top of Big Law Firms?" *New York Times*, Mar. 19, 2006, A4.

91. Boris Groysberg and Katherine Connolly, "Great Leaders Who Make the Mix Work," *Harvard Business Review*, September 2013, 79.

92. See also Karen L. Proudford, "Isn't She Delightful? Creating Relationships That Get Women to the Top (and Keep Them There)," in Kellerman and Rhode, *Women and Leadership*, 431; Ragins, "Gender and Mentoring Relationships," 361–63.

93. Sylvia Ann Hewlett, with Kerrie Peraino, Laura Sherbin, and Karen Sumberg, "The Sponsor Effect: Breaking Through the Last Glass Ceiling," *Harvard Business Review* Research Reports (December 2010).

94. Liza Featherstone, *Selling Women Short: The Landmark Battle for Workers' Rights at Wal-Mart* (New York: Basic Books, 2004).

95. Kathryn E. Jandeska and Maria Kraimer, "Women's Perceptions of Organizational Culture, Work Attitudes, and Role-Modeling Behaviors," *Journal of Managerial Issues* 17 (2005): 461, 465.

96. "Elephant in the Valley."

97. Rivers and Barnett, *The New Soft War on Women*, 21. Women are less likely than men to have level sponsors; see Liz Rappaport, "Networking Isn't Easy for Women, But It Is Crucial," *Wall Street Journal*, Sep. 30, 2015, R8.

98. Rivers and Barnett, *The New Soft War on Women*, 22.

99. Ibid., 22–23.

100. Ibid., 23–24.

101. Ibid., 24.

102. Ella L. J. Edmondson Bell and Stella M. Nkomo, *Our Separate Ways: Black and White Women and the Struggle for Professional Identity* (Cambridge: Harvard University Business Press, 2003), 123–32; Bernardo M. Feldman, "The Color and Culture of Gender in Organizations: Attending to Race and Ethnicity," in Powell, *Handbook of Gender and Work*, 17, 18–26; Catalyst, "Women of Color in Corporate Management: Dynamics of Career Advancement" (New York: Catalyst, 1999), 15; David Wilkins and G. Mitu Gulati, "Why Are There So Few Black Lawyers in Corporate Law Firms? An Institutional Analysis," *California Law Review* 84 (1996): 493; Deborah L. Rhode, *The Unfinished Agenda: Women and the Legal Profession* (Chicago: ABA Commission on Women in the Profession, 2001), 16.

103. Lindsay Gellman, "A Racial Gap in Mentoring at Work," *Wall Street Journal*, Sep. 30, 2015, R2.

104. For general discussion of the problems, see David Thomas, "The Truth about Mentoring Minorities: Race Matters," *Harvard Business Review* (April 2001), 105.

105. Karen S. Lyness and Donna E. Thompson, "Climbing the Corporate Ladder: Do Female and Male Executives Follow the Same Route?" *Journal of Applied Psychology* 85 (2000): 86.

106. Silva et al., "Good Intentions, Imperfect Execution?"

107. Nikki Waller and Joann S. Lublin, "What's Holding Women Back in the Workplace?" *Wall Street Journal*, Sep. 30, 2015, R2.

108. Jamie Rappaport Clark, telephone interview, Mar. 16, 2015.

109. Pew Research Center, "Women and Leadership" (23 percent believed family responsibilities were a major reason, and 35 percent said they were a minor reason).

110. Claire Cain Miller, "More Than Their Mothers, Young Women Plan Career Pauses," *New York Times*, July 22, 2015.

111. Debra Cassens Weiss, "Jack Welch: Women Take Time Off for Kids at Their Peril," *ABA Journal*, July 16, 2009, http://www.abajournal.com/news/article/jack_welch_women_take_time_off_for_kids_at_their_peril.

112. Mara Gay, "Women See Slow Progress in Leadership: Trend Flatlined at New York Companies, Survey Shows," *Wall Street Journal*, Nov. 14, 2013, A23.

113. Miller, "More Than Their Mothers."

114. Elizabeth Bernstein, "In Two-Career Couples, Women Still Bear Most of the Burden at Home," *Wall Street Journal*, Sep. 30, 2015, R6.

115. Ibid.

116. Valerie Young, *The Secret Thoughts of Successful Women: Why Capable People Suffer from the Impostor Syndrome and How to Thrive in Spite of It* (New York: Crown Business, 2011), 188; Families and Work Institute, Catalyst, and Center for Work and Family, "Leaders in a Global Economy: A Study of Executive Women and Men" (New York: Catalyst, 2003).

117. Ann Weisberg, "The Workplace Culture That Flying Nannies Won't Fix," *New York Times*, Aug. 24, 2015.

118. Miller, "More Than Their Mothers."

119. Robin Ely, Pamela Stone, and Colleen Ammerman, "Rethink What You 'Know' About High-Achieving Women, *Harvard Business Review*, December 2014.

120. Crystal L. Hoyt, "Women, Men, and Leadership: Exploring the Gender Gap at the Top," *Social and Personality Psychology Compass* 4 (2010): 484, 488.

121. Julie Coffman and Bill Neuenfeldt, "Everyday Moments of Truth: Front Line Managers Are Key to Women's Career Aspirations" (Boston: Bain & Company, 2014), 7.
122. For discussion of the finding, see Weisberg, "The Workplace Culture That Flying Nannies Won't Fix."
123. Sandrine Devillard, Sandra Sancier-Sultan, and Charlotte Werner, "Why Gender Diversity at the Top Remains a Challenge," *McKinsey Quarterly* (April 2014): 23.
124. Ely et al., "Rethink What You 'Know.'"
125. Erin Reid, "Embracing, Passing, Revealing, and the Ideal Worker Image: How People Navigate Expected and Experienced Professional Identities," *Organization Science* (2015): 1, 13; Erin Reid, "Why Some Men Pretend to Work 80-Hour Weeks," *Harvard Business Review*, Apr. 28, 2015.
126. Claire Cain Miller, "Silicon Valley: Perks for Some Workers, Struggles for Parents," *New York Times*, Apr. 7, 2015 (quoting Zuckerberg).
127. Amy J. C. Cuddy, Susan T. Fiske, and Peter Glick, "When Professionals Become Mothers, Warmth Doesn't Cut the Ice," *Journal of Social Issues* 60 (2004): 701, 709; Kathleen Fuegen, Monica Biernat, Elizabeth Haines, and Kay Deaux, "Mothers and Fathers in the Workplace: How Gender and Parental Status Influence Judgments of Job-Related Competence," *Journal of Social Issues* 60 (2004): 737, 745; Claire Etaugh and Denise Folger, "Perceptions of Parents Whose Work and Parenting Behaviors Deviate from Role Expectations," *Sex Roles* 39 (1998): 215.
128. Michael Judiesch and Karen S. Lyness, "Are Women More Likely to Be Hired or Promoted into Management Positions?" *Journal of Vocational Behavior* 54 (1999): 158.
129. Jay Newton-Small, *Broad Influence: How Women Are Changing the Way America Works* (New York: Time Books, 2016), 129 (quoting Lauer).
130. Madeleine Kunin, *The New Feminist Agenda: Defining the Next Revolution for Women, Work and Family* (White River Junction, VT: Chelsea Green, 2012), 165.
131. Leslie Morgan Steiner, *Mommy Wars: Stay-at-Home and Career Moms Face Off on Their Choices, Their Lives, Their Families* (New York: Random House, 2006), 15.
132. Jennifer Wirjosemito, "Four Imperatives to Increase the Representation of Women in Leadership Positions," Corporate Executive Board, Apr. 10, 2015, 27.
133. Joanna Barsh and Lareina Yee, "Unlocking the Full Potential of Women at Work" (New York: McKinsey & Company, Apr. 30, 2012), 8.
134. Waller and Lublin, "What's Holding Women Back in the Workplace?" R2. Only 12 percent of employees in that study worked a part-time or reduced

schedule. Charlie Wells and Joann Lublin, "Flexibility Is Great, But," *Wall Street Journal*, Sep. 30, 2015, R6.

135. David Leonhardt, "Financial Careers Come at a Cost to Families," *New York Times*, May 27, 2009, at B1; Kenneth Glenn Dau-Schmidt, Marc Galanter, Kaushik Mukhopadhaya, and Kathleen E. Hull, "Men and Women of the Bar: The Impact of Gender on Legal Careers," *Michigan Journal of Gender and Law* 16 (2009): 49, 95–96; Theresa M. Beiner, "Not All Lawyers Are Equal: Difficulties That Plague Women and Women of Color," *Syracuse Law Review* 58 (2008): 317, 326.

136. Williams and Dempsey, *What Works for Women at Work*, 140.

137. Ibid., 139.

138. Shipman and Kay, *Womenomics*, 31.

139. Sheila Wellington and Catalyst, with Betty Spence, *Be Your Own Mentor: Strategies from Top Women on the Secrets of Success* (New York: Random House, 2001), 47–48.

140. Nancy Hirsh, executive director, Northwest Energy Coalition, personal correspondence, Jan. 20, 2015.

141. Sue Shellenbarger, "The XX Factor: What's Holding Women Back," *Wall Street Journal*, May 7, 2012, B7.

142. Adam Bryant, "Executive Women, Finding (and Owning) Their Voice," *New York Times*, Nov. 16, 2014, B6 (quoting Sharon Napier).

143. Shipman and Kay, *Womenomics*, 137.

144. Nancy M. Carter and Christine Silva, "The Myth of the Ideal Worker: Does Doing All the Right Things Really Get Women Ahead?" (New York: Catalyst, 2011), http://www.catalyst.org/knowledge/ myth-ideal-does-doing-all-right-things-really-get-woman-ahead.

145. Herminia Ibarra, *Act Like a Leader, Think Like a Leader* (Boston: Harvard Business Review Press, 2015), 4–5.

146. Susan Herman, email survey, Feb. 20, 2015.

147. Kay and Shipman, *Confidence Code*, 93.

148. Alice H. Eagly and Linda L. Carli, *Through the Labyrinth* (Cambridge: Harvard Business Press, 2007), 164–65.

149. Gail McGovern, telephone interview, Feb. 20, 2015.

150. Cecilia L. Ridgeway, "Interaction and the Conservation of Gender Inequality: Considering Employment," *American Sociological Review* 62 (1997): 218.

151. D. B. Davenport, "Lessons Learned," in J. E. Gustafson, ed., *Some Leaders Are Born Women! Stories and Strategies for Building the Leader Within You* (Anthem, AZ: Leader Dynamics, 2003), 113–14.

152. Patricia S. Parker, *Race, Gender and Leadership: Re-envisioning Organizational Leadership from the Perspectives of African American Women Executives* (Mahwah, NJ: Erlbaum, 2005), 82–84.

153. Eagly and Carli, *Through the Labyrinth*, 168.

154. Patricia A. McBroom, *The Third Sex: The New Professional Woman* (New York: Morrow, 1986), 120.

155. McGovern, telephone interview.

156. Ilene Lang, email survey, Apr. 20, 2015.

157. Kate Wolford, email survey, May 1, 2015.

158. "Born to Be the Boss," *Wall Street Journal*, May 7, 2012, B12 (quoting Denise Morrison).

159. McGovern, telephone interview.

160. Noam Scheiber, "A Woman-Led Law Firm That Lets Partners Be Parents," *New York Times*, May 3, 2015. For the importance of minimizing logistical problems such as an extensive commute, see Bernstein, "In Two Career Couples."

161. Shipman and Kay, *Womenomics*, 198–99.

162. Carol Robles-Roman, email survey, Mar. 7, 2015.

163. Nan Aron, telephone interview, Mar. 13, 2015.

164. Sandra Finely, telephone interview, Apr. 16, 2015.

165. Kathleen Westlock, telephone interview, Apr. 22, 2015.

166. Andrew Ross Sorkin, "Women in a Man's World," New York Times. com, April 2, 2013, http:// dealbook. nytimes.com/ 2013/ 04/ 02/ women- in- a- mans- world/.

167. Adam Bryant, "Four Executives on Succeeding in Business as a Woman," *New York Times*, Oct. 12, 2013 (quoting Amy Shulman).

168. Clark, telephone interview.

169. Barsh and Yee, "Unlocking the Full Potential of Women at Work," 8. See also Waller and Lublin, "What's Holding Women Back in the Workplace?" R2 (fewer than half of employees said that gender diversity was high on their CEO's priority list).

170. Waller and Lublin, "What's Holding Women Back in the Workplace?" R2; Coffman and Neuenfeldt, "Everyday Moments of Truth."

171. Wirjosemito, "Four Imperatives to Increase the Representation of Women in Leadership Positions"; Barsh and Yee, "Unlocking the Full Potential of Women at Work," 11 (only a third thought programs were well implemented).

172. Castilla and Benard, "The Paradox of Meritocracy in Organizations," 551.

173. Aossey, telephone interview.

174. Joann S. Lublin, "Men Enlist in Fight for Gender Equality," *Wall Street Journal*, Mar. 11, 2015, B7.

175. Wolford, email survey.

176. Barsh and Yee, "Unlocking the Full Potential of Women at Work," 12; Ann Pomeroy, "Cultivating Female Leaders," *HR Magazine*, Feb. 1, 2007, and sources cited in Chapter One.

177. This strategy has been effective at eBay. Presentation by Beth Axelrod, senior vice president, human relations, eBay, Gender and Work Conference, Harvard Business School, Apr. 3, 2015.

178. Rivers and Barnett, *The New Soft War on Women*, 231. Brian Welle and Madeline Heilman, "Formal and Informal Discrimination Against Women at Work: The Role of Gender Stereotypes," in Stephen W. Gilliland, Dirk D. Steiner, and Daniel P. Skarlicki, eds., *Managing Social and Ethical Issues in Organizations* (Charlotte, NC: Information Age, 2007), 229.

179. Margaret M. Hopkins, Deborah O'Neil, Angela Passarelli, and Diana Bilimoria, "Women's Leadership Development: Strategic Practices for Women and Organizations," *Consulting Psychology Journal: Practice and Research* 60 (2008): 348, 356; Herminia Ibarra, Nancy M. Carter, and Christine Silva, "Why Men Still Get More Promotions Than Women," *Harvard Business Review*, September 2010, https://hbr.org/2010/09/why-men-still-get-more-promotions-than-women.

180. Alexandra Kaleb, Frank Dobbin, and Erin Kelly, "Best Practices or Best Guesses? Assessing the Efficacy of Corporate Affirmative Action and Diversity Policies," *American Sociological Review* 71 (2006): 589.

181. Wirjosemito, "Four Imperatives," 21–22.

182. Families and Work Institute, National Study of the Changing Workforce (2008), http://www.whenworks.org/be-effective.

183. Rivers and Barnett, *The New Soft War on Women*, 236–37.

184. Jody Greenstone Miller, "The Real Women's Issue: Time," *Wall Street Journal*, Mar. 11, 2013, http://www.wsj.com/articles/SB100014241278 87324678604578342641640982224.

185. Pomeroy, "Cultivating Female Leaders."

186. Shipman and Kay, *Womenomics*, 204.

187. Wirjosemito, "Four Imperatives," 28.

188. Shipman and Kay, *Womenomics*, 41–42; "The Impact of Flexible Working Practices on Performance," Cranfield University School of Management, Apr. 30, 2008.

189. Deloitte and Touche has been a leader. See Susan Sturm, "Second Generation Employment Discrimination: A Structural Approach," *Columbia Law Review* 101 (2001): 458, 493.

190. Shipman and Kay, *Womenomics*, 38.

191. Wirjosemito, "Four Imperatives," 37.

192. Caroline Simard and Denise L. Gammal, "Solutions to Recruit Technical Women" (Anita Borg Institute for Women and Technology, 2012), https://anitaborg.org/wp-content/uplo.

193. Other fields have recognized as much. See Chapter Four and ABA Presidential Initiative, Commission on Diversity, "Diversity in the Legal Profession: The Next Steps" (Chicago: American Bar Association, 2010), 23.

CHAPTER 4

1. This article draws on Deborah L. Rhode, *The Trouble with Lawyers* (New York: Oxford University Press, 2015), 60–86.

2. Deborah L. Rhode, "Perspectives on Professional Women," *Stanford Law Review* 40 (1988): 1163.

3. For new entrants, see Andrew Bruck and Andrew Cantor, "Supply, Demand, and the Changing Economics of Large Firms," *Stanford Law Review* 60 (2008): 2087, 2103; Margaret Rivera, "A New Business and Cultural Paradigm for the Legal Profession," *ACC Docket*, Oct. 2008, 66, 68. For specialties, see Fiona Kay and Elizabeth Gorman, "Women in the Legal Profession," *Annual Review of Law and Social Sciences* 4 (2008): 299, 303.

4. Kay and Gorman, "Women in the Legal Profession," at 316 (summarizing studies); John P. Heinz et al., *Urban Lawyers: The New Social Structure of the Bar* (Chicago: University of Chicago Press, 2006), 260.

5. Report of the Ninth Annual NAWL National Survey on Retention and Promotion of Women in Law Firms (National Association of Women Lawyers, 2015); ABA Women of the Section of Litigation, "Leading, Litigating and Connecting," conference Nov. 5–7, 2014, http://www .americanbar.org/content/dam/aba/administrative/litigation/materials/ 2014_women/2014_womens_conference_brochure.authcheckdam .pdf.

6. National Association for Law Placement, "Women and Minorities at Law Firms by Race and Ethnicity—New Findings for 2015," *NALP Bulletin* (Jan. 2016), http://www/nalp.org/0116research.

7. Theresa M. Beiner, "Not All Lawyers Are Equal: Difficulties That Plague Women and Women of Color," *Syracuse Law Review* 58 (2008): 317, 328; Mary C. Noonan, Mary E. Corcoran, and Paul N. Courant, "Is the Partnership Gap Closing for Women? Cohort Differences in the Sex Gap in Partnership Chances," *Social Science Research* 37 (2008): 156, 174–75.

8. A study of young lawyers by the American Bar Foundation (ABF) found that women attained equity partner status at about half the rate of men. See Ronit Dinovitzer et al., National Association for Law Placement [NALP] Foundation for Law Career Research and Education and the American Bar Foundation, "After the JD II: Second Results from a *National Study* of Legal Careers" (NALP Foundation and American Bar Foundation, 2009), 63. A study by the Federal Equal Employment Opportunity Commission found that male lawyers were five times as likely to become partners as their female counterparts. See U.S. Equal Employment Opportunity Commission, "Diversity in Law Firms" (2003), 9, http://www.eeoc.gov/ eeoc/statistics/reports/diversitylaw/lawfirms.pdf.

9. Mary C. Noonan and Mary Corcoran, "The Mommy Track and Partnership: Temporary Delay or Dead End?" *Annals of the American Academy of Political and Social Science* 596 (2004): 130, 142; Kenneth Dau-Schmidt, Marc Galanter, Kaushik Mukhopadhaya, and Kathleen E. Hull, "Men and Women of the Bar: The Impact of Gender on Legal Careers," *Michigan Journal of Gender and Law* 16 (2009): 49, 96–97, 100–102, 107, 111–12.

10. Jake Simpson, "Only 12 Big Law Firms Have Women Running the Show," Law360, Apr. 21, 2015, http://www.law360.com/articles/645840/only-12-biglaw-firms-have-women-running-the-show.

11. Ninth Annual NAWL Survey; Vivia Chen, "Women Leaders Are," *American Lawyer*, April 2016, 18; Jake Simpson, "Firms Eyeing Gender Equality Should Adopt a Corporate Culture," Law360, Apr. 22, 2014; Nancy Reichman and Joyce Sterling, "Parenthood Status and Compensation in Law Practice," *Indiana Journal of Global Legal Studies* 20 (2013): 1203, 1221; Kim Dougherty and Sofia Bruera, "The Power of Gender Equity," *Trial* (March 2014), 35.

12. Edward S. Adams and Samuel P. Engel, "Gender Diversity and Disparity in the Legal Profession: An Empirical Analysis of the Gender Profile in National Law Firms and Law Schools," *Buffalo Law Review* 63 (2015): 1211, 1220.

13. Ninth Annual NAWL Survey (female equity partners earn 80 percent of what male equity partners earn despite working longer hours). See American Bar Association Commission on Women in the Profession, "Visible Invisibility" (Chicago: American Bar Association, 2006), 28.

14. Marina Angel et al., "Statistical Evidence on the Gender Gap in Law Firm Partner Compensation," *Temple University Legal Studies*, Research Paper No. 2010-24 (2010); Ronit Dinovitzer, Nancy Reichman, and Joyce Sterling, "The Differential Valuation of Women's Work: A New Look at the Gender Gap in Lawyers' Incomes," *Social Forces* 88 (2009): 819, 835–47.

15. Ronit Dinovitzer et al., National Association for Law Placement [NALP] Foundation for Law Career Research and Education, and the American Bar Foundation, "After the JD: First Results of a *National Study* of Legal Careers" (NALP Foundation and American Bar Foundation, 2004), 58; Maria Pabon Lopez, "The Future of Women in the Legal Profession: Recognizing the Challenges Ahead by Reviewing Current Trends," *Hastings Women's Law Journal* 14 (2007): 53, 69; Nancy J. Reichman and Joyce S. Sterling, "Sticky Floors, Broken Steps, and Concrete Ceilings in Legal Careers," *Texas Journal of Women & Law* 14 (2004–05): 27, 47.

16. Nancy Levit and Douglas O. Linder, *The Happy Lawyer: Making a Good Life in the Law* (New York: Oxford University Press, 2010), 14.

17. Kay and Gorman, "Women in the Legal Profession," 317–18.
18. David L. Chambers, "Accommodation and Satisfaction: Women and Men Lawyers and the Balance of Work and Family," *Law and Social Inquiry* 14 (1989): 251, 280.
19. John M. Conley, "Tales of Diversity: Lawyers' Narratives of Racial Equity in Private Firms," *Law and Social Inquiry* 31 (2006): 831, 841–42, and 851–52.
20. Deborah L. Rhode and Lucy Buford Ricca, "Diversity in the Legal Profession: Perspectives from Managing Partners and General Counsel," *Fordham Law Review* 83 (2015): 2483, 2492.
21. Rhode and Ricca, "Diversity in the Legal Profession," 2493.
22. For the failure to invest in mentoring, see Marc Galanter and William Henderson, "The Elastic Tournament: A Second Transformation of the Big Law Firm," *Stanford Law Review* 60 (2008): 1867; Monique R. Payne-Pikus, John Hagan, and Robert L. Nelson, "Experiencing Discrimination: Race and Retention in America's Largest Law Firms," *Law and Society Review* 44 (2010): 553, 576; ABA Commission on Women and the Profession, "Visible Invisibility," 15–16.
23. Lopez, "The Future of Women," at 65.
24. Deepali Bagati, "Women of Color in U.S. Law Firms," Women of Color in Professional Services Series, Catalyst (2009), 37; Tiffani N. Darden, "The Law Firm Caste System: Constructing a Bridge Between Workplace Equity Theory and the Institutional Analyses of Bias in Corporate Law Firms," *Berkeley Journal of Employment and Labor Law* 30 (2009): 85, 125; Lopez, "The Future of Women," at 73.
25. Bagati, "Women of Color," at 13.
26. Simpson, "Firms Eyeing Gender Equality."
27. For competence, see Eli Wald, "Glass Ceilings and Dead Ends: Professional Ideologies, Gender Stereotypes, and the Future of Women Lawyers at Large Law Firms," *Fordham Law Review* 78 (2010): 2245, 2256; Cecilia L. Ridgeway and Paula England, "Sociological Approaches to Sex Discrimination," in Faye J. Crosby, Margaret S. Stockdale, and S. Ann Ropp, eds., *Sex Discrimination in the Workplace: Multidisciplinary Perspectives* (Malden, MA: Wiley-Blackwell, 2007), 189, 195. For women's need to work harder, see Lopez, "Future of Women," 73. Even in experimental situations where male and female performance is objectively equal, women are held to higher standards, and their competence is rated lower. Martha Foschi, "Double Standards in the Evaluation of Men and Women," *Social Psychology Quarterly* 59 (1996): 237. For the special pressures faced by women of color, see Gladys Garcia-López, "Nunca Te Toman en Cuenta" [They Never Take You Into Account], *Gender & Society* 22 (October 2008); 598, 603–4.

28. Deborah L. Rhode and Joan Williams, "Legal Perspectives on Employment Discrimination," in Crosby, Stockdale, and Ropp, *Sex Discrimination in the Workplace*, at 235, 245; Minority Corporate Counsel Association (MCCA), "Sustaining Pathways to Diversity: The Next Steps in Understanding and Increasing Diversity and Inclusion in Large Law Firms," 2009, 32, https://www.mcca.com/_data/global/images/Research/5298%20MCCA%20Pathways%20final%20version%202009.pdf.

29. Monica Biernat, M. J. Tocci, and Joan C. Williams, "The Language of Performance Evaluations: Gender-Based Shifts in Content and Consistency of Judgment," *Social Psychology and Personality Science* 3 (2011): 186.

30. "Written in Black and White: Exploring Confirmation Bias in Racialized Perceptions of Writing Skills," Yellow Paper Series, Nextions (2014).

31. Janet K. Swim and Lawrence J. Sanna, "He's Skilled, She's Lucky: A Meta-Analysis of Observers' Attributions for Women's and Men's Successes and Failures," *Personality and Social Psychology Bulletin* 22 (1996): 507; Jeffrey H. Greenhaus and Saoj Parasuraman, "Job Performance Attributions and Career Advancement Prospects: An Examination of Gender and Race Effects," *Organizational Behavior and Human Decision Processes* 55 (1993): 273, 276, 290.

32. *Harvard Business Review* Staff, "Women in the Workplace: A Research Roundup," *Harvard Business Review*, September 2013, 86.

33. Robin J. Ely, Herminia Ibarra, and Deborah M. Kolb, "Taking Gender into Account: Theory and Design for Women's Leadership Development Programs," *Academy of Management Learning and Education* 10 (2011): 474, 477; Foschi, "Double Standards," 237; ABA Commission on Women in the Profession, "Visible Invisibility," 27.

34. Joan Williams and Rachel Dempsey, *What Works for Women at Work: Four Patterns Working Women Need to Know* (New York: New York University Press, 2014), 228; ABA Commission on Women in the Profession, "Visible Invisibility," 25.

35. Joan C. Williams and Veta T. Richardson, "New Millennium, Same Glass Ceiling? The Impact of Law Firm Compensation Systems on Women," *Hastings Law Journal* 62 (2011): 597, 644 (discussing unequal assignments).

36. Amy J. C. Cuddy, Susan T. Fiske, and Peter Glick, "When Professionals Become Mothers, Warmth Doesn't Cut the Ice," *Journal of Social Issues* 60 (2004): 701, 709; Kathleen Fuegen, Monica Biernat, Elizabeth Haines, and Kay Deaux, "Mothers and Fathers in the Workplace: How Gender and Parental Status Influence Judgments of Job-Related Competence," *Journal of Social Issues* 60 (2004): 737, 745.

37. ABA Commission on Women in the Profession, "Visible Invisibility," 83. For other research, see Reichman and Sterling, "Sticky Floors," at 63–64.

38. Sylvia Ann Hewlett et al., "The Sponsorship Effect: Breaking Through the Last Glass Ceiling," *Harvard Business Review* Research Report (2010): 24; Michele Coleman Mayes and Kara Sophia Baysinger, *Courageous Counsel: Conversations with Women General Counsel in the Fortune 500* (Hastings-on-Hudson, NY: Leverage Media, 2011), 129 (quoting Dana Mayer).

39. Barbara Kellerman and Deborah L. Rhode, *Women and Leadership: The State of Play and Strategies for Change* (San Francisco: Jossey-Bass, 2007), 7; "Women 'Take Care', Men 'Take Charge': Stereotyping of U.S. Business Leaders Exposed" (New York: Catalyst, 2005); Linda L. Carli and Alice H. Eagly, "Overcoming Resistance to Women Leaders: The Importance of Leadership Styles," in Kellerman and Rhode, *Women and Leadership*, at 127–29; Wald, "Glass Ceilings," at 2256.

40. Alice H. Eagly and Steven J. Karau, "Role Congruity Theory of Prejudice Toward Female Leaders," *Psychological Review* 109 (2002): 574; Alice H. Eagly, "Achieving Relational Authenticity in Leadership: Does Gender Matter?" *Leadership Quarterly* 16 (2005): 470; "The Double-Bind Dilemma for Women in Leadership: Damned If You Do, Doomed If You Don't" (New York: Catalyst, 2007); Linda Babcock and Sara Laschever, *Women Don't Ask: The High Cost of Avoiding Negotiation—and Positive Strategies for Change* (New York: Bantam Dell, 2007), 87–89; Mayes and Baysinger, *Courageous Counsel*, 131.

41. Vivia Chen, "Yin and Yang," *American Lawyer*, December 2014, 23.

42. Rick Schmitt, "Prophet and Loss," *Stanford Magazine*, March/April 2009 (quoting Arthur Levitt), https://alumni.stanford.edu/get/page/magazine/article/?article_id=30885; Michael Hirsh, *Capital Offense: How Washington's Wise Men Turned America's Future over to Wall Street* (Hoboken, NJ: Wiley, 2010), 12, 1 (quoting Robert Rubin and unnamed staffer).

43. Schmitt, "Prophet and Loss" (quoting Michael Greenberger).

44. Williams and Richardson, "New Millennium, Same Glass Ceiling?" at 49–50; Ridgeway and England, "Sociological Approaches to Sex Discrimination," at 197; Marilynn B. Brewer and Rupert J. Brown, "Intergroup Relations," in Daniel T. Gilbert, Susan T. Fiske, and Gardner Lindzey, eds., *The Handbook of Social Psychology* (New York: Oxford University Press, 1998), 554–94; Susan T. Fiske, "Stereotyping, Prejudice, and Discrimination," in Gilbert et al., *Handbook of Social Psychology*, 357–414.

45. The term comes from Pierre Bourdieu, "The Forms of Capital," in John G. Richardson, ed., *Handbook of Theory and Research for the Sociology of*

Education (Westport, CT: Greenwood, 1986), 241, 248. For discussion in the legal context, see Cindy A. Schipani, Terry M. Dworkin, Angel Kwolek-Folland, and Virginia G. Maurer, "Pathways for Women to Obtain Positions of Organizational Leadership: The Significance of Mentoring and Networking," *Duke Journal of Gender Law and Policy* 16 (2009): 89; Fiona Kay and Jean E. Wallace, "Mentors as Social Capital: Gender, Mentors, and Career Rewards in Legal Practice," *Sociological Inquiry* 79 (2009): 418.

46. For minorities, see ABA Commission on Women in the Profession, "Visible Invisibility," at 18; David Wilkins and G. Mitu Gulati, "Why Are There So Few Black Lawyers in Corporate Law Firms? An Institutional Analysis," *California Law Review* 84 (1996): 493. For women, see Reichman and Sterling, "Sticky Floors," 65; Timothy O'Brien, "Up the Down Staircase," *New York Times*, Mar. 19, 2006, A4; Williams and Richardson, "New Millennium, Same Glass Ceiling?" 16–17.

47. ABA Commission on Women in the Profession, "Visible Invisibility," 35; Jill Schachner Chanen, "Early Exits," *ABA Journal*, Aug. 6, 2006, 36.

48. Sarah Dinolfo, Christine Silva, and Nancy M. Carter, "High Potentials in the Pipeline: Leaders Pay It Forward" (Catalyst, 2012), 7.

49. See studies cited in Deborah L. Rhode, "From Platitudes to Priorities: Diversity and Gender Equity in Law Firms," *Georgetown Journal of Legal Ethics* 24 (2011); 1071–72.

50. ABA Commission on Women in the Profession, "Visible Invisibility," 14.

51. For the role of sexual concerns see Hewlett et al., "The Sponsorship Effect," 35. For race-related barriers in mentoring, see Payne-Pikus et al., "Experiencing Discrimination," 553, 561.

52. ABA Commission on Women in the Profession, "Visible Invisibility," 27. See also David Lat, "4 Ideas for Advancing Diversity and Inclusion in the Legal Profession," *Above the Law*, May 5, 2016, http://abovethelaw .com/2016/05/4-ideas-for-advancing-diversity-and-inclusion-in-the-legal-profession; David A. Thomas, "The Truth About Mentoring Minorities: Race Matters," *Harvard Business Review* 79 (April 2001): 105; Julie Triedman, "The Diversity Crisis: Big Firms' Continuing Failure," *American Lawyer* (online), May 29, 2014, http:www.americanlawyer .com/id=1202656372552/The-Diversity-Crisis-Big-Firms_Continuing_ failure#ixzz48NF8ny6j.

53. ABA Commission on Women in the Profession, "Visible Invisibility," 21; Wilkins and Gulati, "Why Are There So Few Black Lawyers in Corporate Law Firms?" 565–71.

54. ABA Commission on Women in the Profession, "Visible Invisibility," 21.

55. Williams and Richardson, "New Millennium, Same Glass Ceiling?" 42.

56. Jennifer Smith, "Female Lawyers Still Battle Gender Bias," *Wall Street Journal*, May 4, 2014.

57. ABA Commission on Women in the Profession, "Visible Invisibility," 21; LeeAnn O'Neill, "Hitting the Legal Diversity Market Home: Minority Women Strike Out," *Modern American* 3 (Spring 2007): 10.

58. Linda A. Mabry, "The Token," *California Lawyer*, July 2006, 76.

59. ABA Commission on Women in the Profession, "Visible Invisibility," 26; David B. Wilkins, "From 'Separate Is Inherently Unequal' to 'Diversity Is Good for Business': The Rise of Market-Based Diversity Arguments and the Fate of the Black Corporate Bar," *Harvard Law Review* 117 (March 2004): 1548, 1595.

60. ABA Commission on Women in the Profession, "Visible Invisibility," 26.

61. Rhode and Ricca, "Diversity in the Legal Profession" (quoting Maya Hazell).

62. National Association for Law Placement, "Rate of Part-Time Among Lawyers Unchanged in 2012—Most Working Part-Time Continue to Be Women," Feb. 21, 2013, http://www.nalp.org/part-time_feb2013.

63. Paula A. Patton, "Women Lawyers: Their Status, Influence, and Retention in the Legal Profession," *William & Mary Journal of Women and the Law* 11 (2005): 173, 180. For lower partnership rates, see Beiner, "Not All Lawyers Are Equal," at 326; Dau-Schmidt et al., "Men and Women of the Bar: The Impact of Gender on Legal Careers," *Michigan Journal of Gender and Law* 16 (2009): 49; Mona Harrington and Helen Hsi, "Women Lawyers and Obstacles to Leadership: A Report of MIT Workplace Center Surveys on Comparative Career Decisions and Attrition" (Boston: MIT Workplace Center, 2007), 28–29.

64. David Leonhardt, "Financial Careers Come at a Cost to Families," *New York Times*, May 26, 2009, B1; Dau-Schmidt et al., "Men and Women of the Bar," 95–96; Beiner, "Not All Lawyers Are Equal," 326.

65. Noonan and Corcoran, "The Mommy Track and Partnership," 130, 146.

66. Erin Coe, "Firm Hierarchies Push Women out the Door," Law360, Apr. 22, 2015, http://www.law360.com/articles/644240/fi.

67. See Rhode, "From Platitudes to Priorities," 1056; Deborah L. Rhode, "Balanced Lives for Lawyers," *Fordham Law Review* 70 (2002): 2207, 2213; for stigma, see Holly English, *Gender on Trial: Sexual Stereotypes and Work/Life Balance in the Legal Workplace* (New York: ALM Properties 2003), 212 (reporting perceptions about slackers); Lopez, "Future of Women," 95; Cynthia Thomas Calvert, Linda Bray Chanow, and Linda Marks, "Reduced Hours, Full Success: Part-Time Partners in U.S. Law Firms" (Project for Attorney Retention, 2009) (reporting that even among lawyers who had achieved partnership, about 40 percent feel stigma from taking part-time schedules).

68. Working Mother and Flex-Time Lawyers, "Best Law Firms for Women 2014," Working Mother, July 15, 2014, http://www.workingmother.com/content.

69. Williams and Dempsey, *What Works for Women at Work*, 134, 135.
70. ABA Commission on Women in the Profession, "Visible Invisibility," 16.
71. See Chapter One and Deborah L. Rhode, *What Women Want: An Agenda for the Women's Movement* (New York: Oxford University Press, 2014), 59 (noting that women spend more than twice as much time on care of children as men and more than three times as much on household tasks).
72. Nancy Gertner, *In Defense of Women: Memoirs of an Unrepentant Advocate* (Boston: Beacon Press, 2011), 264.
73. Dinovitzer et al., "After the JD II," 62.
74. Noonan and Corcoran, "The Mommy Track and Partnership," 137.
75. Dau-Schmidt et al., "Men and Women of the Bar," 112–13; Levit and Linder, *Happy Lawyer*, 12–13.
76. Galanter and Henderson, "Elastic Tournament," 1921.
77. Scott Flaherty, Nell Gluckman, and Jennifer Henderson, "What You Need to Hear About Your Firm," *American Lawyer*, March 2016, 65.
78. Noam Scheiber, "A Woman-Led Law Firm That Lets Partners Be Parents," *New York Times*, May 3, 2015 (quoting former Mayer Brown associate).
79. Rhode and Ricca, "Diversity in the Legal Profession," 2500.
80. Calvert, Chanow, and Marks, "Reduced Hours, Full Success."
81. Ibid., at 9, 13, 21.
82. Deloitte and Touche has been a leader. See Susan P. Sturm, "Second Generation Employment Discrimination: A Structural Approach," *Columbia Law Review* 101 (2001): 458, 493.
83. Levit and Linder, *Happy Lawyer*, 170; Calvert, Chanow, and Marks, "Reduced Hours," at 10–12.
84. MP McQueen, "Here Come the Big Law Millennials," *American Lawyer*, March 2016, 53.
85. Rhode and Ricca, "Diversity in the Legal Profession," 2487.
86. Center for Women in Law at University of Texas School of Law, "The Austin Manifesto," Women's Power Summit on Law and Leadership (May 1, 2009).
87. Roderick Palmore, A Call to Action: Diversity in the Legal Profession (Association of Corporate Counsel, October, 2004), http://www.acc.com/vl/public/Article/loader.cfm?csModule=security/getfile&pageid=16074.
88. Christopher J. Whelan and Neta Ziv, "Privatizing Professionalism: Client Control of Lawyers' Ethics," *Fordham Law Review* 80 (2012): 2577.
89. Ibid., at 2597–2600; Claire Tower Putnam, "When Can a Law Firm Discriminate Among Its Own Employees to Meet a Client's Request? Reflections on the ACC's Call to Action," *University of Pennsylvania Journal of Labor and Employment Law* 9 (2007): 657, 660; Karen Donovan, "Pushed by Clients, Law Firms Step Up Diversity Efforts," *New York Times*, July 21, 2006, C6.

90. California Minority Counsel Program, *Diversity Business Matters: Corporate Programs Supporting Business for Diverse Outside Counsel* (California Minority Counsel Program, 2011), 18.

91. Melanie Lasoff Levs, "Carrot Money to Diversify," *Diversity & the Bar*, September/October 2008, 59.

92. Vivia Chen, "Keepers of the Status Quo," *American Lawyer*, March 2015 (quoting Merle Vaughn), 21.

93. Rhode and Ricca, "Diversity in the Legal Profession," 2498.

94. For a sampling of criticism, see Williams and Richardson, "New Millennium, Same Glass Ceiling?" at 51–55.

95. Linda Babcock and Sara Laschever, *Ask for It: How Women Can Use the Power of Negotiations to Get What They Really Want* (New York: Bantam Dell, 2008), 252.

96. Scott Westfahl, "More Women Means More Success," *Women Lawyers Journal* 100 (2015): 26, 30; Adam M. Grant, *Give and Take: Why Helping Others Drives Our Success* (New York: Penguin, 2014).

97. Vivia Chen, "Are Women Allergic to Power?" *American Lawyer*, November 2015, 24.

98. Mayes and Baysinger, *Courageous Counsel*, 82.

99. Ibid., 69.

100. Ibid., 75.

101. Susan A. Berson, "The Rules (for Women): Steps May Be Unspoken But They Are Necessary, Successful Partners Say," *ABA Journal*, Jan. 1, 2012, 28; Linda Bray Chanow and Lauren Stiller Rikleen, "Power in Law: Lessons from the 2011 Women's Power Summit on Law and Leadership," *Center for Women in Law* (2012): 15.

102. Boris Groysberg, Victoria W. Winston, and Shirley Spence, "Leadership in Law: Amy Schulman at DLA Piper," Harvard Business School 9-407-033 (2008), 12.

103. Arin N. Reeves, *From Visible Invisibility to Visibly Successful: Success Strategies for Law Firms and Women of Color in Law Firms* (ABA Commission on Women in the Profession, 2008), 6, http:www.americanbar.org/content/dam/aba/administrative/diversity/Convocation_2013/CWP/VisiblySuccessful-entire-final.authcheckdam.pdf.

104. Gay Gaddis, "Linda Addison Delivers Advice to All with a 'Lawyer's Dozen,'" *Forbes*, Apr. 25, 2014, http://www.forbes.com/sites/gaygaddis/2014/04/25/linda-addison-delivers-advice-to-all-with-a-lawyers-dozen/.

105. Frank Dobbin, Alexandra Kalev, and Erin Kelly, "Diversity Management in Corporate America," *Context*, Fall 2007, at 21; Sheila W. Wellington, *Advancing Women in Business—the Catalyst Guide: Best Practices from the Corporate Leaders* (New York and Hoboken, NJ: Catalyst, Jossey-Bass, 1998), 6, 12–13; Catalyst, "Women of Color in Corporate Management: Three Years Later" (Catalyst, 2002), 69.

106. Rhode and Ricca, "Diversity in the Legal Profession," 2483 (quoting Terri McClure).

107. Chen, "Keepers of the Status Quo"; Rhode and Ricca, "Diversity in the Legal Profession."

108. Frank Dobbin and Alexandra Kalev, "The Architecture of Inclusion: Evidence from Corporate Diversity Programs," *Harvard Journal of Law & Gender* 30 (2007): 279, 283; Jeanine Prime, Marissa Agin, and Heather Foust-Cummings, "Strategy Matters: Evaluating Company Approaches for Creating Inclusive Workplaces" (Catalyst, 2010), 6; Beiner, "Not All Lawyers Are Equal," 333.

109. ABA Presidential Initiative Commission on Diversity, "Diversity in the Legal Profession: The Next Steps" (Chicago: American Bar Association, 2010), 23.

110. Simpson, "Firms Eyeing Gender Equality."

111. Bagati, "Women of Color," 49; Kellerman and Rhode, *Women and Leadership*, 27; Ridgeway and England, "Sociological Approaches to Sex Discrimination," 202; Ely, Ibarra, and Kolb, "Taking Gender into Account," 481; Joanna Barsh and Lareina Yee, *Unlocking the Full Potential of Women at Work* (New York: McKinsey & Company, 2012), 11.

112. Dobbin and Kalev, "The Architecture of Inclusion," 293–94; Dobbin et al., "Diversity Management," 23–24.

113. http://jezebel.com/is-this-the-most-offensively-misguided-office-memo-youv-1568180278.

114. Darden, "The Law Firm Caste System," 85, 100. For the limited research and mixed or negative findings on effectiveness, see Deborah L. Rhode, "Social Research and Social Change: Meeting the Challenge of Gender Inequality and Sexual Abuse," *Harvard Journal of Law & Gender* 30 (2007): 11, 13–14; Elizabeth Levy Paluck, "Diversity Training and Intergroup Contact: A Call to Action Research," *Journal of Social Issues* 62 (2006): 577, 583, 591.

115. Dobbin and Kalev, "The Architecture of Inclusion," 293–95; Dobbin et al., "Diversity Management," 23–25.

116. Darden, "The Law Firm Caste System," at 117; Diane Vaughan, "Rational Choice, Situated Action, and the Social Control of Organizations," *Law & Society Review* 32 (1998): 23, 34.

117. Rhode and Ricca, "Diversity in the Legal Profession" (quoting Nicholas Cheffings).

118. Ibid., 2483, 2495 (quoting Brad Malt and Nicholas Cheffings).

119. Report of the Ninth Annual NAWL National Survey.

120. See Dobbin et al., "Diversity Management," at 25, discussed in Chapter One. See also Alexandra Kalev, Frank Dobbin, and Erin Kelley, "Best Practices or Best Guesses? Assessing the Efficacy of Corporate Affirmative Action and Diversity Policies," *American Sociological Review* 71 (2006): 589, 590.

121. Lauren Stiller Rikleen, "Women Lawyers Continue to Lag Behind Male Colleagues," *Women Lawyers Journal* 100 (2015): 25, 36.

122. Schipani et al., "Pathways," 131.

123. Bob Yates, "Law Firms Address Retention of Women and Minorities," *Chicago Lawyer* (March 2007).

124. Rhode and Ricca, "Diversity in the Legal Profession," 2500.

125. Joan C. Williams, Aaron Platt, and Jessica Lee, "Disruptive Innovation: New Models of Legal Practice" (Center for WorkLife Law, University of California, Hastings College of the Law, 2014); Leigh McMullan Abramson, "Parents in Law: Is It Possible to Be Both an Attorney and a Committed Mom or Dad?" *Atlantic*, Sep. 17, 2015; Scheiber, "A Woman-Led Law Firm That Lets Partners Be Parents."

126. Claire Shipman and Katty Kay, *Womenomics: Write Your Own Rules for Success* (New York: HarperCollins, 2009), 205–6 (quoting Tom Mars).

127. Ibid., 41.

128. Russell G. Pearce, Eli Wald, and Swethaa S. Ballakrishnen, "Difference Blindness vs. Bias Awareness: Why Law Firms with the Best of Intentions Have Failed to Create Diverse Partnerships," *Fordham Law Review* (2015): 2407, 2453.

129. American Bar Association, "Search the Pipeline Diversity Directory," http://apps.americanbar.org/abanet/op/pipelndir/search.cfm. For discussion of such programs, see Jason P. Nance and Paul E. Madsen, "An Empirical Analysis of Diversity in the Legal Profession," *Connecticut Law Review* 47 (2014).

130. Elizabeth Olson, "Many Black Lawyers Navigate a Rocky, Lonely Road to Partner," *New York Times*, Aug. 17, 2015.

131. Elizabeth Olson, "Law Firm's First Latina Partner, with Boost from N.Y.U. Program," *New York Times*, Mar. 3, 2016.

132. Sara Eckel, "Seed Money," *American Lawyer*, September 2008, 20.

133. Ibid. (quoting Ruth Ashby).

134. Rhode and Ricca, "Diversity in the Legal Profession," 2506 (quoting Greg Nitzkowski).

CHAPTER 5

1. Pew Research Center, "Women and Leadership," Jan. 14, 2015, http://www.pewsocialtrends.org/2015/01/14/women-and-leadership/; Audrey Williams June, "Despite Progress, Only 1 in 4 College Presidents Are Women," *Chronicle of Higher Education*, Mar. 20, 2015, A6; Tiffani Lennon, *Recognizing Women's Leadership: Strategies and Best Practices for Employing Excellence* (Santa Barbara: Praeger, 2014), 107. This chapter draws on Barbara Kellerman and Deborah L. Rhode, "Women at the Top: The

Pipeline Reconsidered," in Karen A. Longman and Susan R. Madsen, *Women and Leadership in Higher Education* (Charlotte: Information Age, 2014).

2. Tiffani Lennon, *Benchmarking Women's Leadership in the United States* (Colorado Women's College, University of Denver, 2012), 20.

3. Stacey Patton, "At the Ivies, It's Still All White at the Top," *Chronicle of Higher Education*, June 9, 2013.

4. Angela P. Harris and Carmen G. González, "Introduction," in Gabriella Gutiérrez Muhs, Yolanda Flores Niemann, Carmen G. González, and Angela P. Harris, *Presumed Incompetent: The Intersections of Race and Class for Women in Academia* (Boulder: University Press of Colorado, 2012), 3; Yolanda T. Moses, "Advice from the Field: Guiding Women of Color to Academic Leadership," in Diane R. Dean, Susan J. Bracken, and Jeanie K. Allen, *Women in Academic Leadership: Professional Strategies, Personal Choices* (Sterling, VA: Stylus, 2009), 181, 186.

5. Clayton Spencer, telephone interview, Mar. 2, 2015.

6. Task Force on Women and Leadership, "Findings and Recommendations" (Stanford University, draft, December 2015), 26.

7. Ibid., 8; Katy Murphy, "Stanford and Other Elite Universities Have a Gender Problem: Too Few Women Professors," *San Jose Mercury News*, Feb. 26, 2016.

8. June, "Despite Progress, Only 1 in 4 College Presidents Are Women," A6.

9. Telephone interview with Kathleen McCartney, Mar. 12, 2015.

10. Martha Foschi, "Double Standards in the Evaluation of Men and Women," *Social Psychology Quarterly* 59 (1996): 237; Cecilia L. Ridgeway and Paula England, "Sociological Approaches to Sex Discrimination in Employment," in Faye J. Crosby, Margaret S. Stockdale, and S. Ann Ropp, eds., *Sex Discrimination in the Workplace* (Malden, MA: Blackwell, 2007), 189.

11. Corinne A. Moss-Racusin, John F. Dovidio, Victoria L. Brescoll, Mark J. Graham, and Jo Handelsman, "Science Faculty's Subtle Gender Biases Favor Male Students," *Proceedings of the National Academy of Sciences of the United States of America* 109 (2012): 16474.

12. Frances Trix and Carolyn Psenka, "Exploring the Color of Glass: Letters of Recommendation for Female and Male Medical Faculty," *Discourse and Society* 14 (2003): 191.

13. Sarah-Jane Leslie, Andrei Cimpian, Meredith Meyer, and Edward Freeland, "Expectations of Brilliance Underlie Gender Distributions Across Academic Disciplines," *Science* 347 (2015): 262.

14. Soraya Chemaly, "10 Words Every Girl Should Learn," Alternet, July 2014, http://www.alternet.org/gender/10-words-every-girl-should-learn.

15. Kelly Hannum, Shannon Muhly, Pamela Shockley-Zalabak, and Judith S. White, "Stories from the Summit Trail: Leadership Journeys of Senior

Women in Higher Education" (Higher Education Resource Services, 2014), 16; Janice M. Edwards and Lanthan D. Camblin, "Assorted Adaptations by African-American Administrators," *Women in Higher Education* 7 (November 1998): 33, 46; Mimi Wolverton, Beverly L. Bower, and Adrienne E. Hyle, *Women at the Top: What Women University and College Presidents Say About Effective Leadership* (Sterling, VA: Stylus, 2009); Eugenia P. Gerdes, "Do It Your Way: Advice from Senior Academic Women," *Innovative Higher Education* 27 (2003): 253; Nan-Chi Tiao, "Senior Women Leaders in Higher Education: Overcoming Barriers to Success," doctoral dissertation, Eastern Michigan University, 2006, http://commons.emich.edu/theses/.

16. Penelope M. Huang, "Gender Bias in Academia: Findings from Focus Groups" (Center for Worklife Law University of California, Hastings College of the Law, 2008), 11.

17. Canan Bilen-Green, Karen A. Froelich, and Sarah W. Jacobsen, "The Prevalence of Women in Academic Leadership Positions, and Potential Impact on Prevalence of Women in the Professional Ranks," 2008 WEPAN Conference Proceedings, https://www.ndsu.edu/fileadmin/forward/documents/wepan2.pdf.

18. Debora Spar, email survey, Feb. 20, 2015.

19. Hannum et al., "Stories from the Summit Trail"; 16.

20. Tiao, "Senior Women Leaders." Hannum et al., "Stories from the Summit Trail," 31.

21. Linda Trinh Võ, "Navigating the Academic Terrain: The Racial and Gender Politics of Elusive Belonging," in Muhs et al., *Presumed Incompetent*, 93, 108.

22. Edwards and Camblin, "Assorted Adaptations"; Runae Edwards-Wilson, "You Go, Girl! African American Female Presidents Lead with Style," in Mary Dee Wenniger and Mary Helen Conroy, ed., *Gender Equity or Bust! On the Road to Campus Leadership with* Women in Higher Education (San Francisco: Jossey-Bass, 2001), 43. For women faculty, see Joan C. Williams, Katherine W. Phillips, and Erika V. Hall, "Double Jeopardy? Gender Bias Against Women of Color in Science" (San Francisco: WorkLife Law, University of California Hastings College of the Law, 2014), 5–11.

23. Hannum et al., "Stories from the Summit Trail," 17; Võ, "Navigating the Academic Terrain," 95; Beth A. Boyd, "Sharing Our Gifts," in Muhs et al., *Presumed Incompetent*, 277.

24. Muhs et al., *Presumed Incompetent*.

25. Adrien Katherine Wing, "Lessons from a Portrait: Keep Calm and Carry On," in Muhs et al., *Presumed Incompetent*, 356.

26. Sherri L. Wallace, Sharon E. Moore, Linda L. Wilson, and Brenda G. Hart, "African American Women in the Academy: Quelling the Myth of Presumed Incompetence," in Muhs et al., *Presumed Incompetent*, 431.

27. Yolanda Flores Niemann, "Lessons from the Experiences of Women of Color Working in Academia," in Muhs et al., *Presumed Incompetent*, 476. See also Carmen G. González, "Women of Color in Legal Education: Challenging the Presumption of Incompetence," *Federal Lawyer* 61 (2014): 48, 52–53.

28. Jessica Lavariega Monforti, "*La Lucha*: Latinas Surviving Political Science," in Muhs et al., *Presumed Incompetent*, 402; Wallace et al., "African American Women in the Academy," 423.

29. Edwards and Camblin, "Assorted Adaptations," 47.

30. Brenda Lloyd-Jones, "Implications of Race and Gender in Higher Education Administration: An African American Woman's Perspective," *Advances in Developing Human Resources* 11 (2009): 608, 612.

31. Betsy Metzger, "Lesbian Administrators Make Deeply Personal Choices," in Wenniger and Conroy, eds., *Gender Equity or Bust!* 57.

32. Mildred Garcia, "Moving Forward," in Wolverton et al., *Women at the Top*; Judith Sturnick, "Women Who Lead: Persevering the Face of Skepticism," *The Presidency* 2 (1999): 28; Leila Gonzalez Sullivan, "Informal Learning Among Women Community College Presidents," in Dean et al., *Women in Academic Leadership*, 95, 99.

33. Susan Madsen, *On Becoming a Woman Leader: Learning from the Experiences of University Presidents* (San Francisco: Jossey-Bass, 2008).

34. Dana Dunn, Jeanne M. Gerlach, and Adrienne E. Hyle, "Gender and Leadership: Reflections of Women in Higher Education Administration," *International Journal of Leadership and Change* 2 (2014): 9, 11; June, "Despite Progress, Only 1 in 4 College Presidents Are Women."

35. Drew Faust, email correspondence, Jan. 30, 2015. See Pamela L. Eddy, "Leading Gracefully: Gendered Leadership at Community Colleges," in Dean et al., *Women in Academic Leadership*, 8, 20 (noting that none of surveyed female presidents intentionally planned their career path).

36. Francesca Dominici, Linda P. Fried, and Scott L. Zeger, "So Few Women Leaders," *AAUP Newsletter*, July–August 2009.

37. McCartney, telephone interview.

38. Catalyst, "The Double-Bind Dilemma for Women in Leadership: Damned If You Do, Doomed If You Don't" (New York: Catalyst, 2007).

39. Wolverton et al., *Women at the Top*, 75.

40. Hannum et al., "Stories from the Summit Trail," 16.

41. Dunn et al., "Gender and Leadership," 12, 15.

42. Mary L. Bucklin, "Madame President: Gender's Impact in the Presidential Suite," in Longman and Madsen, *Women and Leadership in Higher Education*, 169, 178.

43. Carol C. Harter, "Still Standing," in Wolverton et al., *Women at the Top*; Tiao, "Senior Women Leaders."

44. Wolverton et al., *Women at the Top*, 61.
45. McCartney, telephone interview.
46. Huang, "Gender Bias in Academia," 2.
47. Kari Lerum, "What's Love Got to Do with It? Life Teachings from Multiracial Feminism," in Muhs et al., *Presumed Incompetent*, 271, 273.
48. Dolly Chugh, Katherine L. Milkman, and Modupe Akinola, "Professors Are Prejudiced, Too," *New York Times*, May 9, 2014, SR 14 (reporting findings that professors were more responsive to mentoring requests from white male students than from female students or students of color).
49. Huang, "Gender Bias in Academia," 7.
50. Ibid.
51. Dominici et al., "So Few Women Leaders"; Dunn et al., "Gender and Leadership," 13. For the phenomena generally, see Sylvia Hewlett, Melinda Marshall, and Laura Sherbin, with Barbara Adachi, "Sponsor Effect 2.0: Road Maps for Sponsors and Protégés" (New York: Center for Talent Innovation, 2012); Belle R. Ragins, "Gender and Mentoring Relationships: A Review and Research Agenda for the Next Decade," in Gary Powell, ed., *Handbook of Gender and Work* (Thousand Oaks, CA: Sage, 1999), 347; Tiao, "Senior Women Leaders."
52. Madsen, *On Becoming a Woman Leader*.
53. Lloyd-Jones, "Implications of Race and Gender," 607; Edward and Camblin, "Assorted Adaptations"; Terry M. Brown, "Mentorship and the Female College President," *Sex Roles* 52 (2005): 659; Katherine L. Milkman, Modupe Akinola, and Dolly Chugh, "Temporal Distance and Discrimination: An Audit Study in Academia," *Psychological Science* 23 (2012): 710.
54. June, "Despite Progress, Only 1 in 4 College Presidents Are Women."
55. Karen Pyke, "Service and Gender Inequity Among Faculty," *PS: Political Science & Politics* 44 (January 2011): 85; Williams, Phillips, and Hall, "Double Jeopardy," 15; Sharon Bird, Jacquelyn Litt, and Yong Wang, "Creating Status of Women Reports: Institutional Housekeeping as Women's Work," *NWSA Journal* 16 (2004): 1.
56. Sara McLaughlin Mitchell and Vicki L. Hesli, "Women Don't Ask? Women Don't Say No? Bargaining and Service in the Political Science Profession," *PS: Political Science and Politics* 46 (2013): 355.
57. Lise Vesterlund, Linda Babcock, Maria Recalde, and Laurie Weingart, "Breaking the Glass Ceiling with 'No': Gender Differences in Declining Requests for Non-Promotable Tasks," University of Pittsburgh Department of Economics, Working Paper No. 15/005 (May 2015), http://www.econ.pitt.edu/sites/default/files/working_papers/WP%20 15-005.pdf. For other research indicating that women faculty spend more time on service and teaching and less on research than their male

colleagues, see Stephen J. Ceci, Donna K. Ginther, Shulamit Kahn, and Wendy M. Williams, "Women in Academic Science: A Changing Landscape," *Psychological Science in the Public Interest* 15 (2014):75, 108.

58. Huang, "Gender Bias in Academia," 10.

59. Ibid., 3.

60. Harris and González, "Introduction," 10; Yolanda Flores Niemann, "The Making of a Token: A Case Study of Stereotype Threat, Stigma, Racism and Tokenism in Academe," in Muhs et al., *Presumed Incompetent*, 345; Boyd, "Sharing Our Gifts," 279; Monforti, "*La Lucha*," 395.

61. Huang, "Gender Bias in Academia," 9.

62. Michelle M. Jacob, "Native Women Maintaining Their Culture in the White Academy," in Muhs et al., *Presumed Incompetent*, 245.

63. Spar, email survey.

64. Lewis A. Coser, *Greedy Institutions: Patterns of Undivided Commitment* (New York: Free Press, 1974).

65. Spar, email survey.

66. Spencer, telephone interview.

67. Rita Bornstein, "Women and the Quest for Presidential Legitimacy," in Dean et al., *Women in Academic Leadership*, 208, 213–14.

68. Dominici et al., "So Few Women."

69. Madsen, *On Becoming a Woman Leader*; Dominici et al., "So Few Women Leaders." Women's disproportionate family burdens are reflected in their disproportionate use of parental leaves. Steven E. Rhoads and Christopher H. Rhoads, "Gender Roles and Infant/Toddler Care: Male and Female Professors on the Tenure Track," *Journal of Social, Evolutionary, and Cultural Psychology* 6 (2012): 13.

70. Dunn et al., "Gender and Leadership," 17.

71. Huang, "Gender Bias in Academia," 12.

72. June, "Despite Progress, Only 1 in 4 College Presidents Are Women," A6 (quoting Tilghman).

73. Janet Napolitano, telephone interview, Feb. 17, 2015.

74. Alice H. Eagly and Linda L. Carli, *Through the Labyrinth: The Truth About How Women Become Leaders* (Boston: Harvard Business School Press, 2007).

75. Madsen, *On Becoming a Woman Leader*; Tiao, "Senior Women Leaders", Denise A. Bonebright, Anitra D. Cottledge, and Peg Lonnquist, "Developing Women Leaders on Campus: A Human Resources–Women's Center Partnership at the University of Minnesota," *Advances in Developing Human Resources* 14 (2012): 79.

76. Martha T. Nesbitt, "A Perfect Fit," in Wolverton et al., *Women at the Top*, 87.

77. Sharon Shinn, "At the Top of Her Game" (on Donna Shalala), *BizEd*, July/August 2002, http://www.e-digitaleditions.com/i/63429/2.

78. Sturnick, "Women Who Lead."
79. For authoritative styles, see Margaret Jablonski, "The Leadership Challenge for Women Presidents," *Initiatives* 57 (1996); Paula Young, "Leadership and Gender in Higher Education: A Case Study," *Journal of Further and Higher Education* 28 (2004): 95. For androgynous styles, see Madsen, *On Becoming a Woman Leader.*
80. Mary D. Wenniger, "Tips to Circumvent Alien Gatekeepers," in Wenniger and Conroy, *Gender Equity or Bust!* 114; Williams, Phillips, and Hall, "Double Jeopardy," 26.
81. June, "Despite Progress, Only 1 in 4 College Presidents Are Women," A6 (quoting Faust).
82. Nannerl Keohane, email survey, Mar. 12, 2015.
83. Linda Babcock and Sara Laschever, *Ask for It: How Women Can Use the Power of Negotiation to Get What They Really Want* (New York: Bantam Dell, 2008), 253.
84. Edwards-Wilson, "You Go, Girl!" 46.
85. Bornstein, "Women and the Quest for Presidential Legitimacy," 223–24.
86. Madsen, *On Becoming a Woman Leader,* 249.
87. Daniel Goleman, "Leadership That Gets Results," *Harvard Business Review* (March/April 2000): 78.
88. Madsen, *On Becoming a Woman Leader*; James M. Kouzes and Barry Z. Posner, *The Jossey-Bass Academic Administrator's Guide to Exemplary Leadership* (San Francisco: Jossey-Bass, 2003); Adena W. Loston, "Leadership Survival Strategies in the Vacuum of Upheaval," in Wenniger and Conroy, *Gender Equity or Bust!* 268; Nesbitt, "A Perfect Fit," in Wolverton et al., *Women at the Top.*
89. Tiao, "Senior Women Leaders."
90. Madsen, *On Becoming a Woman Leader,* 259.
91. Loston, "Leadership Survival Strategies"; Madsen, *On Becoming a Woman Leader.*
92. Madsen, *On Becoming a Woman Leader*; Tiao, "Senior Women Leaders."
93. Kouzes and Posner, *Jossey-Bass Academic Administrator's Guide,* 101.
94. Hannum et al., "Stories from the Summit Trail," 39, 41.
95. Brown, "Mentorship and the Female College President," 659. Gerdes, "Do It Your Way," 253; Hewlett et al., "Sponsor Effect."
96. McCartney, telephone interview.
97. Brown, "Mentorship and the Female College President"; Hannum et al., "Stories from the Summit Trail," 41.
98. Dunn et al., "Gender and Leadership," 15.
99. Bornstein, "Women and the Quest for Presidential Legitimacy," 208 (quoting Shalala).

100. See Kenneth R. Melchin and Cheryl A. Picard, *Transforming Conflict through Insight* (Toronto: University of Toronto Press, 2008), 79–80; Craig E. Runde and Tim A. Glanagan, *Becoming a Conflict Competent Leader* (San Francisco: Jossey Bass, 2013); David L. Bradford and Allan R. Cohen, "Power Talk: A Hands-on Guide to Supportive Confrontation," Appendix A, in Allan R. Cohen and David L. Bradford, eds., *Power Up: Transforming Organizations through Shared Leadership* (Hoboken, NJ: Wiley, 1998), 340.

101. Dunn et al., "Gender and Leadership," 14.

102. Sarah G. Cook, "How Women Administrators Choose Their Battles," in Wenniger and Conroy, eds., *Gender Equity or Bust!* 96.

103. Niemann, "Lessons from the Experiences of Women of Color Working in Academia," 490.

104. Gerdes, "Do It Your Way," 266.

105. Barbara Douglass, "Having Fun," in Wolverton et al., *Women at the Top*, 32.

106. Bornstein, "Women and the Quest for Presidential Legitimacy," 224. See also *Robert Gates, A Passion for Leadership* (New York: Knopf, 2016), 26–27, 63.

107. Thomas McDaniel, "Special Caveats for New Women Presidents," in Wenniger and Conroy, *Gender Equity or Bust!* 132.

108. Kevin Carey, "The Decline and Fall of a Public University: How Status Anxiety Doomed the University of Virginia," New Republic.com, June 12, 2012, https://newrepublic.com/article/104204/kevin-carey-decline-and-fall-public-university-how-status-anxiety-doomed-university. See also Andrew Rice, "Anatomy of a Campus Coup," *New York Times Magazine*, Sep. 11, 2012.

109. Rice, "Anatomy of a Campus Coup."

110. Douglass, "Having Fun," 32.

111. Madsen, *On Becoming a Woman Leader*, 260.

112. McDaniel, "Special Caveats for New Women Presidents."

113. Shinn, "At the Top of Her Game," 19.

114. Suzanna McCorkle and Jane Oldenburger, "Humor as a Management Tool Helps Women Lighten Up," in Wenniger and Conroy, *Gender Equity or Bust!* 279; Nesbitt, "A Perfect Fit"; Tiao, "Senior Women Leaders."

115. McCorkle and Oldenburger, "Humor as a Management Tool."

116. Gerdes, "Do It Your Way."

117. McCorkle and Oldenburger, "Humor as a Management Tool."

118. Vesterlund et al., "Breaking the Glass Ceiling with 'No'"; Judith D. Singer, "Fostering the Advancement of Women in Academic Statistics," in Amanda L. Golbeck, Ingram Olkin, and Yulia R. Gel, *Leadership and Women in Statistics* (Boca Raton, FL: CRC Press, 2016), 413, 425.

119. Moses, "Advice from the Field," 199.

120. Ibid., 189. See also Niemann, "Lessons from the Experiences of Women of Color Working in Academia," 498.
121. Niemann, "Lessons from the Experiences of Women of Color Working in Academia," 498.
122. Nannerl Keohane, email survey.
123. Karin Klenke, *Women and Leadership: A Contextual Perspective* (New York: Springer, 1996). For the need to address structures in the academic context, see Sharon R. Bird, "Unsettling Universities' Incongruous, Gendered Bureaucratic Structures: A Case-Study Approach," *Gender Work & Organization* 18 (2011): 202.
124. Task Force on Women and Leadership, "Findings and Recommendations," 21.
125. Lennon, *Benchmarking Women's Leadership in the United States*, 27.
126. William E. Kirwan, "Diversifying the American College Presidency," *The Presidency* 11 (2008): 4–5.
127. Task Force on Women and Leadership, "Findings and Recommendations," 17.
128. Damon Hack, "The NFL Spells Out New Hiring Guidelines," *New York Times*, Dec. 9, 2003, at D3. During the first seven years after the rule was adopted in 2003, the number of black head coaches in the NFL increased from 6 percent to 22 percent. Douglas M. Branson, "Initiatives to Place Women on Corporate Boards of Directors: A Global Snapshot," *Journal of Corporate Law* 37 (2012): 793.
129. McCartney, email survey.
130. Singer, "Fostering the Advancement of Women in Academic Statistics," 421–23.
131. Robert Drago et al, "The Avoidance of Bias Against Caregiving," *American Behavioral Scientist* 49 (2006): 1222.
132. Williams, Phillips, and Hall, "Double Jeopardy," 52; Sabine Girod et al., "Reducing Implicit Gender Bias in Academic Medicine with an Educational Intervention," *Academic Medicine* 20 (2015): 1.
133. Diane R. Dean, "Resources, Role Models, and Opportunity Makers: Mentoring Women in Academic Leadership," in Dean et al., *Women in Academic Leadership*, 128, 144.
134. Ibid. Caroline Sotello Viernes Turner and Janelle Kappes, "Preparing Women of Color for Leadership: Perspectives on the American Council on Education Fellows Program," in Dean et al., *Women in Academic Leadership*, 149, 152–56 (describing programs).
135. Sandra Lee Gupton, "Leadership Role of Academic Chairpersons in Higher Education," in Genevieve H. Brown, Beverly J. Irby, and Shirley A. Jackson, *Women Leaders: Advancing Careers* (Charlotte: Information Age, 2012), 55.

136. Nannerl Keohane, email survey.

137. Pyke, "Service and Gender Inequity," 86–87; Niemann, "The Making of a Token," 352; Niemann, "Lessons from the Experiences of Women of Color Working in Academia," 474; González, "Women of Color in Legal Education," 55–56.

138. Boyd, "Sharing Our Gifts," 281 (noting that such efforts are often not valued in promotion).

139. Iris Bohnet, *What Works: Gender Equality by Design* (Cambridge, MA: Harvard University Press, 2016), 108 (describing Harvard Kennedy School's efforts to monitor the gender composition of such programs).

140. Jay Newton-Small, *Broad Influence: How Women Are Changing the Way America Works* (New York: Time Books, 2016), 104.

141. Princeton University Steering Committee on Undergraduate Women's Leadership, Report of the Steering Committee on Undergraduate Women's Leadership (2011), http://www.princeton.edu/reports/2011/leadership/download.

CHAPTER 6

1. Michael D. Goldhaber, "Bye-Bye, Boys' Club," *American Lawyer*, June 14, 2015, 23 (quoting Ansgar Gabrielsen). This article draws on Deborah L. Rhode and Amanda Packel, "Diversity on Corporate Boards: How Much Difference Does 'Difference' Make?" *Delaware Journal of Corporate Law* 39 (2014): 377.

2. Goldhaber, "Bye-Bye, Boys' Club" (quoting Une Amundsen).

3. Susan Franceschet and Jennifer M. Piscopo, "Equality, Democracy, and the Broadening and Deepening of Gender Quotas," *Politics & Gender* 9 (2013): 310, 311. Often the quotas refer to the underrepresented sex, which is always women.

4. Lisa M. Fairfax, "Board Diversity Revisited: New Rationale, Same Old Story?" *North Carolina Law Review* 89 (2011): 855, 867. For increasing attention to the issue of women on boards, see Franceschet and Piscopo, "Equality, Democracy," 310.

5. For the importance of boards, see Aaron A. Dhir, *Challenging Boardroom Homogeneity: Corporate Law, Governance, and Diversity* (New York: Cambridge University Press, 2015), 30–31; Stephen J. Lubben, "Separation and Dependence: Explaining Modern Corporate Governance," *Seton Hall Law Review* 43 (2013): 893, 903.

6. Troy A. Paredes, "Enron: The Board, Corporate Governance, and Some Thoughts on the Role of Congress," in Nancy B. Rapoport et al., *Enron and Other Corporate Fiascos: The Corporate Scandal Reader*, 2nd ed. (New York: Foundation Press, 2009), 495, 495–538.

7. Lawrence J. Trautman, "The Matrix: The Board's Responsibility for Director Selection and Recruitment," *Florida State University Business Review* 11 (2012): 75, 111–12; Tim Smedley, "Diversity at the Top Pays Dividends," *Financial Times*, Mar. 8, 2016, 1.

8. Claire Cain Miller, "Women on Boards: Where the U.S. Ranks," *New York Times*, Mar. 10, 2015; Catalyst, "Still Too Few: Women of Color on Boards," Catalyst, March 17, 2015, http:www.catalyst.org/know/still-too-few. Women hold 20 percent of the seats on S&P 500 boards; see Spencer Stuart Board Index (2015), 16.

9. Dan Marcec et al., "Gender Diversity in the Boardroom," Equilar, Apr. 2, 2015.

10. Melanne Verveer and Kim K. Azzarelli, *Fast Forward: How Women Can Achieve Power and Purpose* (Boston: Houghton, Mifflin and Harcourt, 2015), 57.

11. Charles A. O'Reilly and Brian G. M. Main, *Women in the Boardroom: Symbols or Substance?* (Stanford Graduate School of Business, 2012, citing studies regarding gender disparities); "Women Progress on Corporate Boards, But Going Is Slow" (finding women account for 6 percent of board leadership roles and 26 percent of positions on key committees).

12. See Lisa M. Fairfax, "Clogs in the Pipeline: The Mixed Data on Women Directors and Continued Barriers to Their Advancement," *Maryland Law Review* 65 (2006): 579, 586.

13. See Douglas M. Branson, "Initiatives to Place Women on Corporate Boards of Directors: A Global Snapshot," *Journal of Corporation Law* 37 (2012): 793, 800 ("Women may be serving on four, five, six, or seven boards of directors").

14. Branson, "Initiatives to Place Women," 800; Douglas M. Branson, *No Seat at the Table: How Corporate Governance and Law Keep Women out of the Boardroom* (New York: New York University Press, 2007), 98–101, 155.

15. House of Lords, European Union Commission, "Women on Boards: Report" (Nov. 9, 2012, UK: 13–14.

16. See James A. Fanto et al., "Justifying Board Diversity," *North Carolina Law Review* 89 (2011): 901, 932; Julie C. Suk, "Gender Parity and State Legitimacy: From Public Office to Corporate Boards," *International Journal of Constitutional Law* 10 (2012): 449, 452 (noting that the moral case is insufficient to drive diversity initiatives); Lisa M. Fairfax, "Board Diversity Revisited: New Rationale, Same Old Story?" *North Carolina Law Review* 89 (2011): 864 (noting the business community's embrace of the business case); Lissa Lamkin Broome and Kimberly D. Krawiec, "Signaling Through Board Diversity: Is Anyone Listening?" *University of Cincinnati Law Review* 77 (2008): 431, 446–47.

17. Lawrence J. Trautman, "Corporate Boardroom Diversity: Why Are We Still Talking About This?" *The Scholar: St. Mary's Law Review on Race and Social*

Justice 17 (2015): 219, 226–27 (reviewing studies); Smedley, "Diversity at the Top," 1 (reviewing studies); SB Policy and Impact Committee of the Commission for Economic Development, "Fulfilling the Promise: How More Women on Corporate Boards Would Make America and American Companies More Competitive" (Commission for Economic Development (2012), 11, 13–14, http://perma.cc/A57Y-8JWA (concluding that women directors help deliver "measurable economic gains" and that the presence of women directors may be the key differentiator in future global success); D. Champion, "Women and Profits," *Harvard Business Review* 79 (2001): 30 (reporting Roy Adler's study finding a positive relationship); "The Bottom Line: Corporate Performance and Women's Representation on Boards" (New York: Catalyst, 2007, finding a positive relationship); Anthony F. Jurkus, Jung Chul Park, and Lorraine S. Woodard, "Women in Top Management and Agency Costs" (Working Paper, March 2011), http://perma.cc/PV38-UM6W (finding a positive relationship), 11. Researchers have also looked at gender diversity and nonprofit boards. At least one study of nonprofit boards finds that equal representation of sexes enhanced social performance (i.e., an organization's ability to fulfill its mission). Julie I. Siciliano, "The Relationship of Board Member Diversity to Organizational Performance," *Journal of Business Ethics* 15 (1996): 1313, 1317.

18. Marcus Noland, Tyler Moran, and Barbara Kotschwar, "Is Gender Diversity Profitable? Evidence from a Global Survey" (Peterson Institute for International Economics, Working Paper WP 16-3, February 2016), https://piie.com/publications/wp/wp1; Frank Dobbin and Jiwook Jung, "Corporate Board Gender Diversity and Stock Performance: The Competence Gap or Institutional Investor Bias?" *North Carolina Law Review* 89 (2010): 809, 833–36; Dan R. Dalton et al., "Meta-Analytic Reviews of Board Composition, Leadership Structure, and Financial Performance," *Strategic Management Journal* 19 (1998): 269, 282; Kassim Hussein and Bill Kiwia, "Examining the Relationship Between Female Board Members and Firm Performance—A Panel Study of U.S. Firms" 14 (June 27, 2009), http://perma.cc/9AGC-UTVQ; Toyah Miller and Maria del Carmen Triana, "Demographic Diversity in the Boardroom: Mediators of the Board Diversity–Firm Performance Relationship," *Journal of Management Studies* 46 (2009): 755, 777; Renée B. Adams and Daniel Ferreira, "Women in the Boardroom and Their Impact on Governance and Performance," *Journal of Financial Economics* 94 (2009): 291, 292, 305–7.

19. Corinne Post and Kris Byron, "Women on Boards and Firm Financial Performance: A Meta-Analysis," *Academy of Management Journal* 58 (2015): 1546, 1559.

20. Fairfax, "Board Diversity Revisited," 862; Kathleen A. Farrell and Philip L. Hersch, "Additions to Corporate Boards: The Effect of Gender," *Journal of Corporate Finance* 11 (2005): 85, 101. In a sample of three hundred nonregulated Fortune 1000 firms from 1990 to 1999, the authors found a positive relationship between ROA and the likelihood of adding a female director. But the addition of female directors showed no subsequent effect on performance, which indicates reverse causation. Farrell and Hersch, "Additions to Corporate Boards," 86, 89, 101–2; Renée B. Adams and Daniel Ferreira, "Gender Diversity in the Boardroom," 16, 19 (ECGI, Working Paper No. 57/2004, 2004, finding a positive impact on Tobin's Q when the percentage of women directors was the dependent variable, although ROA was not significant, and that firms with greater variability in stock returns had fewer women directors).

21. Broome and Krawiec, "Signaling Through Board Diversity," 434.

22. Ibid., Siri Terjesen et al., "Women Directors on Corporate Boards: A Review and Research Agenda," *Corporate Governance: An International Review* 17 (2009): 320, 327–28; Farrell and Hersch, "Additions to Corporate Boards," 85, 102 (hypothesizing either that women directors select high-performing or low-risk firms, or that well-functioning firms are more able to focus on adding diversity).

23. Amy J. Hillman et al., "Organizational Predictors of Women on Corporate Boards," *Academy of Management Journal* 50 (2007): 941, 944–45 (finding that organizational size, industry type, firm diversification strategy, and network effects, i.e., links to other boards with women directors, have significant effects on the likelihood of board gender diversity).

24. Joseph A. Grundfest, "Diversity on Corporate Boards: When Difference Makes a Difference," speech to Rock Center for Corporate Governance, Stanford University, Sep. 10, 2009, http://perma.cc/9K4Q-Z8MG; see also Byron J. Hollowell, "Examining the Relationship Between Diversity and Firm Performance," *Journal of Diversity Management* 2 (2007): 51–52 (examining the four-year relationship between diversity reputation and shareholder value for a sample of Fortune 500 firms designated as diversity leaders and finding a significant positive relationship, but noting that there is little empirical research on the relationship between diversity and long-term stock price performance).

25. Fairfax, "Clogs in the Pipeline," 592–93.

26. Ibid., 593; Alison M. Konrad, Vicki Kramer, and Sumru Erkut, "The Impact of Three or More Women on Corporate Boards," *Organizational Dynamics* 37 (2008): 145.

27. Marleen A. O'Connor, "Women Executives in Gladiator Corporate Cultures: The Behavioral Dynamics of Gender, Ego, and Power," *Maryland Law Review* 65 (2006): 465, 468; Fairfax, "Clogs in the Pipeline," 592–93.

28. Hedvig Bugge Reiersen and Beate Sjåfjell, "Report from Norway: Gender Equality in the Board Room," *European Company Law* 7(23), (2008), http://www.ft.com/intl/cms/s/0/792384e4-8591-11dc-8170-0000779fd2ac.html#axzz3lTHSZ3zY (quoting Lynda Gratton and Lamia Walker, "Gender Equality: A Solid Business Case At Last," *Financial Times*, Oct. 28, 2007, finding corporate insiders believe that groups with gender balance deliver optimal performance in most areas that "drive innovation").

29. See Fairfax, "Clogs in the Pipeline," 586; John M. Conley, Lissa L. Broome, and Kimberly D. Krawiec, "Narratives of Diversity in the Corporate Boardroom: What Corporate Insiders Say About Why Diversity Matters," UNC Legal Studies Research Paper No. 1415803 (2009), 24, http://perma .cc/4Q95-SVHT; Scott E. Page, *The Difference: How the Power of Diversity Creates Better Groups, Firms, Schools, and Societies* (Princeton: Princeton University Press, 2007); Zena Burgess and Phyllis Tharenou, "Women Board Directors: Characteristics of the Few," *Journal of Business Ethics* 37 (2002): 39.

30. Post and Byron, "Women on Boards," 1548; Donald C. Hambrick, "Upper Echelons Theory: An Update," *Academy of Management Review* 32 (2007): 334.

31. Irving L. Janis, *Victims of Groupthink* (Boston: Houghton Mifflin, 1972), 3. See Branson, "Initiatives to Place Women," 795; Seletha R. Butler, "All on Board! Strategies for Constructing Diverse Boards of Directors," *Virginia Law & Business Review* 7 (2012): 61, 76; Fanto et al., "Justifying Board Diversity," 928; Steven A. Ramirez, "A Flaw in the Sarbanes-Oxley Reform: Can Diversity in the Boardroom Quell Corporate Corruption?" *St. John's Law Review* 77 (2003): 837, 839.

32. National Association of Corporate Directors Blue Ribbon Commission, "The Diverse Board: Moving from Interest to Action" (National Association of Corporate Directors, 2012).

33. Nancy Ammon Jianakoplos and Alexandra Bernasek, "Are Women More Risk Averse?" *Economic Inquiry* 36 (1998): 620, 629; Elsa Ermer et al., "Relative Status Regulates Risky Decision Making about Resources in Men: Evidence for the Co-Evolution of Motivation and Cognition," *Evolution and Human Behavior* 29 (2008): 106, 116.

34. See Nicholas D. Kristof, "Mistresses of the Universe," *New York Times*, Feb. 7, 2009, at WK 12; Branson, "Initiatives to Place Women," 795–97. Norway's minister of trade similarly claimed that women board members reduce excessive risk taking. Kate Swe, "How Women Have Changed Norway's Boardrooms," *Harvard Business Review* Blog Network, July 27, 2009, http://perma.cc/57JX-9GKZ.

35. Katrin Bennhold, "Where Would We Be If Women Ran Wall Street?" *New York Times*, Feb. 1, 2009.

36. See Michael Cohn, "Women on Corporate Boards Encourage Better Financial Reporting," *Accounting Today*, Nov. 14, 2012.

37. Ajay Palvia, Emilia Vahamaa, and Sami Vahamaa, "Are Female CEOs and Chairwomen More Conservative and Risk Averse? Evidence from the Banking Industry During the Financial Crisis," *Journal of Business Ethics* 131 (2015): 577, 592.

38. Sheelah Kolhatkar, "What If Women Ran Wall Street?" *New York Magazine*, Mar. 21, 2010, http://perma.cc/6P5K-VCD7.

39. For trustworthiness, Joan MacLeod Heminway, "Sex, Trust, and Corporate Boards," *Hastings Women's Law Journal* 18 (2007): 173, 181; Rachel Croson and Nancy Buchan, "Gender and Culture: International Experimental Evidence from Trust Games," *American Economic Review* 89 (1999): 386, 389–90; Alessandro Innocenti and Maria Grazia Pazienza, "Altruism and Gender in the Trust Game" (Labsi Working Paper No. 5/2006, 2006): 13–14, http://ssrn.com/abstract=884378; Jana Vyrastekova and Sander Onderstal, "The Trust Game Behind the Veil of Ignorance: A Note on Gender Differences" (CentER Discussion Paper No. 2005-96, 2005), http://ssrn.com/abstract=807724. For collaborative styles, see Vicki W. Kramer, Alison M. Konrad, and Sumru Erkut, *Critical Mass on Corporate Boards: Why Three or More Women Enhance Governance* (Wellesley Centers for Women, 2006), 11. For board dynamics, see Credit Suisse Research Institute, "Gender Diversity and Corporate Performance" (Credit Suisse Research Institute, 2012), 18 (discussing mentoring and concern with the needs of others).

40. Kramer et al., *Critical Mass*, 12.

41. Fairfax, "Clogs in the Pipeline," 590; Kramer et al., *Critical Mass*, 9; Ramirez, "A Flaw in the Sarbanes-Oxley Reform," 840–41 (arguing diversity alters the functioning and deliberative style of boards and would lead to a new culture of scrutiny and reduce corporate corruption).

42. Post and Byron, "Women on Boards," 1548.

43. Nabil A. Ibrahim and John P. Angelidis, "Effect of Board Members' Gender on Corporate Social Responsiveness Orientation," *Journal of Applied Business Research* 10 (1994): 35, 36.

44. Catalyst, "Companies Behaving Responsibly: Gender Diversity on Boards" (New York: Catalyst, 2015), 1.

45. Lynne L. Dallas, "The New Managerialism and Diversity on Corporate Boards of Directors," *Tulane Law Review* 76 (2002): 1363, 1391; Frances J. Milliken and Luis L. Martins, "Searching for Common Threads: Understanding the Multiple Effects of Diversity in Organizational Groups," *Academy of Management Review* 21 (1996): 402, 416; Erica Beecher-Monas, "Marrying Diversity and Independence in the Boardroom: Just How Far Have You Come, Baby?" *Oregon Law Review* 86 (2007): 373, 394.

46. Dobbin and Jung, "Corporate Board Gender Diversity," 814–15; Lisa M. Fairfax, "The Bottom Line on Board Diversity: A Cost-Benefit Analysis of the Business Rationales for Diversity on Corporate Boards," *Wisconsin Law Review* (2005): 795, 831–34; Susan E. Jackson, "Consequences of Group Composition for the Interpersonal Dynamics of Strategic Issue Processing," *Advances in Strategic Management* 8 (1992): 345, 355–59; Cass R. Sunstein, "Deliberative Trouble? Why Groups Go to Extremes," *Yale Law Journal* 110 (2000): 71, 75.

47. Ramirez, "A Flaw in the Sarbanes-Oxley Reform," 841.

48. Kramer et al., *Critical Mass*, 9, 12.

49. Post and Byron, "Women on Boards," 1560.

50. Page, *The Difference*, 324–35; Dobbin and Jung, "Corporate Board Gender Diversity," 814–15.

51. Fairfax, "The Bottom Line on Board Diversity," 832–36.

52. O'Reilly and Main, *Women in the Boardroom*, 23; O'Connor, "Women Executives in Gladiator Corporate Cultures," 465, 468.

53. Sabina Nielsen and Morten Huse, "The Contribution of Women on Boards of Directors: Going Beyond the Surface," *Corporate Governance: An International Review* 18 (2010): 136, 138. For a review of the research, see Deborah L. Rhode and Barbara Kellerman, "Women and Leadership: The State of Play," in Barbara Kellerman and Deborah L. Rhode, eds., *Women and Leadership: The State of Play and Strategies for Change* (San Francisco: Jossey-Bass, 2007), 16–20.

54. Dobbin and Jung, "Corporate Board Gender Diversity," 817; Page, *The Difference*, 325; O'Reilly and Main, *Women in the Boardroom*, 24; Karen A. Jehn, Gregory B. Northcraft, and Margaret A. Neale, "Why Differences Make a Difference: A Field Study of Diversity, Conflict, and Performance in Workgroups," *Administrative Science Quarterly* 44 (1999): 741, 756.

55. Page, *The Difference*, 328.

56. Katherine W. Phillips, "How Diversity Works," *Scientific American* (October 2014), 43, 44.

57. Darren Rosenblum and Daria Roithmayr, "More than a Woman: Insights into Corporate Governance after the French Sex Quota," *Indiana Law Review* 48 (2015): 889.

58. Adams and Ferreira, "Gender Diversity in the Boardroom," 2 (attendance); Adams and Ferreira, "Women in the Boardroom," 298–301 (attendance and monitoring); Anita Williams Woolley, Christopher F. Chabris, Alex Pentland, Nada Hashmi, and Thomas W. Malone, "Evidence for a Collective Intelligence Factor in the Performance of Human Groups," *Science Express* 330 (Sep. 30, 2010), 686, 688 (monitoring and openness to diverse viewpoints); Aarti Maharaj, "Do Women on Boards Improve Governance?" *Corporate Secretary* (Dec. 14, 2011), http://

www.corporatesecretary.com/articles/boardrooms/12089/do-women-boards-improve-governance/ (attendance and oversight).

59. David A. H. Brown, Debra L. Brown, and Vanessa Anastasopoulos, "Women on Boards: Not Just the Right Thing . . . But the 'Bright' Thing" (Conference Board of Canada, 2002), 11, http://www.utsc.utoronto .ca/~phanira/WebResearchMethods/women-bod&fp-conference%20 board.pdf.

60. Ibid.

61. Morten Huse and Anne Grethe Solberg, "Gender-Related Boardroom Dynamics: How Women Make and Can Make Contributions on Corporate Boards," http://perma.cc/4yxw-s9ts; Joan MacLeod Heminway, "Women in the Crowd of Corporate Directors: Following, Walking Alone, and Meaningfully Contributing," *William & Mary Journal of Women and the Law* 21 (2014): 59, 82.

62. Broome and Krawiec, "Signaling Through Board Diversity," 434; Dhir, *Challenging Boardroom Homogeneity*, 64.

63. Lois Joy, "Advancing Women Leaders: The Connection Between Women Board Directors and Women Corporate Officers" (New York: Catalyst, 2008), 9, http://perma.cc/37BC-FR65; Fairfax, "The Bottom Line on Board Diversity," 852; Fanto et al., "Justifying Board Diversity," 931; European Commission, "The Costs and Benefits of Diversity," Directorate-General for Employment, Industrial Relations, and Social Affairs (2003).

64. Catalyst, "First Steps: Gender Diversity at the Top Pays Off from the Board Room to the C-Suite" (New York: Catalyst, 2013).

65. Broome and Krawiec, "Signaling Through Board Diversity," 447; Lissa L. Broome, John M. Conley, and Kimberly D. Krawiec, "Dangerous Categories: Narratives of Corporate Board Diversity," *North Carolina Law Review* 89 (2011): 759, 763–64; Miller and Triana, "Demographic Diversity in the Boardroom," 756, 762–63.

66. Claire Cain Miller, "Curtain Is Rising on a Tech Premier with (as Usual) a Mostly Male Cast," *New York Times*, Oct. 4, 2013. Men and women use Twitter almost equally. Twitter has since appointed a woman to its board of directors. Vindu Goel, "Twitter Appoints Marjorie Scardino as First Female Board Member," *New York Times*, Dec. 5, 2013.

67. Fanto et al., "Justifying Board Diversity," 934; Rushworth M. Kidder, "Diversity on Corporate Boards—Why It Matters," Minority Business Roundtable, http://perma.cc/46ZX-PBDA; Steven Brammer et al., "Gender and Ethnic Diversity Among UK Corporate Boards," *Corporate Governance: An International Review* 15 (2007): 393, 393–94.

68. David A. Matsa and Amalia R. Miller, "Chipping Away at the Glass Ceiling: Gender Spillovers in Corporate Leadership," *American Economic Review* 101 (2011): 635, 636; Cook and Glass, "Women and Top

Leadership Positions: Towards an Institutional Analysis," *Gender, Work and Organization* 21 (2014): 91, 100.

69. Matsa and Miller, "Chipping Away at the Glass Ceiling," 639.
70. Brammer et al., "Gender and Ethnic Diversity," 394–95.
71. Credit Suisse Research Institute, "Gender Diversity and Corporate Performance," 18.
72. PricewaterhouseCoopers, *Governing for the Long Term: PWC's 2015 Annual Corporate Directors Survey* (New York: PricewaterhouseCoopers, 2015), 3.
73. Antonio Perez, "Diversity on Corporate Boards: When Difference Makes a Difference," Eastman Kodak, Sep. 10, 2009.
74. PricewaterhouseCoopers, "Governing for the Long Term," 4.
75. Fairfax, "Clogs in the Pipeline," 595–96.
76. Ibid., 600–602.
77. See Alexandra Kalev et al., "Best Practices or Best Guesses? Assessing the Efficacy of Corporate Affirmative Action and Diversity Policies," *American Sociology Review* 71 (2006): 589, 595.
78. Ibid., 595.
79. Fairfax, "Clogs in the Pipeline," 599–600 (finding a "dearth" of women among the executive ranks); Fairfax, "Board Diversity Revisited," 880 (stating that executive experience is the most common characteristic of Fortune 1000 directors).
80. PricewaterhouseCoopers, "Governing for the Long Term," 3.
81. Lissa Lamkin Broome, "The Corporate Boardroom: Still a Male Club," *Journal of Corporate Law* 33 (2008): 665, 665–67; Heidrick & Struggles International, *Board Monitor: Four Boardroom Trends to Watch* (New York: Heidrick & Struggles, 2015). See Jayne W. Barnard, "More Women on Corporate Boards? Not So Fast," *William & Mary Journal of Women and Law* 13 (2007): 703, 707 ("the primary source of board members traditionally has been CEOs and former CEOs"); "Getting on Board: Women Join Boards at Higher Rates, Though Progress Comes Slowly," Ernst & Young (2012), 4 (reporting that 80 percent of female directors have executive experience).
82. National Association of Corporate Directors and Center for Board Leadership, 2009 NACD Public Company Governance Survey (2009).
83. Pew Research Center, "Women and Leadership," Jan. 14, 2015, http://www.pewsocialtrends.org/2015/01/14/women-and-leadership/; Claire C. Miller, "An Elusive Jackpot," *New York Times*, June 8, 2014; Rachel Soares, Liz Mulligan-Ferry, Emily Fendler, and Elijah Wai Chun Kun, "2013 Catalyst Census: Fortune 500 Women Executive Officers and Top Earners" (New York: Catalyst, 2013): 1, http://perma.cc/W56A-XEZU.
84. Fairfax, "Clogs in the Pipeline," 600–601.

85. Boris Groysberg and Deborah Bell, "2012 Board of Directors Survey (2012)," 3, http://perma.cc/QWC3-LXLY (survey facilitated by Heidrick & Struggles and WomenCorporateDirectors (WCD); Carmen Nobel, "Few Women on Boards: Is There a Fix?" (2013), Harvard Business School, http://perma.cc/82AG-QP66.

86. Barnard, "More Women on Corporate Boards?" 708–10.

87. David Larcker and Brian Tayan, *A Real Look at Real World Corporate Governance* (San Bernardino, CA: Larcker-Tayan, 2013).

88. Ibid., 30.

89. *2011 Corporate Board of Directors Survey* (Heidrick & Struggles and Stanford Rock Center for Corporate Governance, 2011); Larcker and Tayan, *A Real Look*, 30–31.

90. See Michelle R. Clayman, "Diversity on Corporate Boards: When Difference Makes a Difference," Sep. 10, 2009, archived at http://perma .cc/5D45-RE23; Larcker and Tayan, *A Real Look* ("Although respondents value the strategic and operating experience of CEO directors, when asked about their undesirable attributes, a full 87 percent believe that active CEOs are too busy with their own companies to be effective"); David Larcker and Brian Tayan, "Are Current CEOs the Best Board Members?" Stanford Closer Look Series: Topics, Issues, and Controversies in Corporate Governance, Aug. 17, 2011, 30; Heidrick & Struggles and Stanford Rock Center for Corporate Governance, *Corporate Board of Directors Survey* (Stanford: Stanford Rock Center for Corporate Governance, 2011), 11 (reporting that responding directors felt active CEOs were "too busy with their company to be effective directors," 87 percent; "too interested in networking/promoting their own company to be effective directors," 21 percent; "too bossy/used to having their own way," 33 percent; and "not good collaborators," 28 percent; emphasis omitted).

91. Jeff Green, "Men Seeking Women for Boards: Looking in All the Wrong Places," *Bloomberg*, April 5, 2016, http://www.blomberg.com/news/ articles/2016/04/05/men-seeking-women-for-boards-looking-inall-the-wrong-places.

92. Ibid.

93. Dhir, *Challenging Boardroom Homogeneity*, 38; Spencer Stuart, "Boardrooms Uncertain About Economic Outlook, with Few Predicting Growth," Feb. 16, 2016, https://www.spencerstuart.com/who.

94. Milliken and Martins, "Searching for Common Threads," 420–21; Barbara F. Reskin, "Rethinking Employment Discrimination and Its Remedies," in Mauro F. Guillen et al., eds., *The New Economic Sociology: Developments in an Emerging Field* (New York: Russell Sage Foundation, 2002), 218, 221–22; Marilyn B. Brewer and Rupert J. Brown, "Intergroup

Relations," in Daniel T. Gilbert, Susan T. Fiske, and Gardner Lindzey, eds., *The Handbook of Social Psychology*, vol. 2, 4th ed. (New York: Oxford University Press, 1998); Susan T. Fiske, "Stereotyping, Prejudice, and Discrimination," in Gilbert et al., *The Handbook of Social Psychology*, vol. 2 (review of social stereotyping studies), 357.

95. Belle Rose Ragins, "Gender and Mentoring Relationships: A Review and Research Agenda for the Next Decade," in Gary N. Powell, ed., *Handbook of Gender and Work* (New York: Russell Sage, 1999); "Women in Corporate Leadership: Progress and Prospects" (New York: Catalyst, 1996), 39–40; Timothy L. O'Brien, "Up the Down Staircase," *New York Times*, Mar. 19, 2006.

96. Branson, *No Seat at the Table*, 14–15.

97. U.S. Government Accountability Office, *Corporate Boards: Strategies to Address Representation of Women Include Federal Disclosure Requirements* (Washington, DC: GAO, December 2015), 13.

98. Ibid.

99. Groysberg and Bell, "2012 Board of Directors Survey," 3.

100. John F. Dovidio and Samuel L. Gaertner, "Stereotypes and Evaluative Intergroup Bias," in Diane M. Mackie and David L. Hamilton, eds., *Affect, Cognition, and Stereotyping* (New York: Academic Press, 1993), 167, 170–71; Martha Foschi, "Double Standards in the Evaluation of Men and Women," *Social Psychology Quarterly* 59 (1996): 237, 237–38.

101. Dovidio and Gaertner, "Stereotypes," 170–71; Foschi, "Double Standards in the Evaluation of Men and Women," 237–39.

102. See Jennifer Crocker et al., "Social Stigma," in Gilbert et al., *The Handbook of Social Psychology*, vol. 2, 508–9; Dovidio and Gaertner, "Stereotypes," 170–71; Martha Foschi, "Double Standards for Competence: Theory and Research," *Annual Review Sociology* (2000): 21, 31–32; Linda Hamilton Krieger, "The Content of Our Categories: A Cognitive Bias Approach to Discrimination and Equal Employment Opportunity," *Stanford Law Review* 47 (1995): 1161, 1187–88, 1204–5; Cecilia L. Ridgeway, "Interaction and the Conservation of Gender Inequality: Considering Employment," *American Sociology Review* 62 (1997): 218, 221.

103. Allison Sheridan and Gina Milgate, "Accessing Board Positions: A Comparison of Female and Male Board Members' Views," *Corporate Governance: An International Review* 13 (2005): 6.

104. Maria C. González Menendez, Colette Fagan, and Silvia Gómez Ansón, "Introduction," in Colette Fagan, Maria C. González Menendez, and Silvia Gómez Ansón, eds., *Women on Corporate Boards and in Top Management: European Trends and Policy* (New York: Palgrave Macmillan, 2012), 1, 3.

105. Boris Groysberg and Deborah Bell, "Dysfunction in the Board Room," *Harvard Business Review*, June 2013, 94.

106. Rhode and Kellerman, "Women and Leadership," 6–15; Sylvia Ann Hewlett et al., *The Sponsor Effect: Breaking Through the Last Glass Ceiling* (*Harvard Business Review* Research Report, December 2010). A survey of upper-level American managers found that almost half of women of color and close to a third of white women cite lack of influential mentors as a major barrier to advancement. Catalyst, "Women of Color in Corporate Management" (New York: Catalyst, 1999), 10–15.

107. See Michael L. McDonald and James D. Westphal, "Access Denied: Low Mentoring of Women and Minority First-Time Directors and Its Negative Effects on Appointments to Additional Boards," *Academy of Management Journal* 56 (2013): 1169, 1175–84.

108. See Ella L. J. Edmondson Bell and Stella M. Nkomo, *Our Separate Ways: Black and White Women and the Struggle for Professional Identity* (Cambridge, MA: Harvard Business School Press, 2001), 122–32; Bernardo M. Ferdman, "The Color and Culture of Gender in Organizations: Attending to Race and Ethnicity," in Powell, *Handbook of Gender and Work*, 17, 23; "Women of Color in Corporate Management" (New York: Catalyst, 1999), 15; Lisa Fairfax, "Some Reflections on the Diversity of Corporate Boards: Women, People of Color and the Unique Issues Associated with Women of Color," *St. John's Law Review* 79 (2005): 1105, 1113; David B. Wilkins and G. Mitu Gulati, "Why Are There So Few Black Lawyers in Corporate Law Firms? An Institutional Analysis," *California Law Review* 84 (1996): 493, 557–58, 568, 570, 579.

109. Diane Brady, "To Get Women on Company Boards, Make Men Leave," *Bloomberg Businessweek*, Sep. 20, 2012, http://perma.cc/LWX3-M6K2.

110. National Association of Corporate Directors, "The Diverse Board," 11–14.

111. Holly J. Gregory, "Board Composition, Diversity, and Refreshment," *Practical Law*, June 2013, http://perma.cc/W5VL-X7HY. As more directors near retirement age, a higher proportion of companies (88 percent) have retirement age set at seventy-two years or older as compared to a decade ago, when the majority of companies with a mandatory retirement age set it at seventy or younger. Spencer Stuart Board Index 2013, 16.

112. Spencer Stuart Board Index 2012, 7, 10, http://perma.cc/B7E4-X5C7.

113. Government Accountability Office, *Corporate Boards*, 15.

114. Spencer Stuart Board Index, 16.

115. Rosabeth Moss Kanter, *The Problems of Tokenism* (Wellesley: Center for Research on Higher Education and the Professions, 1974); Joan MacLeod Heminway and Sarah White, "WANTED: Female Corporate Directors," *Pace Law Review* 29 (2009): 249, 257–64. See also Cook and Glass, "Women and Top Leadership Positions," 101.

116. Terjesen et al., "Women Directors on Corporate Boards," 328. One study "found that directors who were the sole woman on a board had to struggle to be heard in board discussions, while being one of two or three women on the board dramatically changed the situation." Beate Elstad and Gro Ladegard, "Women on Corporate Boards: Key Influencers or Tokens?" *Journal of Management and Governance* 16 (2012): 595, 598.

117. Groysberg and Bell, "Dysfunction in the Boardroom," 94.

118. William B. Stevenson and Robert F. Radin, "Social Capital and Social Influence on the Board of Directors," *Journal of Management Studies* 46 (2009): 16, 33 ("As one CEO said . . . 'Don't confuse board actions with board decisions. Board decisions don't take place in the boardroom. Board actions take place in the boardroom.'"); Gonzalez Menendez et al., "Introduction," in Fagan et al., *Women on Corporate Boards*, 5 (discussing women's exclusion from informal socializing).

119. Groysberg and Bell, "Dysfunction in the Boardroom," 94.

120. Heminway and White, "WANTED: Female Corporate Directors," 261.

121. Menendez et al., "Introduction," in Fagan et al., *Women on Corporate Boards*, 5.

122. Heminway and White, "WANTED, Female Corporate Directors," 261.

123. Ibid., 259 (quoting Branson); Edward S. Adams, "Using Evaluations to Break Down the Male Corporate Hierarchy: A Full Circle Approach," *University of Colorado Law Review* 73 (2002): 117, 170–71 (defining the "queen bee" syndrome).

124. Konrad, Kramer, and Erkut, "The Impact of Three or More Women on Corporate Boards."

125. Seletha R. Butler, "'Financial Expert': A Subtle Blow to the Pool and Current Pipeline of Women on Corporate Boards," *Georgetown Journal of Gender and Law* 14 (2013): 1, 31–32.

126. Fairfax, "Clogs in the Pipeline," at 603–5. The most systematic large-scale study to date has found that mentoring programs are correlated with modest gains in female representation in managerial positions and that women of color benefit most. Kalev et al., "Best Practices or Best Guesses?" 611. Other smaller-scale studies suggest that executives identify influential mentors as an important success strategy and that having more mentors increased the number of women's promotions. Catalyst, "Women and Men in U.S. Corporate Leadership: Same Workplace, Different Realities?" (New York: Catalyst, 2004), 11–13; Catalyst, "Women of Color in Corporate Management: Three Years Later" (New York: Catalyst, 2002), 12–15; Rhode and Kellerman, "Women and Leadership," 21 (discussing the need to combat barriers to self-promotion among women); Gordon C. C. Liao, *Diversity on Corporate Boards: When Difference Makes a Difference* (Baird Capital Partners, Sept. 10, 2009).

127. Fairfax, "Clogs in the Pipeline," 603–4.
128. Thomas Lee Hazen and Lissa Lamkin Broome, "Board Diversity and Proxy Disclosure," *University of Dayton Law Review* 37 (2011): 39, 42–43.
129. Alison Damast, "Program Aims to Prepare Women for Board Service," *Bloomberg Businessweek*, July 16, 2012, http://perma.cc/TP9M-ZFHZ (describing a mentoring program through George Washington University's Business School, and citing initiatives at Stanford, Harvard, and Northwestern).
130. Rhode and Kellerman, "Women and Leadership," 31.
131. Ibid.; Kate Grosser and Jeremy Moon, "Gender Mainstreaming and Corporate Social Responsibility: Reporting Workplace Issues," *Journal of Business Ethics* 62 (2005): 327, 330–31 (discussing Australian legislation).
132. Luis A. Aguilar, "Board Diversity: Why It Matters and How to Improve It," speech by commissioner at SEC Agenda Luncheon Program (Nov. 4, 2010; transcript archived at http://perma.cc/7YCY-HLQC).
133. The countries include Austria, Belgium, Denmark, Finland, France, Greece, Iceland, Ireland, Israel, Italy, Malaysia, the Netherlands, Norway, Spain, Switzerland, and South Africa. Franceschet and Piscopo, "Equality, Democracy," 310–11. For support of this approach, see Bruce Kogut, Jordi Colomer, and Mariano Belinky, "Structural Equality at the Top of the Corporation: Mandated Quotas for Women Directors," *Strategic Management Journal* 35 (2014): 891.
134. Nicola Clark, "Getting Women into Boardrooms, by Law," *New York Times*, Jan. 27, 2010. Spanish companies that achieve a "balanced presence of women and men," defined as at least 40 percent of both sexes, are eligible to receive a "corporate equality mark" that they can use in promotional materials. Netherlands companies that do not achieve at least 30 percent of both sexes must disclose the reasons in their annual reports, as well as the measures they have taken to attain gender balance. Dhir, *Challenging Boardroom Homogeneity*, 72–73.
135. *Women in the Boardroom: A Global Perspective*, 3rd ed. (Deloitte and Touche, 2013), 19, 23. For Germany, see Alison Smale and Claire Cain Miller, "Germany Sets Gender Quota in Boardrooms," *New York Times*, Mar. 6, 2015.
136. *Women in the Boardroom*, 20.
137. Sara Hamdan, "U.A.E. Promotes Women in the Boardroom," *New York Times*, Dec. 19, 2012 (reporting that the UAE has made it mandatory for every company and government agency in the country to have female board members); David A. Katz and Laura A. McIntosh, "Corporate Governance Update: Developments Regarding Gender Diversity on Public Boards," AmericanBar.Org (2013), http://perma.cc/P6K2-D4QQ ("[India's] August 2013 Companies Act now requires every listed

company to have at least one female director within one to three years of its listing, depending on the size of the company").

138. Clark, "Getting Women into Boardrooms," 1; "Committee on the Elimination of Discrimination Against Women Examines Reports of Sweden," United Nations Press Release, Feb. 18, 2016, http://www.ohchr.org/ EN/NewsEvents/Pages/DisplayNews.aspx?NewsId=17068&LangID=E (noting that the Swedish government plans to introduce legislating quotas for women on boards if 40 percent female representation is not achieved); Bryce Covert, "Sweden May Establish Quotas If Companies Don't Have More Female Board Members," *ThinkProgress*, Feb. 13, 2014.

139. Amy Dittmar et al., "Using Quotas to Raise the Glass Ceiling," *New York Times*, Mar. 22, 2010.

140. "Women on Company Boards: La Vie en Rose," *Economist*, May 6, 2010.

141. See Dittmar et al., "Using Quotas to Raise the Glass Ceiling" (discussing the Norway numbers); David M. Matsa and Amalia R. Miller, "A Female Style in Corporate Leadership: Evidence from Quotas," *American Economic Journal: Applied Economics* 5 (2013): 136.

142. Smale and Miller, "Germany Sets Gender Quota." See also Bryce Covert, "It's Time to Fix the Very Pale, Vey Male Boardroom," *New Republic*, July 8, 2014; John D. Stoll, "Norway's Exemplary Gender Quota? Just Don't Ask About CEOs," *Wall Street Journal*, May 22, 2014.

143. Smale and Miller, "Germany Sets Gender Quota" (quoting Federation of German Industries).

144. Victor E. Sojo, Robert E. Wood, Sally A. Wood, and Melissa A. Wheeler, "Reporting Requirements, Targets, and Quotas for Women in Leadership," *Leadership Quarterly* (forthcoming in print; online Jan. 14, 2016, http:// www.sciencedirect.com/science/article/pii/S1048984315001514), 15.

145. Nielsen and Huse, "The Contribution of Women on Boards of Directors," 143–45. Another study, however, found that most corporate decisions were unaffected by increased representation of women on the board, but that firms affected by the quota conducted fewer employee layoffs after female board representation increased, leading to higher relative labor costs and reduced short-term profits). David A. Matsa and Amalia R. Miller, "A Female Style in Corporate Leadership? Evidence from Quotas," *American Economic Journal: Applied Economics* 5 (2013): 136, 137–38 (comparing Norwegian firms affected by the quota to other public and private Nordic firms unaffected by the legislation).

146. Dhir, *Challenging Boardroom Homogeneity*, 101.

147. Ibid.

148. Ibid., 143–144.

149. Ibid., 144.

150. Rosenblum and Roithmayr, "More than a Woman."

151. Ibid.
152. See "Civil Rights Act Veto—Bush Turns His Back on American Workers," *Seattle Times*, Oct. 25, 1990 (vetoing the Civil Rights Act of 1990 on the grounds that it would impose quotas on employers); Anthony Lewis, "The Case of Lani Guinier," *New York Review of Books*, Aug. 13, 1998 (withdrawing the nomination of Lani Guinier to head the Justice Department's Civil Rights Division after she was labeled a "quota queen").
153. Ken Auletta, "A Woman's Place: Can Sheryl Sandberg Upend Silicon Valley's Male-Dominated Culture?" *New Yorker*, July 11, 2011 (quoting Mark Zuckerberg).
154. Meghan Casserly, "Sheryl Sandberg Named to Facebook Board, Finally," *Forbes*, June 25, 2012. See also Brian Womack, "Facebook Adds COO Sandberg to Board as First Female Director," *Bloomberg News*, June 26, 2012.
155. House of Lords, European Union Commission, *Women on Boards: Report* (Nov. 9, 2012), 27 (noting that quotas would be unpopular among many potential beneficiaries and would risk fostering the perception that women appointed were not there on their merit); Dhir, *Challenging Boardroom Homogeneity*, 80–81 (summarizing objections).
156. One study shows that 39 percent of women directors opposed quotas, although 51 percent believed that they are an effective tool for increasing board diversity. Groysberg and Bell, "2012 Board of Directors Survey," 4 (noting also that 25 percent of men believe quotas to be an effective tool and that 18 percent of men support use of quotas).
157. The California State Senate passed this resolution:

> Within a three-year period from January 2014 to December 2016, inclusive, every publicly held corporation in California with nine or more director seats [should] have a minimum of three women on its board, every publicly held corporation in California with five to eight director seats [should] have a minimum of two women on its board, and every publicly held corporation in California with fewer than five director seats [should] have a minimum of one woman on its board. . . . S. Con. Res. 62 (Cal. 2013) (enacted) (introduced July 11, 2013, and passed Aug. 26, 2013), http://perma.cc/7NJV-AH4D.

158. See Rachel Sanderson and Kate Burgess, "Directors Must Be Re-Elected Annually," *Financial Times*, May 28, 2010.
159. "How to Build Diversity on Boards: A Voluntary 30% Quota for Women Would Signal Intent," *Financial Times*, May 19, 2009, 12.
160. Jennifer S. Lerner and Philip E. Tetlock, "Accounting for the Effects of Accountability," *Psychological Bulletin* 125 (1999): 255, 263; Foschi, "Double Standards in the Evaluation of Men and Women," 251;

Stephen Benard, In Paik, and Shelley J. Correll, "Cognitive Bias and the Motherhood Penalty," *Hastings Law Journal* 59 (2008): 1359, 1381.

161. Sanderson and Burgess, "Directors Must Be Re-Elected Annually."

162. Ibid.

163. Ibid.

164. *Corporate Governance Principles and Recommendations with 2010 Amendments*, 2nd ed. (ASX Corporation Governance Council, 2010), 11.

165. Ibid.; Branson, "Initiatives to Place Women," 807–8; Hazen and Broome, "Board Diversity and Proxy Disclosure."

166. *Directive 2014/95/EU of the European Parliament and of the Council of 22 October 2014 amending Directive 2013/34/Eu as regards disclosure of non-financial and diversity information by certain large undertakings and groups*; Dhir, *Challenging Boardroom Homogeneity*, 242–43.

167. *Directive 2014/95/EU of the European Parliament and of the Council of 22, October 2014, amending Directive 2013/34/Eu as regards disclosure of non-financial and diversity information by certain large undertakings and groups.*

168. Sarbanes-Oxley Act of 2002, Publ. L. No. 107–204, §§ 406 and 407, 116 Stat. 745 (2002).

169. Dodd-Frank Wall Street Reform and Consumer Protection Act, Publ. L. No. 111–203, § 972, 124 Stat. 1376 (2010).

170. 17 C.F.R. § 229.407(c)(2)(vi) (2012).

171. Ibid.

172. Proxy Disclosure Enhancements, Release No. 33-9089, SEC Docket S7-23-09, at 39 (Dec. 16, 2009).

173. Dhir, *Challenging Boardroom Homogeneity*, 189.

174. Ibid., 190 (quoting proxy statements).

175. Ibid., 200.

176. Sojo et al., "Reporting Requirements," 5 (compiling data suggesting that the rule may have had some positive impact but noting that for most companies, increases in the percentage of women on their boards occurred before the reporting requirements).

177. Aguilar, "Board Diversity: Why It Matters and How to Improve It," https://www.sec.gov/news/speech/2010/spch110410laa.htm.

178. "A Conversation with [SEC] Chair Mary Jo White," Keynote Session, 43rd Annual Securities Regulation Institute (San Diego, Jan. 26, 2016), 5–6, 11 https://www.sec.gov/news/speech/securities-regulation-institute-keynote-white.html.

179. See David Seidl, Paul Sanderson, and John Roberts, "Applying the 'Comply-or-Explain' Principle: Discursive Legitimacy Tactics with Regard to Codes of Corporate Governance," *Journal of Management and Governance* 17 (2013): 791, 797–804 (finding substantial rates of noncompliance).

180. Iris Bohnet, *What Works: Gender Equality by Design* (Cambridge: MA: Harvard University Press, 2016), 274.

181. Sandeep Gopalan and Katherine Watson, "An Agency Theoretical Approach to Corporate Board Diversity," *San Diego Law Review* 52 (2015): 1, 6.

182. For arguments about expanding the pool of candidates beyond CEOs, see Trautman, "Corporate Boardroom Diversity," 251. For the need to develop a board culture that values dissent, see Post and Byron, "Women on Boards," 2015. For strategies to increase the number of women with relevant credentials, see Rhode and Kellerman, "Women and Leadership," 27–30 (discussing strategies such as well-designed mentoring programs and accountability structures); Frank Dobbin, Alexandra Kalev, and Erin Kelly, "Diversity Management in Corporate America," *Contexts* 6 (2007): 21, 25 (discussing mentoring programs for women and minorities); Kalev et al., "Best Practices or Best Guesses?" 590 (discussing accountability structures).

183. Branson, *No Seat at the Table*, 144 (noting the relative ease and flexibility of board structures).

184. Clarence Otis, Jr., "Diversity on Corporate Boards: When Difference Makes a Difference," speech by chairman and CEO of Darden Restaurants, Rock Center for Corporate Guidance, Stanford University, Sep. 10, 2009.

185. Butler, "All on Board!" 85–86.

186. Ilene Lang, email survey, Apr. 20, 2015.

187. Fairfax, "Clogs in the Pipeline," 605–7; Trautman, "Corporate Boardroom Diversity," 251; Government Accountability Office, *Corporate Boards*, 18 (noting that all stakeholders who expressed an opinion supported expanding board searches).

188. Barnard, "More Women on Corporate Boards?" 703, 708–9; Virtcom Consulting, "Board Diversification Strategy: Realizing Competitive Advantage and Shareholder Value," white paper on behalf of CalPERS, 2008, 23 (discussing practices that help board diversification).

189. Jay Newton-Small, *Broad Influence: How Women Are Changing the Way America Works* (New York: Time Books, 2016), 111. The Thirty Percent Coalition lists such organizations on its webpage: http://www.30percentcoalition.org.

190. Virtcom Consulting, "Board Diversification Strategies," 23–24.

191. Barnard, "More Women on Corporate Boards," 709–10.

192. National Association of Corporate Directors, "The Diverse Board," 13.

193. Steven A. Ramirez, "Games CEOs Play and Interest Convergence Theory: Why Diversity Lags in America's Boardrooms and What to Do About It," *Washington and Lee Law Review* 61 (2004): 1583, 1598–99. However, one recent study suggests that women directors may be more

generous than their male counterparts in setting compensation policy. See O'Reilly and Main, *Women in the Boardroom*, 5. If that pattern is confirmed in further research, CEOs might find women to be more attractive candidates.

194. Richard A. Bernardi, David F. Bean, and Kristen M. Weippert, "Minority Membership on Boards of Directors: The Case for Requiring Pictures of Boards in Annual Reports," *Critical Perspectives on Accounting* 16 (2005): 1019, 1029.

195. Dhir, *Challenging Boardroom Homogeneity*, 20.

196. Jeff Elder, "What Silicon Valley's Diversity Reports Say About the Tech Workforce," Wall Street Journal Online, June 19, 2014, blogs .wsj.com/digits/2014/06/19/what-silicon-valley-diversity-reports-say-about-the-tech-workforce.

197. Alison Griswold, "When It Comes to Diversity in Tech, Companies Find Safety in Numbers," *Slate*, June 27, 2014, http://perma.cc/439G-FJPL.

198. Maxine Williams, "Building a More Diverse Facebook," Facebook Newsroom, June 25, 2014, newsroom.fb.com/news/2014/06/building-a-more-diverse-facebook; Laszlo Bock, "Getting to Work on Diversity at Google," Google Official Blog, May 28, 2014, http://perma.cc/M5AR-F7MW; Jacqueline Reses, "Workforce Diversity at Yahoo," Yahoo, June 17, 2014, http://perma .cc/3UWC-8488; Pat Waldors, "LinkedIn's Workforce Diversity," LinkedIn Official Blog, June 12, 2014, http://perma.cc/H5ZX-LSPJ.

199. National Association of Corporate Directors, "The Diverse Board," 16 (noting that large public pension funds such as CalPERS and CalSTRS have used shareholder proposals and the threat of those proposals to negotiate with companies whose stock they own regarding board diversity); Barbara Black, "Stalled: Gender Diversity on Corporate Boards," *University of Dayton Law Review* 37 (2011): 7, 10 (noting that CalPERS and CalSTRS are working with a panel of leading corporate governance experts to create a digital database aimed at increasing board diversity).

200. "About," Thirty Percent Coalition, http://perma.cc/97NG-BSCL.

201. "Institutional Investors Note Progress as Eight Companies Appoint Women to Their Boards," Thirty Percent Coalition, Sep. 18, 2013.

202. Jenny Anderson, "Aiming at Glass Ceilings," *New York Times*, Jan. 27, 2015, B1; Peter Grauer and Michael Milken, "Male Executives Need to 'Lean in' Too," *Wall Street Journal*, Apr. 27, 2015, A11.

203. Bohnet, *What Works*, 260.

204. "2020 Gender Diversity Index: 2013 Key Findings," 2020 Women on Boards, http://www.2020wob.com/sites/default/files/2020GDI-2013 Report.pdf.

205. ASX LtD, ASX Listing Rule 4.10.3, http://perma.cc/VDH5-UNDM (requiring listed Australian companies to disclose their diversity policies,

including measurable objectives and progress, or to explain why they do not disclose the information); NZX Ltd., NZSX/NZDX Listing Rule 10.5.5(j), http://perma.cc/JB9K-MTWG (requiring a "quantitative breakdown" of New Zealand officers and directors as well as a comparison from the year before); Black, "Stalled," 17–18; Katz and McIntosh, "Corporate Governance Update," 5.

206. Richard Milne, "Fund to Invest in Gender Diversity," *Financial Times*, Oct. 26, 2009, http://www.ft.com/cms/s/0/ada6d18c-c1ce-11de-b86b-00144feab49a.html#axzz3lTRtgK7G; Julia Werdigier, "Fund Plans to Invest in Companies with Women as Directors," *New York Times*, Oct. 26, 2009, http://www.nytimes.com/2009/10/27/business/global/27fund.html?_r=0; Linda Tarr-Whelan, *Women Lead the Way: Your Guide to Stepping Up to Leadership and Changing the World* (Oakland: Berrett-Koehler, 2011), 140.

207. *Women in the Boardroom*, 1; Dhir, "Challenging Boardroom Homogeneity," 57.

208. "Proxy Preview 2013," As You Sow, 2013, http://www.asyousow.org/ays_report/proxy-preview-2013/.

209. See Dhir, *Challenging Boardroom Homogeneity*, 264–65.

210. "2012 Boardroom Diversity Survey: Summary Report," Spencer Stuart, 2012, http://perma.cc/A6VH-E9V8 (reporting only 11.3 percent of surveyed firms received contact from investors within the previous three years on issues of racial or gender diversity on the board).

211. Tarr-Whelan, *Women Lead the Way*, 140 (finding corporations responded positively when an investment firm made the proposal).

212. "About the DiversityInc Top 50 Process," DiversityInc, http://perma.cc/3A72-8SRL.

213. "2012 Best Companies for Diversity," *Black Enterprise*, July 11, 2012, http://perma.cc/G57V-BRA2. An Ethical Investment Research Service survey found the majority of women want their pension funds to favor companies with good records on equal opportunity. Grosser and Moon, "Gender Mainstreaming," 333–35. See also studies cited in Amanda K. Packel, "Government Intervention into Board Composition: Gender Quatas in Norway and Diversity Disclosures in the U.S.," *Stanford Journal of Law, Business, and Finance* (forthcoming, 2016).

214. ABA, Commission on Women in the Profession, Business Law Section, Commission on Disability Rights, Commission on Sexual Orientation and Gender Identity, *Report to the House of Delegates on Resolution 116* (2016).

CHAPTER 7

1. Kim Parker and Wendy Wang, "Modern Parenthood: Roles of Moms and Dads Converge as They Balance Work and Family" (Pew Research Center, 2013).

2. Sheryl Gay Stolberg, "He Breaks for Band Recitals," *New York Times*, Feb. 12, 2010, S1, S11.

3. Ibid., S10.

4. Bob Sherwin, "Why Women Are More Effective Leaders Than Men," *Business Insider*, Jan. 24, 2014. See also Brian S. Moskal, "Women Make Better Managers," *Industry Week*, Feb. 3, 1997, 17; Rochelle Sharpe, "As Leaders, Women Rule: New Studies Find That Female Managers Outshine Their Male Counterparts in Almost Every Measure," *Businessweek*, Nov. 20, 2000.

5. Deborah L. Rhode and Lucy Ricca, "Diversity in the Legal Profession: Perspectives from Managing Partners and General Counsel," *Fordham Law Review* 83 (2015): 2483.

6. Anne-Marie Slaughter, *Unfinished Business: Women, Men, Work, Family* (New York: Random House, 2015), 233.

7. Deborah L. Rhode, *What Women Want: An Agenda for the Women's Movement* (New York: Oxford University Press, 2015).

8. Laura Nash and Howard Stevenson, *Just Enough: Tools for Creating Success in Your Work and Life* (Hoboken, NJ: Wiley, 2004), 120.

9. Christopher P. Niemiec, Richard M. Ryan, and Edward L. Deci, "The Path Taken: Consequences of Attaining Intrinsic and Extrinsic Aspirations in Post-College Life," *Journal of Research in Personality* 73(3) (2009): 291.

10. Martin E. P. Seligman, *Authentic Happiness: Using the New Positive Psychology to Realize Your Potential for Lasting Fulfillment* (New York: Free Press, 2002), 49; Ed Diener, Richard E. Lucas, and Christie Napa Scollon, "Beyond the Hedonic Treadmill: Revising the Adaptation Theory of Well-Being," *American Psychologist* 61 (2006): 305.

11. Robert H. Frank, "How Not to Buy Happiness," *Daedalus* 133 (2004): 69, 69–71; David G. Myers, *The Pursuit of Happiness: Who Is Happy, and Why?* (New York: Morrow, 1992), 39.

12. Myers, *The Pursuit of Happiness*, 32–38; David G. Myers and Ed Diener, "Who Is Happy?" *Psychological Science* 6 (1995): 10, 17; Christopher Peterson and Martin E. P. Seligman, *Character Strengths and Virtues: A Handbook and Classification* (New York: Oxford University Press, 2004); William C. Compton, *Introduction to Positive Psychology* (Belmont, CA: Wadsworth, 2004), 48–49, 53–54; Ed Diener et al., "Subjective Well-Being: Three Decades of Progress," *Psychological Bulletin* 125 (1999): 276.

13. Air Vice-Marshal Sir Norman Duckworth Kerr MacEwen, http://www.quotatio.com/m/macewen-norman-quotes.html.

14. Laura Nash and Howard Stevenson, "Success That Lasts," *Harvard Business Review* 82 (2004): 102, 104.

15. Carolyn Miles, email survey, Feb. 13, 2015.

16. Jonathan Haidt, *The Happiness Hypothesis: Finding Modern Truth in Ancient Wisdom* (New York: Basic Books, 2006), 53.

17. J. Patrick Dobel, "Managerial Leadership and the Ethical Importance of Legacy," in Denis Saint-Martin and Fred Dalton Thompson, *Public Ethics and Governance, Volume 14: Standards and Practices in Comparative Perspective*, Research in Public Policy Analysis and Management (Oxford: Elsevier, 2004): 179, 200–203.

18. Ibid., 201.

19. Patricia Harrison, email survey, Feb. 4, 2015.

20. Ingrid Newkirk, email survey, Feb. 3, 2015.

21. Condoleezza Rice, Leadership Presentation, Stanford University, May 9, 2015.

22. Madeleine Albright, keynote speech, Celebrating Inspiration Luncheon with the NBA's All Decade Team, 2006.

23. Albright herself acknowledged that "I absolutely believe what I said, that women should help one another, but this was the wrong context and the wrong time to use that line." She did not "mean to argue that women should support a particular candidate based solely on gender." Madeleine Albright, "My Undiplomatic Moment," *New York Times*, Feb. 13, 2016, A21.

24. Elizabeth Cady Stanton, "The Ballot—Bread, Virtue, Power, Revolution," Jan. 8, 1868, 1. See Deborah L. Rhode, *Justice and Gender* (Cambridge, MA: Harvard University Press, 1991), 16.

INDEX